The . .
SOUTH AFRICANS
WITH GENERAL SMUTS
IN GERMAN EAST AFRICA
1916
■

AUTHOR'S NOTE

By the kindness of the Historical Section of the Committee of Imperial Defence, the author has been afforded the opportunity of perusing the draft chapters of the Official History of the Campaign in German East Africa which cover the period dealt with in this Volume. He would take this opportunity of expressing his grateful appreciation of this act of courtesy.

. The .
SOUTH AFRICANS WITH GENERAL SMUTS IN GERMAN EAST AFRICA
1916

By

BRIGADIER-GENERAL J. J. COLLYER
C.B., C.M.G., D.S.O.

Formerly Chief of the General Staff, Union Defence Forces
Author of "The Campaign in German South West Africa, 1914-1915"

WITH A FOREWORD BY GENERAL THE
RIGHT HONOURABLE J. C. SMUTS

THE IMPERIAL WAR MUSEUM
Department of Printed Books

In Association With
THE BATTERY PRESS
Nashville

Originally Published 1939

Published jointly by
The Imperial War Museum, London
Department of Printed Books
ISBN: 1-904897-03-7
and
The Battery Press, Inc.
P. O. Box 198885
Nashville, Tennessee 37219
Eighty-sixth in The Battery Press Great War Series
2004
ISBN: 0-89839-334-5
Printed in the United States of America

FOREWORD

This BOOK is a very interesting and instructive account of the East African Campaign during the period covered by my command. It is a careful critical study by the very able and experienced officer who was my chief of the General Staff and who was therefore in a special position to know or to learn the circumstances and difficulties of the task which faced us.

The book is written particularly for students who are interested in warfare under the unusual tropical conditions of East Africa, but it is in no sense a merely technical military account of the campaign. It is a full story of a great human performance, and as such is certain to prove of deep interest to the general public as well as to students of war. I have read it with much interest, not only because it revived memories of an unusual and arduous task, but also because it reproduces so well the African atmosphere and setting of an extraordinary undertaking. The East African Campaign is and may—one hopes—long remain the outstanding example of tropical African warfare, and as such is deserving of the attention of all who take an interest in this continent and its future. A large literature has already gathered round this campaign, and it is still growing. But of all the books on it that I have seen—English, German, South African, Belgian —this is the best informed, the most carefully written and accurate, and I have therefore great pleasure in commending it to the reading public.

The East African Campaign started shortly after the outbreak of the Great War and was carried on—in British territory—with many ups and downs until my arrival in February, 1916, and after I left in January, 1917, it continued till the Armistice. But during the

*eleven months of my command the greatest effort on
the Allied Side was made, most of the fighting on the
various fronts took place, and almost the entire enemy
territory was occupied. Thereafter the campaign
continued for a while in the extreme south of German
East Africa, and subsequently passed on to Portuguese
East Africa, and finally to Northern Rhodesia. But
although in this later phase much territory was covered
in endless marches, the military performance and its
significance were on a comparatively minor scale.
General Collyer is therefore right in having concentrated attention on the central period covered by my
command. It is this period which is specially typical
of African campaigning and fruitful in instructive
lessons for the future. His book deals fully with this
period and is valuable not only for its admirable
account of this part of the campaign, but also because
it is throughout critical in its outlook, drawing attention
to mistakes made, opportunities missed, and defects and
faults in the necessary administrative, transport, and
medical arrangements. It is on this critical examination that the constructive lessons for the future are
rightly based.*

*A specially welcome aspect of General Collyer's
account is that there is nothing in it of a one-sided
Allied story. Full justice is done to the brilliant
performance of General von Lettow Vorbeck, his
German officers, and his African Askari army. It is
indeed an extraordinary performance. Outnumbered
most of the time, during my command greatly outnumbered and continuously outfought, this black
army under highly trained white officers put up a fight
so skilful, so prolonged under the most discouraging
conditions of continuous retreat, that it stands out in
my memory of seven years' war experience as one of
the most striking military feats I have known. Indeed*

there is a significance in the achievement to which far too little attention has hitherto been given. Among the lessons of the Great War this is one to be specially pondered in all its bearings. To the indomitable von Lettow himself I have on other occasions paid my tribute. General Collyer here does justice to his military leadership. Undoubtedly some of the most instructive lessons of this campaign are to be learnt from the German side. Mobility of men on foot, the dexterous use of the African bush, repeated night fighting, the skilful handling of reserves, counter-attacks whenever the opportunity offered : of all these invaluable arts of war we had repeated exhibitions which won the admiration of the most hardened veterans among us. Von Lettow made some grave mistakes, to several of which General Collyer draws attention. But in spite of them all his record as a whole remains a fine one, in which his old opponents also take great pleasure.

Having praised our opponents, let us not forget our own. On the Allied side the brave Belgian army which, timing its advance with mine, swept the Kagera basin, cleared Ruanda and Urundi provinces, and finally occupied Tabora, has every right to be proud of its performance. Our ancient Portuguese allies in the south did their best, but could not stem the German retreat into Mozambique under our attack from the north. General Northey's small force in the west proved not only a sure shield to Northern Rhodesia up to near the very end, but advanced successfully eastwards towards Iringa, putting up some specially brilliant attacks in the process. The Indians in my army proved themselves gallant and skilful soldiers and in many a hardwon fight earned the respect and admiration of their European colleagues.

To these, one and all, officers and men, I would respectfully pay my grateful tribute. Thousands of them sleep in East African soil.

But to me the real hero of the East African campaign is the South African citizen soldier. I know my other comrades will not mind my saying so.

They were mostly young men, civilian volunteers from the veld and the towns, from the open country and the unrivalled climate of their native land, with scanty military training, with no knowledge or thought in any quarter of what awaited them in East Africa, either in the manner of fighting or in the climatic or biotic conditions of nature. Immediately on arrival they were flung against military positions skilfully prepared for more than a year; they had to face a well-led army, skilled in bush-fighting; they had to make acquaintance with unknown devastating tropical diseases. As they fought their way through, and lines of communication rapidly lengthened, hospital equipment, transport, and supply arrangements proved inadequate, reduced rations became an effective ally to malaria and the host of other tropical diseases. Bush and forests, mountains, rivers and deserts proved far more formidable than the enemy army. The Equatorial sun blazed on them from above, disease and hunger sapped them from within. All around spread the endless bush, cutting off vision, full of lurking invisible danger, fear-inspiring, heart-breaking. With this went hard labour in long marches, in road and bridge-making, in cutting their way through endless obstacles. And all this immense exertion under conditions of intolerable lassitude and weakness from disease. It was their greatness of spirit, the high tension of their effort that kept them going, kept them from faltering. And supporting them there was the *immense drive which was necessary to keep so great a machine from slowing down in the face of such obstacles. They kept marching and fighting on. From the Lumi to the Rufiji, from the Indian Ocean to the Great Lakes they fought their way through, and in eleven months had mastered a huge stretch of primeval Africa. They stood a test almost beyond human endurance. East Africa is in line with the effort of the Great Trek and of the Boer War.*

They have received scant recognition. After all, was East Africa not one of the little side-shows of the Great War ? The honours have gone to those of their comrades who went to the Western Front. Delville Wood, Marrières Wood and other battle centres in France are the high lights in the South African War record.

Let us not grudge the heroes of the Western Front the glory that is theirs, and that is South Africa's. But equally, let us not forget that there was no less heroism in East Africa, no less endurance to the utmost limit of human nature, no less a contribution to the heroic record of South Africa.

Thousands of them lie there, in the furthest north of our African Trek. This book, with its ample record of their achievement, will help to keep the memory of their service green.

J. C. SMUTS.

PREFACE

> *" It is therefore with a fully equipped mind that one ought to start in order to make and even understand war . . . The truth is no study is possible on the battle field; one does what one can in order to apply what one knows. Therefore in order to do even a little, one has to know a great deal and to know it well."*
>
> FOCH.

> *" In peace time history becomes the true means of learning war and of determining the fixed principles of the art of war."*
>
> DE PEUCKER.

HISTORY has been defined as " philosophy teaching by experience ".

Official military histories are, as a rule, bulky volumes dealing with high politics, the broad principles of strategy, and operations and movements on a large scale, and are necessarily full of much statistical matter. They are mainly useful to the general historian or the military student with ample time at his disposal.

The experiences upon which such histories are based are very rarely described in enough detail to enable the soldier, who is compelled to learn his profession while he practises it, to derive from a study of them the benefit which a more circumstantial account would afford him.

Yet, unless he is aware of the experience of those who have preceded him and can clearly appreciate the factors which made for their success or failure—and for this full knowledge is essential—he is placed at a great disadvantage in learning the ground work of his profession.

The campaign against the German forces in German East Africa, which was one of the theatres of operations in the Great War of 1914-15, lasted throughout the whole period of that struggle.

It falls naturally into three phases:—

(i) The period from the outbreak of war in 1914 until the end of the year 1915 during which the British forces sustained some severe set-backs—including a heavy repulse at Tanga in November, 1914—and were forced into the assumption of a strictly defensive attitude.

(ii) The year 1916, during which, under the command of General the Right Honourable J. C. Smuts, the British Forces very strongly reinforced, especially from the Union of South Africa, by continuous movement and with Belgian co-operation, occupied the greater portion of the territory of the enemy and captured all his railways and sea ports.

(iii) The period from the beginning of the year 1917 until the Armistice when, as a consequence of the disappearance of the strategic objectives mentioned just above, the operations took the form of guerilla warfare.

This volume deals in detail only with phase (ii), i.e. the year 1916.

This period was that of the employment of the great bulk of the 48,565 Europeans who were sent to East Africa from the Union of South Africa.

Before 1916 only a detachment of Union troops had been sent to Nyasaland, where they remained, with some small additions, with General Northey, and, by the end of that year, many thousands of South Africans had become casualties from disease and unfit for further service in any tropical area and were invalided to South Africa, and the employment of native troops was largely resorted to.

With the exception of the comparatively small strength of South Africans who served in the south and entered German East Africa from Nyasaland, all the forces from the Union—two Divisions, each comprising one mounted and one infantry brigade, with Artillery and Service Corps, Medical and other formations, under Generals van Deventer and Brits, respectively, advanced under the direct control of General Smuts from Taveta in the north to the Rufiji River.

It is this advance with which this volume deals in detail as being of special interest and importance to the forces of the Union, seeing that invaluable experience of campaigning in an abnormally difficult country was gained.

General Smuts, of course, in addition to commanding personally the largest and most important British forces in the field in East Africa, with which he remained throughout 1916, exercised chief command over the whole Expeditionary Force there and generally controlled all movements in the campaign.

Only such reference has been made to events and operations of detachments, other than that which the Commander-in-Chief commanded on the spot, as is necessary to a proper conception of the course of the operations as a whole and of the full measure of General Smuts' responsibility.

Any possible stage of active military operations in the continent of Africa must be a factor in the calculations of the Union General Staff, and any such theatre of war, if south of the Equator, assumes an added importance as the potential scene of the employment of South African troops on active service in the defence of their country.

A highly important pronouncement by the Minister of Defence of South Africa was made on October 13, 1937, to the effect that the Defence Department was basing its military measures on the assumption that the Union would remain a member of the British Commonwealth.

As a member of this association of free states South Africa has much to offer by maintaining her territory and seaboard intact, for the Cape of Good Hope, always a strategic point of much importance, has, in consequence of comparatively recent happenings in Africa, become more important than ever before, and, indeed, vital to any scheme of defence common to those states.

In return, South Africa gains an advantage equally vital to her own safety in time of general war or in the event of attack directed against her, viz.: the safety—as far as it is possible to guarantee it—of her ocean trade routes which she is quite unable to protect herself.

That some strong alliance of this nature is indispensable if the Union is not to be at the mercy of any powerful predatory enemy is obvious.

With the ocean trade routes reasonably secure, the Union military authorities may eliminate a successful direct invasion of the Union by a descent and landing upon the seaboard of South Africa as a probability, if not as a possibility; such an event would place the Union in the hopeless position of the two South African republics in 1899.

There remains, however, the possibility of an invasion overland, and this by a strong Power based in Africa and able to maintain its army by means of a comparatively short and safe sea-route. Such a possibility is distinct, and only absolute command of the sea by the British Commonwealth—a highly improbable condition—could prevent it from materialising, if a potential enemy had made preparations for such an invasion.

In the event of attack of this nature, and in view of the likelihood of such an attack by air, the defence of Union territory might have to be undertaken in country the counterpart (if not actually on the identical terrain) of that over which the campaign in East Africa was fought in 1916.

The troops of South Africa would in all probability be inferior in numbers and, quite possibly, in war material to their opponents, and would have to supplement the want by superior tactical efficiency.

In view of the first class fighting material which the Union possesses, this might not prove to be so difficult as might be expected, if advantage were taken of a full knowledge of the climatic conditions and topography of the theatre of operations.

To use again the words of the Minister of Defence on the occasion already referred to : " African warfare is of a type peculiarly its own, and the army that could turn the bush into a friend and ally instead of an enemy and obstacle should be invincible ".

To give some indication as to how the bush and other physical features may aid a carefully prepared defensive—offensive strategy is one of the purposes of this book.

We read in Field Service Regulations, Volume II—

> " The instructions laid down herein cover a war of the first magnitude, but are to be modified in their application to other forms of warfare."

and again in Infantry Training, Volume II—

> " Conditions of battle vary according to the climate and physical features of the country and to the relative strength, armament, physical condition, and fighting spirit of the opposing forces. It is therefore not possible to lay down definite rules for the handling of troops in battle. Nevertheless there are certain guiding principles, the application of which has been proved by experience to be essential to victory. These principles are set forth in Field Service Regulations, Volume II, on which this book is based."

The British Army may have to face " a war of the first magnitude " which will probably be largely static and present many of the features familiar on the Western Front in Europe in 1914-18, but may also find itself participating in what is commonly called a " small war ", in which case the instructions in Field Service Regulations and in Training Manuals based on those Regulations " are to be modified ".

Such a war as that last referred to will be a war of movement, and it is for mobile warfare—bearing in mind the probable scenes of their employment on active service—that the Union Defence Forces, generally, should be trained.

They will presumably fight on the continent of Africa, and potential theatres of operations, so far as they are concerned, present the varied terrain which is to be found from the Cape to the Equator.

Conditions of warfare in Europe have undergone radical change in consequence of the introduction of modern appliances, but those in less civilised countries of sparse population, great distances, and vast tracts of undeveloped territory have not altered to anything like the same extent.

A tendency to assume that innovations possess a uniform tactical value may perhaps be occasionally corrected by reflection on some of the natural hindrances which a country may present.

The approved text books, based, as they are, on the conditions of war in Europe, make scant reference to the circumstances which will attend war in other theatres, and the necessary modifications referred to above must be arrived at in the light of experience gained in less closely settled countries.

These modifications may be considerable, alike in number and scope.

We read, for example, in Field Service Regulations, on the subject of tanks that "certain types of terrain limit their movements. Deep water, cuttings, swamps, boggy or heavily shelled ground, rocky mountainous country and thick woods *present serious obstacles to them* ".

Anyone who has campaigned in Africa will recognise terrain of this type as characteristic of many scenes of conflict on the continent where hostilities may well occur again, and it is plain that in such country the tactical value of the tank (one of the important innovations) will be seriously diminished.

Again observation from the air is infinitely more difficult in country covered with dense bush than elsewhere, and the observation of artillery fire, unless high eminences are available for the purpose—which, judging from past experience, will often not be the case—is in such country far less simple than in more open terrain.

There are many other respects in which much adaptation of modern means of warfare, of which the use in uncivilised territories may be possible, will be essential.

With a knowledge of the obstacles which have hampered military operations in Africa in the past, those charged with the task of training the troops of the Union for war will be in a position to judge of the extent to which the use of newer appliances and more recent methods may be possible in the country in which those troops may be expected to fight, and to decide the measure of adaptation of such appliances and methods required for local needs.

From the account which follows it will be possible to appreciate how physical and climatic conditions combined to retard the advancing and attacking forces of General Smuts, whilst very materially aiding the retiring and defending troops of General von Lettow.

Tropical Africa, as a consequence of the experience in German East Africa in this campaign, has acquired a sinister reputation as essentially unhealthy and the view has been formed that any European troops must necessarily be decimated after a comparatively short spell of active service in that part of the world.

Endemic tropical disease must remain a menace, but in estimating its effect in the light of this campaign in German East Africa, it must always be remembered that *practically no preparation whatever was made* before the troops were committed to the venture, and that, in future, intelligent preparation and precautions should tend *most substantially* to reduce casualties from disease and prevent much unnecessary suffering to those who may succumb to it.

Clausewitz wrote: " By the word ' Information ' we denote all the knowledge which we have of the enemy and his country; therefore, in fact the foundation of all our ideas and actions ", and as another military writer lays down: " It is a great error to believe that a suitable organisation of the various services which help to render an army victorious can be set on foot at a moment's notice ".

Prominent among the " services " referred to are those of transport and medical assistance, the legitimate demands of which were completely underestimated by those who were responsible for sending the British Expeditionary Force to East Africa in 1914, with the gravest consequences to the fighting troops.

8,000 Troops were originally estimated to be enough for the reduction of the German Protectorate, whereas the ration state of the British forces there at the Armistice, when General von Lettow surrendered with a gallant handful of his compatriots and 1,100 Askaris, showed a strength of 111,731!

It is difficult to understand upon what information this amazing miscalculation can have been based.

As Chief of the General Staff to General Smuts during the campaign the author had ample opportunity to study the difficulties that surround campaigning in the African bush. His observations on the course of events and the lessons for the future to which he draws attention are all based on his experience in that campaign. His object in writing this account is largely practical and utilitarian, and his comments and criticisms are incidental to this practical aim, and must not be taken as having any official sanction.

J. J. COLLYER.

Capetown, May, 1939.

CONTENTS

CHAPTER I

CHAPTER II

CHAPTER III

CHAPTER IV

CHAPTER V

CHAPTER VI

CHAPTER VII

LIST OF MAPS
(see end of book)

Map
No.

CHAPTER I

(i) THE ACQUISITION OF GERMAN EAST AFRICA BY THE GERMANS.

IN THE YEAR 1875 many Germans were doing their utmost to develop the idea of a German Colonial Empire, and among them was Vice-Admiral Livonius, who emphasised the desirability of taking the island of Zanzibar under German protection and establishing a Great German protectorate on the opposite, east, coast of Africa.

The greater part of those who at this time endeavoured to awaken German national feeling in response to their views devoted their attention to the Far East and the South Pacific, and comparatively few advocated colonial enterprise in Africa.

Among the latter was Moldenhauer who, three years after Livonius' suggestion, urged that Africa might well repay consideration. He asked whether Germany was prepared to do anything else than send scientific missions to Africa and strew that continent with the bones of her explorers.

At this time the German Government, under the control of Bismarck, had little sympathy with the aims of its colonial party.

In the following years, however, after the formation of the Deutsche Kolonialgesellschaft in 1881, the Hamburg Senate, in 1883, forwarded a long report to the German Foreign Office recommending among other things " The establishment of a German Protectorate over all independent territories frequented by German merchants ".

German South-West Africa was the first German colony, established after careful preparation by the establishment of merchants and their agreements with adjoining native tribes, and became so on April 25, 1884, when the German Imperial Government officially declared that Herr Lüderitz, who had hoisted the German flag a year earlier at Angra Pequena (afterwards Lüderitzbucht) was under the protection of the German Empire.

The efforts of Dr. Karl Peters to establish German authority on the eastern side of the continent were not at first so warmly received.

For many centuries the eastern coasts of Africa had been under various civilising influences which had not been operative on the western seaboard.

There had been continuous commercial intercourse with Arabia, the Persian Gulf and India, and Zanzibar was the rendezvous of the Arab and Indian traders who frequented the coasts and was also the headquarters of the slave trade.

Gums, ebony, ivory, hides, oil seeds, cloves and many other kinds of produce, including, in the earlier days, gold, had been conveyed from Africa to the east by Persians, Arabians and Indians, and the inhabitants of the east coast of Africa had come under the influence of these people.

One of the results of this contact was the existence of natives on the east coast far superior to those on the west.

Large and important native towns were situated on the east coast, and their rulers carried on trade with the uncivilised tribes of the interior and the eastern countries.

A later consequence was the commercial dependence of Zanzibar on Great Britain and her Indian traders.

In 1885 the German Imperial Government, which had so far refused any official backing to Dr. Peters, became more ready to support his schemes, should he prove successful in their execution.

The change of attitude was very largely due to the fact that at the time Great Britain was confronted by difficulties in the Soudan and Afghanistan where Russian intrigue was proving an embarrassment.

The idea of a great German dependency in Africa, to be gained mainly at the expense of Great Britain, apparently took definite shape about this time, a scheme which was to be largely aided by local trouble to be fomented *ad hoc* in South Africa.

Whatever may be thought of Peters' methods, and a full description of them is to be obtained from " The Germans in Africa ", by Evans Lewin, his resolution and persistence were beyond doubt. His efforts gained impetus and purpose from a deep hatred of Great Britain.

Dr. Karl Peters, to whose initiative the occupation of German East Africa was mainly due, founded in 1884 " The Society for German Colonisation ", and issued an appeal to the German people emphasising the fact that Germany was without a voice in the partition of the world, and that his Society was founded to remedy " this deplorable state of affairs " and " to undertake the execution of colonial projects ".

The strength of British influence—ably upheld by the British Consul—at Zanzibar, the delicacy of the situation, and the fact that Peters' projects involved totally ignoring the claim of the Sultan of Zanzibar to sovereignty on the mainland up to Lake Tanganyika, combined to make caution imperative on the part of the apostle of German colonisation.

Accordingly he acted with secrecy and with two companions, Dr. Jühlke and Count Joachim Pfeil, gave it as his intention to proceed from Liverpool to West Africa. Embarking, however, under false names at Trieste for Zanzibar, they reached the latter place on November 4, 1884.

Crossing six days later to the mainland, the party, at Sadani, concluded the first of many " treaties " by which the German Colonisation Society established itself in East Africa.

By December 2, by a repetition of the procedure at Sadani, Peters had obtained similar documents from various chiefs—who understood nothing of their effect—which gave him " rights " over Nguru, Usagara, Ukami, Umvomero and Umkondokiva, a block of territory of more than 60,000 square miles north of Bagamoyo.

Rapidly making his way back to Berlin, Peters, on February 17, 1885, obtained a charter of protection from the German Emperor for the German Colonisation Society in respect of the territory thus acquired.

Soon after this the British East Africa Association was founded to confirm " rights " obtained from chiefs in the neighbourhood of Taveta by Mr. Harry Hamilton Johnston.

During 1885 eleven German expeditions were organised at Zanzibar and treaties were concluded with native chiefs in Usambara, Tanga, Wilhelmstal and other districts up to Moschi. Uhehe, Ubena and the neighbourhood of Lake Nyasa and the Rovuma river were also reached, and by the end of the year a large portion of German East Africa had been opened up.

In October, 1885, a joint commission with a representative of Great Britain (Lieut.-Colonel—afterwards Earl—Kitchener), France and Germany met at Zanzibar to decide the exact extent of the dominion of the Sultan of Zanzibar who claimed sovereignty far into the interior on the mainland.

As the outcome of this commission, in an agreement between the British and German Governments (October 29-November 1, 1886), the islands of Zanzibar and Pemba and certain lesser

3

islands including Lamu and Mafia were assigned to the Sultan, while on the mainland the latter was allowed the coast line from Cape Delgado and the Rovuma river to Kipini at the mouth of the Tana river with an internal depth of ten miles.

Among a variety of arrangements and undertakings Great Britain and Germany agreed each to respect the boundaries of the other and not to make acquisitions of territory or accept protectorates within the respective spheres of influence.

Great Britain received advantages in East Africa, but the Germans gained the rich district of Kilimanjaro, the first objective of the campaign which will be described.

The northern boundary of British East Africa followed the line of the Tana river to the point of intersection of the Equator and the 38th degree of east longitude and thence direct to the point of intersection of the 1st degree of north latitude with the 37th degree of east longitude. Access to Lake Victoria Nyanza was thus assured to Great Britain.

Native risings followed, and in May, 1889, the administration of the Protectorate passed to the Imperial Government.

Dr. Peters meantime had further ideas as to the extension of German colonial territory, and early in 1889, evading the blockade established by Great Britain and Germany against the slave trade, landed at Pasa in Kwaihu Bay and started upon yet another expedition by way of Witu and the Tana river, the then northern boundary of British East Africa.

Though he had been refused permission to lead an expedition through the British sphere, he proceeded to do so, ostensibly, though quite unnecessarily, for the relief of Emin Pasha who was supposed to be in imminent danger of death at the hands of the fanatical savages of the Soudan.

His real intention was to prevent any further extension of British territory to the north and deny the British East Africa Company access to the upper Nile.

He accordingly concluded more " treaties ", hoisted the German flag at Malalulu on the north of the Tana to show the English that their " sphere of interests extended only to the southern side of the river ", and did the same near Mount Kenya and at Kwa Sakwa near Lake Victoria Nyanza and at other places.

When Peters returned to Europe after these activities he found the stage set for the conclusion of the Anglo German

4

agreement of 1890, and that his own particular game was finished.

Incidentally, this ardent coloniser, after having been appointed Imperial Commissioner for German East Africa, was tried on April 24, 1897, on charges of cruelty and the hanging of natives and was dismissed from the colonial service. He appealed but did not appear before the appeal court which confirmed the first decision.

The whole story of the circumstances and negotiations which led up to the conclusion of the Anglo German Agreement is to be found in " The Germans and Africa ", by Evans Lewin, which has already been referred to, and from which all the information, contained in the preceding pages, has been drawn.

Here it is enough to say that so far as East Africa is concerned it fixed the boundaries of German East Africa in the form in which they remained up to the outbreak of the Great War, and, as a consequence of the abandonment of any German claims north of the Tana river, eliminated all danger of the encirclement of British East Africa by German territory.

The agreement also recorded Germany's willingness to recognise a British protectorate over the dominions of the Sultan of Zanzibar.

For these and other concessions in Africa, Lord Salisbury— in the face of opposition from his naval advisers, though the soldiers apparently regarded the act as of little importance—made the fateful cession of Heligoland of which the full effect may remain yet to be determined.

From map number one the situation of German East Africa in August, 1914, may be realised.

The Protectorate was surrounded on land by enemy territory, British, Belgian, and Portuguese, and its coast was blockaded though, as will be seen, not with complete effect, by the British Navy.

Circumstances were, however, favourable in some important respects to a prolonged defence by the German forces which were in German East Africa at the outbreak of the Great War, despite their isolated position.

The physical features of the country and its climate were formidable obstacles to anything like rapid movement by forces new to the terrain against local troops to whom the ground was familiar, as may be gathered from the following description of the theatre of operations.

(ii) THE CLIMATE.

There are three types of climate in German East Africa—now Tanganyika Territory.

The trade wind type which prevails over the greater part of the country.

The monsoon type in the north-east.

The equatorial type in the north-west.

So far as General Smuts' operations were concerned, the two first mentioned types were encountered.

The first of these is influenced by the south-east trade winds. It has one rainy season in the year and its hottest period is at the end of November just before the rainy season begins. The coolest and driest period is from June to August. It then becomes warmer until the rainy season which lasts from December till April.

The second type (monsoon) is that in which the bulk of General Smuts' operations were carried out.

The hottest month is February just before the great rainy season begins. There is a " little " rainy season in the mountainous regions in July.

From March to May a heavy rainfall occurs and is experienced within an area bounded by a line from the mouth of the Rufiji through the Protectorate to the north-west. In this area are included the Uluguru and Nguru districts through which his major operations were carried out by General Smuts in his advance southwards and by General van Deventer on his right and under his general direction.

The effect of these rains may perhaps be gauged from the following episode which occurred late in the campaign.

General Smuts, anxious to move a force south of the Central Railway at a time when rain might be expected, came to a drift some 30 yards wide and asked a native *jumbe* (headman) standing by how wide it would become in the rainy season. This occurred in the direction of Mahenge and Iringa.

The native gravely replied " 60 miles! "

He meant to convey that for 60 miles the whole country would be covered with water, at varying depths and often superficially, but to an extent which at once ruled out the project.

6

Commander Whittall, R.N., who commanded the Naval armoured cars for a time with General Smuts and has recorded his own experiences, writes describing a movement which he had been ordered to undertake with his cars: " We had been just five weeks in covering the distance from Mbuyuni, a distance we could have easily covered in a day over roads worthy of the name . . . I really do not know how we ever got through at all."

These two instances of the effect of tropical rain may give an idea of its influence on movement by a large force, accompanied by the quantity of mechanical, or even animal, transport necessary for its proper subsistence. It was such a force that General Smuts commanded in 1916.

The account of General van Deventer's movement on Kondoa Irangi in April, 1916, will show later how General von Lettow took advantage of climatic conditions, of the full import of which he was of course well aware, to concentrate against van Deventer, confident that nature would assist him by keeping General Smuts immobile for a clearly defined length of time.

The vegetation of the country is the result, in the main, of the rainfall, and consequently varies greatly throughout the whole territory from tropical forest to desert.

We read in Volume II of " Infantry Training, 1931 " that conditions of battle vary according to the physical features of the country and to . . the physical condition and fighting spirit of the troops ".

Throughout the year 1916 General Smuts conducted his operations in country where " the climate and physical features " were factors of supreme importance in their effect upon the " physical fitness " and, if not on the " spirit ", emphatically on the fighting capacity of his troops, as may be realised from the following general description of the scene of hostilities.

(iii) GENERAL TOPOGRAPHY.

The area of what is now Tanganyika Territory (formerly German East Africa) is some 385,000 square miles, roughly twice the size of the German Empire in Europe in 1914, with a coast line of 470 miles bordered by a maritime plain of from 10 to 40 miles in width.

From this plain the country rises gradually to the plateau which forms the greater part of the hinterland and is bordered on the east by the Pare, Nguru, Uluguru and Uhehe mountains, the last-named bending to the north of Lake Nyasa.

This plateau falls sharply to the west to the level of Lake Tanganyika (2,590 feet) and Lake Nyasa (1,607 feet).

The Great Rift Valley inland runs across the plateau, at a height of some 2,000 to 4,000 feet, from Lake Rukwa near the south of Lake Tanganyika to Lake Naivasha in British territory (1914).

The great lakes Victoria Nyanza, Tanganyika and Nyasa, with Kivu and Rukwa, formed the western boundary of the German Protectorate in 1914.

The greatest rivers in the territory, unfordable and infested with crocodile, Pangani, Wami, Ruwu, Rufiji, Matandu, Mbemkuru, Lukuledi and Rovuma flow into the Indian Ocean. All these rivers are within the area of General Smuts' operations, as are the great massifs of the Nguru and Uluguru mountains, as well as the Pare and Usambara.

The important Kigera and Mlagarasi empty themselves into Victoria Nyanza and Tanganyika, respectively.

While in the temperate zone of the sub-alpine heights, such as the Usambara, Nguru and Uluguru mountains, the temperature is comfortably cool, and at night even occasionally chilly, in the country in which the South Africans and their comrades fought in 1916, viz.: between the coast region and the hills bordering the eastern side of the central plateau, the heat was trying in the extreme and it was always dangerous to omit to wear a helmet from sunrise to sunset.

The scene of operations was either steppe covered with grass which, springing up to man's height during the rains, quickly died down afterwards, or parkland grass steppe covered with bushes or trees—isolated or in groups—affording a good measure of visibility, or dense bush in which only objects close at hand may be discerned.

This last condition predominated, and prevailed on almost every occasion of close touch with the enemy, and invariably in all tactical contact when, as will be seen, the opposing commander took full advantage of his knowledge of the ground.

Elephant grass, long and tough, grew in profusion by the rivers and in moist places.

The huge ranges of the Nguru and Uluguru and the smaller, but no less effective, Pare and Usambara were additional difficulties to the advance and advantages to the defence.

From time to time the German Commander derived much help from the power of observation of his antagonist's laborious advance through the almost impenetrable bush below which possession of the heights gave him.

Game abounded, and lion, elephant, rhinoceros and hippopotamus were always to be found in their special haunts, and occasional rhinoceros charges at patrols, and once through the lines of a brigade, as well as the upsetting of boats by hippopotamus at river crossings were features of the campaign.

It was found necessary to place the insulators of the telegraph lines at an unusual height to obviate breakage by giraffe.

(iv) ENDEMIC DISEASES.

Tropical diseases were general.

Malaria of severe type extends over the whole country except in its highest parts, as does its frequent consequence, black water fever.

African relapsing fever, caused by a tick which lurked in the roof of every native hut and every rest-house, was another scourge.

Dysentery of a grave nature with often very serious results and hook-worm disease (helminthiasis) were also rife.

Less serious, if irritating, inconveniences were prickly heat and the jigger flea. The female flea burrows under the skin near the toe-nail, and, unless the egg-sac which it deposits is quickly removed, a painful wound ensues. A native with an ordinary sewing needle will remove the sac dexterously and—this is essential—intact. Loss of toes from this cause is not uncommon among the natives of the country.

So far as the animals were concerned, tsetse fly was deadly, and every horse or ox bitten by the fly died in about six weeks.

Thousands of animals—28,000 oxen alone—died from tsetse bite which was inevitable when they passed through a tsetse zone.

Fly was found in bush country wherever there was stagnant water and followed the game, and, during the campaign, the animals of the mounted units and transport.

9

(v) DIFFICULTIES ATTENDING AN ADVANCE.

Tropical disease, enervating climate, dense bush, huge mountains and, in the rainy season, appalling seas of thick, slimy mud, were weighty considerations in determining the strategy and course of the campaign.

The forces under General Smuts, of which the personnel (with its animals) was extremely susceptible to the pests which have been described, shrank steadily throughout its entire advance, independently of any action by the enemy, whose askaris were immune from the consequences of the diseases which decimated their opponents, and who moved with great rapidity on foot.

During all the operations in 1916 the German forces fell back on magazines and prepared positions in their movements against which their adversaries were seriously hampered by the necessity for cutting every path and road that they used for tactical purposes.

Tactical surprise was practically impossible, while any strategic movement, if any good result were to be achieved, called for the nicest timing in the light of, and with due regard to, climatic conditions.

The susceptibility of the invading force to disease held good from the firing line to the base, and the toll of casualties from this cause was constant and relatively enormous.

Tactically—after any sustained advance—there was often little practical disparity of strength.

The laborious cutting of roads for every tactical venture of importance, the steady decrease from disease of the strength originally intended to be brought into action seriously aggravated by shortage of transport and, consequently, of necessary supplies continually hampered the operations of General Smuts.

(vi) ADVANTAGES OF THE DEFENCE.

His opponent, General von Lettow Vorbeck, invariably made the utmost possible use of the advantages which nature extended to him, and to this good fortune joined a powerful personality—always a potent weapon in the hands of a leader of native troops —together with the soldierly virtues of courage, endurance and leadership.

(vii) THE NEED FOR CAREFUL PREPARATION.

In the conditions which have been described as peculiar to the theatre of operations any shortcomings in respect of the medical, supply or transport services were bound to react with tremendous effect on the health, and therefore the fighting efficiency and mobility, of the British troops.

The campaign in East Africa, after military operations there involved anything more than a passive defence of British territory, was what was called in the parlance of the day a " side show ".

In other words it was decided upon chiefly as the result of pressure from individuals influential enough to carry their point, and not as a carefully considered diversion in a general plan of campaign. A diversion, strategical or tactical, is useless unless it is designed to achieve a clearly understood effect in a larger scheme.

However, this is not the place to debate the wisdom of embarking on the venture.

It *was* undertaken, without any real preparation and, apparently, with scant consideration of what the task involved; and, probably, with little enthusiasm except on the part of its advocates.

Consequently, there was no attempt to prepare for the campaign in its larger aspect until hurried hand to mouth arrangements were started, and in no direction was the evil of unreadiness more prominent or more productive of avoidable hardship to the force engaged than in the matter of transport.

The feeding and medical care of the troops and the evacuation of casualties and their treatment as speedily as possible, all essential services for the maintenance of the fighting strength, were most seriously affected by the lack of preparation and, apparently, a faulty appreciation of the demand upon the vitality of the personnel engaged which the campaign was bound to entail.

The narrative which follows will make this clear.

(viii) COMMUNICATIONS.

Another factor of extreme importance in the conduct of offensive operations was the nature of the communications in the country. In order properly to estimate the influence of this factor, it must be remembered that the British forces contained troops from all parts of the Empire, and, in 1916, large numbers were European. In May, 1916, there were 23,300 such troops from South Africa *alone* and 3,000 more were being trained in the Union. Only a small, if valuable, proportion was found from local native troops.

Such a force required supplies of all kinds in large quantities and their provision and distribution called for the use of much mechanical transport, as well as carriage by porters, and the employment of animal drawn vehicles where possible in view of the absence of tsetse. A dearth of roads therefore complicated this distribution.

The bulk of the enemy forces, on the other hand, was composed of local askaris, used to the food grown, and to be found, in the country, and their needs in the way of medical and other assistance for the preservation of bodily efficiency were infinitely less than those of their opponents. Whatever supplies were available to the German Commander were in the country, and he could, and did, so arrange his movements as to fall back upon depots and fertile districts where sustenance for his askaris was procurable.

His transport was virtually entirely by porters, and the inadequacy of the few lines which were possible for an advance in force by the British Commander was a very distinct advantage to General von Lettow. The latter was well aware of all these lines which were of a nature seriously to interfere with anything but a slow rate of movement.

Roads were to all intents and purposes non-existent.

At best they were broad tracks cut in the bush which in fine weather allowed of the passage of motor transport. The soil was black or red cotton soil, and in no instance was a road metalled, and, as a consequence, the rainy season converted these roads into their worst condition. In the case of the black soil the tracks became stretches of liquid mud rendering any movement of transport impossible; the red soil, if on high ground, would occasionally allow of the passage of light vehicles. Heavy transport, and indeed any continuous flow of transport, would reduce the soil in dry weather to powder, and all kinds of devices had to be resorted to to get vehicles along.

A " road " in East Africa usually was determined, in respect of lay out, by the track made by advancing troops in and out of tree trunks and bush, and was at first merely a winding track.

A rough removal of the greater obstacles to straight forward movement reduced the bends and twists, and, if the route was to be used to any great extent, a further obliteration of obstacles and a rough levelling produced the finished article. Between 3,000 and 4,000 miles of such tracks, which would serve motor traffic, were made in the course of the war. Occasionally some far more elaborate engineering work was needed to surmount special physical difficulties, and some fine work was done in this respect.

A month or so, however, if the route were abandoned, would see the work all undone by the rapid growth of the bush, and sometimes an effort to find a track along which hundreds of troops and waggons had passed was futile.

This was specially the case w'th native paths shown on the maps. The removal of a tribe and the abandonment of the path led to its complete disappearance.

Such an experience was encountered in the Uluguru mountains by Brigadier-General Nussey, for example.

Three railway systems were made use of during 1916.

The Uganda railway in British territory from Mombasa, the original sea base, and, in German territory the Usambara railway from Moschi to Tanga and the Central railway from Dar-es-Salaam in the east to the western boundary of the German Protectorate at Kigoma on Tanganyika.

The last-named railway became of the utmost help when the sea base was switched to Dar-es-Salaam after the occupation of Morogoro.

The sea bases available were Mombasa (Kilindini): Tanga, which was only used for a short time: Dar-es-Salaam, which, after its occupation, remained for the duration of the war the principal base on the coast: Kilwa and Lindi were used as subsidiary to Dar-es-Salaam for operations in the south.

There were of course other ports on the coast but those mentioned were actually made use of as bases.

(ix) LOCAL RESOURCES.

(a) Food.

Many of the products of German East were of great value from the supply point of view for the native troops who found in fertile districts all that was necessary for their subsistence.

13

The German movements were largely based at first in their retirements by the consideration that certain districts were fertile and well adapted for the sustenance of the forces. Later on, when such districts had been occupied by the enemy many devices were resorted to with success to convert local products for useful purposes. For example material was made for bandages from a bark, and quinine was obtained from a similar source. The fat of elephant and hippopotamus furnished lard, and the use of fruit and honey supplied a deficiency of sugar.

This, however, was for a native army accustomed to the country.

On the British side the question of supply was—as has been indicated—far more difficult.

Supplies locally obtainable were fresh meat, bacon, mealies, coffee and ground nuts.

The United Kingdom, India, South Africa and Sumatra were the sources of other supplies.

It is of interest to observe that an unlimited supply of biscuits and preserved meat could have been furnished from South Africa but for the lack of any tinning plant in the Union.

The varied nationalities of the troops, in the case of some of which religious scruples had to be respected, complicated the question.

Broadly, while in the case of the German forces their country yielded at first plentiful supplies of food for the rank and file, only a few of the necessary articles could be procured locally for the British troops.

(b) Transport.

One of the methods of transport was peculiar to the country and used to a very great extent, that by porters.

The German transport—there were only 3 motor cars and 3 motor lorries available for military work—was almost entirely effected by porters.

A military porter service was a feature of the Protectorate system and an average of 250 porters was allotted to each Askari company. This, incidentally, formed a most valuable reservoir of potential askaris and was so used to advantage by General von Lettow. He says " hundreds of thousands of carriers worked for the troops ".

14

The system was also adopted very largely in the end by the British forces, though it was sometimes difficult to procure the numbers required, or to keep them occasionally when any unpleasant situation arose.

Except for the rolling stock on the railways—and in the case of the Germans much of this was destroyed as the campaign progressed—there was no other local transport on land available.

(c) War Material.

General von Lettow's first action with regard to arms and ammunition which " were lying unprotected " in the harbour of Dar-es-Salaam, was to distribute them among various places in the interior along the railway line in depots.

Neither in German East Africa nor in adjacent British territory did any facilities exist for producing any warlike stores to supplement those in the possession of each contesting force at the outbreak of hostilities. These will be enumerated later.

While sea-power would enable the British Government to send any additional war material which it was desired to convey to East Africa, the German Commander would have to rely upon an evasion of the blockade on the coast by such German ships as should survive the hazards of a long and risky voyage, or upon captures from his enemy for aid in the above respect.

In point of fact, he was well served by his fortune so far as help from oversea was concerned, while his own skilful generalship came to his assistance on several occasions when he succeeded in securing welcome material from his enemies.

Two store ships reached him. The first reached Mansa Bay north of Tanga in April, 1915, where she was fired upon by a British cruiser and her captain was compelled to beach her. This resulted in an addition of ammunition and other valuable supplies, though it was necessary to remake the ammunition in consequence of damage by sea water.

The second ship arrived at Ssudi Bay while the Kilimanjaro operations were 'in progress. This was a much more important event, for, in addition to arms and ammunition (several thousand rounds for the Königsberg guns were included) four field howitzers and two mountain guns—all particularly useful for the bush—had been brought.

It was some time, for some reason or other, before General Smuts was informed of this last mentioned occurrence, but, before he was apprised of the event, an increased volume of fire from the enemy in different engagements, had caused some speculation.

15

(x) THE NATIVES AND THEIR MILITARY VALUE.

The climate and the physical features of the theatre of war were two powerful allies for the German Commander in a defence of territory with which he and his troops were familiar, and he had a third in the possession of well trained askaris (native soldiers) who were able to resist the many diseases to which the great bulk of their opponents were an easy prey.

In 1912 the total native population of German East Africa was recorded as 7,495,800.

It is from time to time suggested that hordes of native soldiers may be trained in Equatorial Africa and its adjacent territories to the north, and that they may prove to be a grave menace to European civilisation on the continent of Africa.

Whatever the future may hold, and a sane policy by all the states of the British Commonwealth in the said continent, based on common defence precautions and mutual support, should go far to prevent such a catastrophe as that adumbrated, it is well to realise that in 1914, and even to-day, nearly a quarter of a century later, the numbers of natives fit to be trained to arms was, and is, strictly limited both as regards their strength and their location. The askaris, British, Belgian or German, came from clearly defined districts of the different territories in which they were recruited. Some even came from comparatively far afield, e.g. from the Soudan.

In order to support this assertion, it is necessary briefly to consider the ethnography of the native tribes.

In an attempt to discover their historical origin speculation must figure largely.

It would appear that the aboriginal inhabitants were akin to some extent to the Bushmen and Hottentots, being of comparatively light colour and small in stature.

Traces of this type remain in the pygmy tribes and in others whose language bears a resemblance to that of the Bushmen.

Considerably later than the establishment of the aboriginals an invasion of Bantu (tall and dark-skinned) is supposed to have taken place from Southern Asia. People of this stock are to be found principally in the coastal region and the mountainous country adjacent to it, Wilhelmstal, Pangani, Tanga, Bagamoyo, Dar-es-Salaam, Lindi, Kilwa, Rufiji and Morogoro, and in the Nguru and Uluguru mountains. These districts were all the scene of General Smuts' operations.

Much later a second influx of Bantu occurred. The later Bantu are supposed to have been pushed southwards by Hamitic people in the north. From this stock the natives in the Pare and Usambara ranges, on Kilimanjaro and in the districts of Moschi and Aruscha are supposed to be descended.

Two groups of Hamitic natives in the Protectorate are entirely distinct in appearance from the other tribes in German East Africa. Their features bear out an assumption of their Nilotic origin and are much closer to those of Europeans.

They are the Wahuma and the Masai.

The former are considered to have come from Arabia through Egypt some 600 years ago. They are lighter in colour than the other natives of the country and settled in the north-west where they are to-day known by different tribal names. Probably the best known of them are the Watussi in Ruanda. They are a tall well made people of fine physique, and their high foreheads and oval-shaped faces denote their foreign strain. By virtue of a far superior intelligence they have always dominated all other tribes within their sphere of influence.

The Masai are also much apart from the other natives. Following the Wahuma they present some of the same features. Until the introduction of European administration the Masai were the terror of all who were within striking distance of them, raiding the tribes continuously and carrying off their women and cattle and exterminating the men.

In 1914 they were located in the Masai Steppe lying in the north-eastern corner of the Protectorate in the districts of Mwanza, Aruscha and Kondoa Irangi. The steppe is wide and covered with grass and acacia bush. It is for the most part open with good visibility and grass knee-high. Here the Masai raised cattle, for which the country is well suited, served by the Wandorobbo tribe whom they had dispossessed of the country on the occasion of their first invasion, and who had never emerged from a state of subjection the consequence of their defeat.

An admixture of Zulus was effected from the south about the middle of the sixteenth century. Migrations of Zulus continued. They spread over the eastern coast districts, but their penetration into German East Africa only took place in the middle of the nineteenth century. The intervention of the Germans prevented any serious clash between the Zulus and the Masai, and the

17

former remained largely in the southern part of the Protectorate where they reared cattle and engaged in slave hunting.

Even such a cursory examination as the above of the origin and influence of various immigrations of foreign tribes into German East Africa would be incomplete without a consideration of the effect of the slave trade upon the natives of the country. This is specially important in its relation to the martial qualities of the latter.

In the latter part of the 17th century Arabs from Oman and Muskat deprived the Portuguese of almost all the places where the latter had effected a lodgment in East Africa, and Arab domination became well established.

The peak of the slave trade was reached in the first half of the 19th century when the Arabs made their way into the interior, and, in the process of taking slaves from the native tribes, treated the latter with much brutality and cruelty. Such action entailed the use of armed forces sufficient to attack and overwhelm the tribes selected for the attention of the slave dealers, and, naturally enough, soldiers for this purpose were selected from such tribes as exhibited the qualities of ruthlessness and courage of a far higher order than that possessed by their victims.

The more virile natives of Wahuma, Masai and Zulu descent were calculated to fill the role required to which they were familiar. They were, necessarily, far fewer than the thousands of unfortunates on whom they practised their brutal trade, and this fact seems to account for the comparatively small proportion of natives in, and adjacent to, German East Africa who could be regarded in 1914 as first class fighting material or can be so regarded to-day.

From this very general ethnographical review of the native races it may be accepted that the Bantu form their basic element with the addition of Wahuma and Masai, who have kept their distinctive racial appearance and habits, and of Zulu who have merged into different tribes and whose characteristics are perpetuated merely by the greater virility of the latter.

The difference in bearing and physique between the askari class and the ordinary native of the country was most remarkable. The native soldier who, receptive of the military cult as a consequence of his life spent in the exercise of force, bore himself as one of a higher caste, under the careful tutelage of the German

officers in the application of strict discipline, was a vastly
different mortal from the ordinary native in whose demeanour
the sense of inferiority and the timidity engendered by years of
oppression was very noticeable.

At the inception of the German Protectorate Force in 1889 it
was raised almost entirely from native tribes beyond the
Protectorate borders, and consisted chiefly of Soudanese or Zulus,
but when war broke out in 1914 it was practically entirely
composed of natives recruited in German East Africa.

Zulus, quâ Zulus, had disappeared into the local tribes and,
as may be well understood, political considerations tended to
prevent a regular or substantial recruitment of Soudanese.

In view of the opinions expressed above as to the limited
number of natives who may be regarded as fit to become good
soldiers and the reason for such limitation, it is interesting to
observe that the following districts were those which supplied
the great majority of the recruits.

In the north-west—the home of the Wahuma already
mentioned—from Tabora came Manyema, composed of former
slaves of the Wanyamwezi and deserters from the Congo forces
and other refugees, Wangoni, an offshoot of the Zulu tribe, and
Wanyamwezi, accustomed to cattle and slave raids who had
been able to maintain their independence against the Arabs.
From the district of Mwanza were drawn Wasukuma, accustomed
to repel incursions by their neighbours the Masai and therefore
habituated to war.

From southern districts, e.g. Lindi and Ssongea, were obtained
soldiers from the Wangoni already mentioned as of Zulu descent
and Wayao who were also strongly mixed with a Zulu strain.

The mass of the natives in the interior will have to undergo
a great change in physique and temperament before they can
become promising material for first class soldiers.

Incidentally, the European power—Italy—which has just
deprived the Ethiopians of their country and their independence,
has the best means on the continent of Africa for the rapid
preparation of a native army formidable in numbers and military
spirit, for the Abyssinians who fought for Haile Selasse—ill-
equipped and lacking war material—are people of a martial
spirit.

Prior to 1914 the German authorities had assiduously
encouraged their Askaris, carefully picked from one or two

districts, to consider themselves in every way superior to the mass of non-military natives and as a class apart from their fellows.

Years of preparation during the slave trade had made these few special tribes apt disciples of the cult of force.

The Masai were found to be good irregular soldiers of the guerilla type, but they would not put up with constant discipline, a failing from the point of view of the strict disciplinarian of all such troops. It may have been this defect which prevented the Germans from raising native forces in their territory in German South-West Africa where the natives were fine shots—which the Askaris were not—and in their own country guerilla fighters of a high order.

From the foregoing review it will be realised that General von Lettow had at his disposal a disciplined force of good native soldiers. They were soldiers of fortune, and true to their salt and loyal to those under whom they served.

After the Central Railway was reached, some 1,000 German Askaris were collected at Morogoro, the weaker members, strays, and prisoners who had fallen behind in the German retreat, but desertion from the German lines was practically unknown, and efforts to tamper with the loyalty of serving German Askaris were conspicuously barren of result.

CHAPTER II

(i) SITUATION FROM THE GERMAN POINT OF VIEW AT THE OUTBREAK OF WAR.

THE geographical position of German East Africa in 1914 has been described in the foregoing Chapter, and, as it was a factor of much importance in determining the German Commander's plan of campaign, map number one should be consulted again.

The situation from General von Lettow's point of view may best be given from his own account.

As he says, it was clear that the fate of German East Africa would be settled—as would that of all Germany's oversea possessions—in Europe.

Could the German military authorities in East Africa with their " small forces prevent considerable numbers of the enemy from intervening in Europe, or in other more important theatres, or inflict on their enemies any loss of personnel or war material worth mentioning? "

He answered " this question in the affirmative ".

He formed the opinion that the British troops " would allow themselves to be held only if we attacked them or at least threatened them at some really sensitive point "; that " protection of the Colony (G.E.A.) could not be ensured even by purely defensive tactics "; that it followed that " it was necessary not to split up our small available forces in local defence, but, on the contrary, to keep them together, to grip the enemy by the throat and force him to employ his forces for self-defence ".

He at once decided that the vital point for a successful attack, or the threat of it, was the Uganda railway, " the main artery of the British territory, an object, which, with a length of quite 440 miles, was extremely difficult for the enemy to protect, and would, therefore, if effectively threatened, require a large part of his troops for the purpose ".

His first plan contemplated the concentration of all the troops at his disposal for the purpose in the north near Kilimanjaro, where he regarded the numerous German settlers as " already deployed for the object " of " tackling the enemy at a sensitive point, the Uganda railway ".

21

The Governor, Dr. Schnee, however, who, as a consequence of some mistaken interpretation of an instruction from his Government as to the command of the forces, at first seems to have been a considerable hindrance to his military commander, disagreed with the proposal, and Pugu, a day's march west of Dar-es-Salaam, was selected as the point of concentration.

An offensive against the British forces with the Uganda railway as its first objective was the broad strategic plan of General von Lettow.

(ii) SITUATION FROM THE BRITISH POINT OF VIEW.

The British authorities were quite alive to the danger involved by the proximity of the Uganda railway to the enemy frontier 60 miles away from it, a danger accentuated by the intrusion of the great salient of Kilimanjaro into British territory.

Several lines of advance from the German Protectorate were available, notably the road from Moschi to Taveta and thence to Voi by the Tsavo river to Tsavo railway bridge, and to the north-west of Kilimanjaro via Longido and Kadjiado. Native tracks, too, provided a means by which small raiding parties could approach the railway.

The protection of the line from Voi to Tsavo became accordingly a matter of instant importance on the outbreak of hostilities.

Defence, then, was the main consideration governing the first military arrangements in British territory.

(iii) THE GERMAN FORCES.

General von Lettow gives the numbers of those enrolled during the war on the German side as 3,000 Europeans and 11,000 askaris, and states that in this total were included all non-combatants serving with the troops.

14 Field companies* formed the permanent troops of the Protectorate on the outbreak of war.

Of these 6 were concentrated at Pugu, 2 were at Mwanza in the west on Lake Victoria and 2 in the Kilimanjaro area.

---

* Von Lettow states that each field company was brought up to a strength of " about 16 Europeans, 160 Askaris and 2 machine guns ".

The carriers, of which there were some 250 attached to each company, formed a regular source of reinforcements to a certain extent.

With some of the Police natives who were placed at the disposal of the military authorities and old askaris who were recalled to the colours four new companies were at once formed, bringing the total number up to 18.

Extra machine guns and small field guns were added as necessary and as the supply permitted.

The tactical value of the field companies was impaired by the fact that, of the 14 original units, 8 were armed with 1871 pattern rifles firing smoky powder.

The white personnel not needed for the field companies was formed into " Schützen " (sharpshooter or rifle) companies.

These latter were later broken up and their personnel used to replace European casualties in the field companies.

Various rifle clubs had been formed shortly before the war, but the variety of patterns of sporting rifles owned by the members and the consequent impossibility of standardising the ammunition had become the subject of suggestions to arm these clubs with " a uniform military weapon " which, when hostilities began, had not been brought to completion.

Companies were grouped as necessary in detachments which bore the names of their commanders.

Except for the guns of the Königsberg, used later in the campaign, the German artillery was of old pattern and not numerous.   Von Lettow mentions " our two 1873 pattern field guns " at Tanga and the impossibility of " a prolonged fire for effect " as the smoke disclosed the positions of the guns at once.

As will be seen, however, artillery, in which by the beginning of 1916 the British were preponderantly superior, exercised no effect upon the tactics of the campaign.

(iv) THE BRITISH FORCES.

The military forces of British East Africa, Uganda and Nyasaland, were dangerously weak for the protection of their long frontiers against such a plan of offence as that contemplated by General von Lettow.   Their weakness was aggravated by their distribution at the outbreak of war, as will appear.

In British East Africa and Uganda were two battalions of the King's African Rifles, the 3rd (East Africa) and 4th (Uganda) strengthened for the purpose of certain punitive operations by four companies of the 1st Battalion (Nyasaland).

These units were recruited from local native tribes and officered by British regular officers seconded for the purpose.

Approximately the full strength of the regular forces of the two opposing nations in East Africa was the same until 1914.

At the end of July six companies were near the river Juba engaged with the Marehan tribe, others were scattered along the northern frontier or remote from communication. One company was at Zanzibar.

Garrisoning the protectorates proper were two weak companies at Bombo and Entebbe, half a company at Nairobi, half a company of Abyssinian recruits being trained as mounted infantry and another half company marching back from relief on outpost work.

The three battalions contained in all twenty companies of infantry of a strength varying from 125 to 75. To each company was allotted one machine gun, 20 in all.

There was no artillery.

The battalions had no organised reserve. 100 ex askaris were re-enrolled after the commencement of the war.

No regular organisation for the employment of such Europeans as might be available for war service was in existence, though some training had been possible in one or two semi-military associations.

Some 3,000 European males were available for service, and some of the Indian population had undergone some military training.

An advantage possessed by the German Protectorate Forces, but which was lacking on the other side, was the presence of the Commander of the forces in the Protectorate throughout his period of command. This meant constant supervision, the existence of a staff, and such preparation for war as was possible.

The value of these circumstances was at once apparent in the immediate assumption of the initiative by General von Lettow.

The King's African Rifles were supervised by an Inspector General whose headquarters were in London and who visited the Protectorate from time to time during his period of office for the purposes of inspection.

There was thus no local chief command, and the advantages just mentioned as resting with the German Commander were absent on the British side.

On the declaration of war martial law was proclaimed in the British territories and the formation of a volunteer force ensued.

The senior officer of the King's African Rifles assumed command of the forces, and efforts were made to form a staff and to extemporise some of the services for which a regular staff exists.

The volunteer force was organised in various units and services, some for general and some for local (district) service.

The same difficulty as confronted the German commander-in-chief in arming his white personnel arose here.

The Europeans of British East Africa possessed many sporting weapons but of different types, and standardisation of ammunition was here also impossible.

Delay and disappointment ensued.

Two instances of what may occur to any country which in present day conditions has to rely upon oversea sources of supply of war material.

(v) THE CHARACTER OF GENERAL VON LETTOW VORBECK.

The campaign in German East Africa is influenced during the whole of its course by the remarkable and forceful personality of the leader of the German forces.

The original plan, its prosecution, the whole conduct of operations from the German side reflect the character of this fine soldier, and before proceeding to note the initial dispositions and movements of the two sides, an attempt to estimate that character must be made.

General von Lettow had reached German East Africa in January, 1914.

His book " My Reminiscences of East Africa " is, quite spontaneously and with no intention to that end, for it is characterised by extreme modesty so far as his own predominant share in the success of his troops is concerned, a revelation of his military talent.

25.

It shows a commander who, by his personal character, courage, example and professional skill, maintained his native troops throughout the Great War as an efficient body of fighting soldiers. During the whole of that period, though constantly on the retreat, the German forces never failed under the guidance of their officers whenever an opportunity was offered to them, to inflict severe losses, and, from time to time, defeats, on their opponents.

General von Lettow surrendered after the armistice with some 1,400 rifles a force which he describes as then " still maintaining itself proudly and victoriously in the field ".

If victory had eluded him, there cannot be two opinions as to the pride and the justice of it, and its commander's further description of it as " always ready for action and possessed of the highest determination " is no more than fair tribute.

Natives, as is well known, react sensitively to the personality of any white man who aspires to lead them, and General von Lettow's ascendancy and influence over his askaris was remarkable to a degree.

He had had experience of native and bush warfare which he gained in the Herero and Hottentot campaign of 1904-06 where he was wounded. He served on the staff of General von Trotha and as a company and detachment commander. Here he formed a high opinion of the fighting capacity of certain of the native tribes of Africa and was to test his theories to some effect ten years later.

He had qualified at the Staff College, had seen other service in China in the Boxer Rebellion, and his peace service had alternated between regimental duty and the General Staff.

Determined, courageous, professionally efficient and impervious to fatigue, he was an ideal leader for such a campaign.

Though there were of course some failures, generally speaking, the leadership of his subordinates was worthy of their chief.

The generalship of von Lettow will be referred to from time to time, but enough has been recorded here to show that his presence was a source of great strength to his soldiers.

(vi) THE INITIAL DISTRIBUTIONS OF BOTH SIDES FOR WAR.

As has been pointed out, it was no passive defence that the German commander had in mind.

If he had had his way, there would have been a considerably greater concentration of strength in the Kilimanjaro area.

Such a bold policy did not, however, commend itself to the Governor nor indeed to many others, and only sound professional soldiers seem to have supported the Chief Command in its proposals.

The concentration at Pugu already mentioned represented the influence of the less venturesome spirits with whom the preservation of what had been achieved in the process of colonisation in the Protectorate weighed more than purely military considerations.

There was, however, a considerable strength collected in the north in the Aruscha and Moschi districts under the command of Captain von Prince, a retired officer, a former associate at the Military College of General von Lettow of whose forward policy he thoroughly approved. He was later killed at Tanga and von Lettow mentions the loss there of " the splendid Captain von Prince ".

Under Captain von Prince at Himo were two field companies, another police company and a force of local white volunteers.

At Mwanza in the west on Lake Victoria were 2 field companies.

In the south were a field company at Masoko near Neu Langenburg and a platoon, from another field company at Ujiji, at Bismarckburg on Lake Tanganyika.

So far as the British local forces were concerned, at the beginning of August, 1914, no offensive action was in contemplation, and the defence of British territory and the vulnerable Uganda railway was the first consideration in the north.

Voi was occupied by a very small force which was subsequently strengthened. This place became the junction of the railway line to Taveta with the main line and a place of much importance.

Companies of the King's African Rifles were recalled from outlying situations nearer to the centre of future activity, the

27

Masai border was watched by hastily raised formations, and by the second week in August the frontier was under observation by white volunteers or native scouts.

Efforts to establish some defence at Mombasa included the use of old saluting guns and muzzle loaders as artillery.

The real defence of Mombasa and of Zanzibar at this time, however, rested with the Royal Navy.

In the south measures of a similar kind had been taken in Nyasaland.

Here by the 10th August energetic measures had produced a force, assembled at Fort Johnston on the south of Lake Nyasa, consisting of 4 companies of the 1st K.A.R. and 2 reserve companies with four 7 pdr. muzzle loading guns as artillery.

After the German steamer " Hermann von Wissmann " had been put out of action by the British steamer " Gwendolen " at Sphinxhaven, the Nyasaland Field Force was transported by lake steamers to Karonga where the defence of the 70 mile frontier formed by the river Songwe was necessary.

The Belgians, whose Government had at this time adopted a strictly defensive attitude, watched their frontier from Mount Sabinio to Lake Kivu and from the south of this lake along the Russisi valley to the northern end of Lake Tanganyika.

It is impossible, and, for the special purpose of the present record, unnecessary, to give more detail than is required for a general idea of the situation existing at this time.

(vii) THE OPENING MOVEMENTS.

In pursuance of his general plan General von Lettow, on August 13, ordered von Prince at Himo to capture Taveta. This instruction the latter carried out on the 15th and Taveta remained in enemy occupation until it was reoccupied by the British force under General Smuts in March, 1916.

The German Commander-in-Chief also ordered Captain Schulz from Moschi to destroy the (Uganda) railway line and a similar instruction was conveyed to Captain Bock von Wulfingen at Mwanza.

Both these efforts failed.

The occupation of Taveta apparently put heart into the Governor and his advisers, for, immediately afterwards, his

28

objection to any forward movement seems to have been overcome, and the force at Pugu was transferred to the Usambara area which it reached at the end of August.

Leaving three field companies for the protection of the coastal area, the bulk of the German forces were concentrated in the Kilimanjaro districts.

General von Lettow followed, reaching Moschi, where he established his headquarters, in early September.

Before his arrival patrol encounters had taken place in consequence of his orders that the Uganda railway should be destroyed at various spots.

The most important event at this time was an insurrection in the Giriama country some 50 miles north of Mombasa on the coast. This called for the detachment of K.A.R. at a time when no troops could be spared from the centre of activity.

(viii) THE FIRST BRITISH REINFORCEMENTS.

After preliminary negotiations between the departments of state concerned, the Government of India had agreed to send help to the small forces in East Africa.

It was decided that one force, a Brigade, should be sent to capture and occupy the ports of German East Africa, while three battalions of infantry were to be sent to help in the defence of British East Africa.

Brigadier General Stewart, in command of these reinforcements, reached Mombasa with the leading portion of his forces on September 1.

The troops from India were sent with a view to offensive action, and it would appear that their strength was based on the assumption that it would take a force of 8,000 to reduce German East Africa.

In view of the numbers which were eventually employed, it may be well here to consider the administrative problems involved in such an enterprise as that contemplated. Seeing that a force of 8,000 was originally considered adequate, even a cursory examination of the local obstacles to campaigning argues much misconception behind the estimate.

(ix) CONSIDERATION OF THE ADMINISTRATIVE PROBLEMS CONNECTED WITH OFFENSIVE ACTION AGAINST GERMAN EAST AFRICA.

The climate, physical features, and endemic tropical diseases of German East Africa have been described in the previous chapter.

Ignorance or neglect fully to appreciate their consequences caused much waste of money, man power, and effort, and great suffering to the troops, much of which could have been avoided, if a carefully worked out scheme of action had been planned in advance.

Since an adequate strength is essential for the successful prosecution of military operations in war, the basic problem in East Africa in view of the general prevalence of tropical disease was the maintenance of the fighting strength.

The chief means of resistance to the tropical diseases which have been mentioned—in addition to prophylactic measures as to the efficiency of which opinion was not unanimous—is the maintenance of the body in a well nourished condition and so best able to withstand infection or shake off its consequences. As to this there was no divergency of view.

Normally, as explained by General von Lettow in his " Reminiscences of East Africa ", an official on a long journey took with him " from eleven to thirteen bearers in addition to two or three personal servants ".

This staff was regarded as essential to convey supplies in such quantities and of such kind as would enable the traveller to proceed with reasonable safeguard for his health.

Von Lettow makes this observation in explanation of a " storm of indignation " aroused by his action—under pressure of his supply difficulties—in reducing the attendants of each of his European personnel to five.

Regular and adequate supplies, in the quantity judged by competent authority to be required to keep the troops in good heart and bodily comfort, were absolutely indispensable to the maintenance of the fighting force at a strength enough for the performance of its role and at a figure which might be relied upon when calculating the conditions of its tactical employment.

For this was required a carefully arranged system and allowance of transport based on the minimum amount of rations and other means of maintaining the health of the troops at a normal level.

Transport was thus a consideration of the first importance.

It was necessary that enough transport should be made available to ensure as good and plentiful a ration as might be necessary reaching the forces regularly.

Transport in the East African campaign of 1914-18 was by rail, motor vehicles, animal-drawn vehicles and native carriers or porters.

In the case of all these methods, except in that of the railways which, when in going order, could be relied upon for regular work along their lines, a variety of difficulties attended the employment of the three remaining means of conveyance.

The use of animal drawn transport was restricted to areas which were free from tsetse fly, and where this pest was rife, mechanical transport or porters were the two alternatives.

Mechanical transport became useless while the heavy rains lasted, and porters remained then the sole means of transport.

As the forces grew, enormous quantities of native carriers were needed and, while they could be worked in any kind of weather in which movement was possible, as the campaign proceeded they became more and more difficult to procure, and what amounted to compulsion was resorted to from time to time.

The conditions in which native carriers worked frequently involved close proximity to the enemy, and hastily raised porter units which had not been under competent direction for some time often stampeded and were lost.

There was no real difficulty in getting enough supplies to the bases at the scene of war, but to get them from the depots to the fighting troops was, as will be seen, constantly well nigh impossible.

As the advance went on, the lines of communication became steadily longer, and a difficult situation was made far more troublesome by the fact that all along these lines the personnel of the transport medical and supply services was just as liable to disease as anyone in the firing line. As the lines lengthened,

31

so did the incidence of disease increase and the situation become less favourable to the prospect of a regular supply of even reduced rations reaching the advanced formations.

Roads, as has been explained, were virtually non-existent and when some kind of track had been prepared it was always rough and difficult and often quite impassable in wet weather.

The effect of these difficulties will appear in the course of the account of the campaign, and remedies for future consideration will be considered, but enough perhaps has here been outlined to give an idea of what obstacles exist to prevent free and rapid movement in a campaign in tropical Africa.

CHAPTER III

(i) THE DESTRUCTION OF " PEGASUS " AND " KÖNIGSBERG ".

AS HAS BEEN* stated in the preceding chapter, the first reinforcements from India reached British East Africa in early September, 1914.

Their arrival made possible some welcome readjustment of the British Forces which, on September 4, represented approximate strengths distributed as follows:—

Uganda	650
Kisumu	200
Nairobi (Headquarters)	1,100
Masai Frontier	20
Magadi Railway	150
Voi-Tsavo	1,000 (of these 600 were at Voi).
Variously distributed posts	320
Mombasa	250

while between Jubaland, Northern Uganda and Zanzibar was distributed a strength of some 600.

The ensuing weeks were spent in various advances by the German forces up the Tsavo river valley, against the Magadi line, and from the south in the coastal area against Gazi.

None of these enterprises succeeded, though in the north-west the Germans succeeded in capturing Kwijwi island in Lake Kivu from the Belgians.

One of the most important events at this time was the sinking of H.M.S. " Pegasus " by the " Königsberg " at Zanzibar on September 20.

The remainder of General Stewart's force (India Expeditionary Force " C ") reached the scene of hostilities and was employed to reinforce the troops at Kadjiado on the Magadi line, Voi and Mombasa, the balance being sent to Nairobi.

After the mishap to the " Pegasus " the " Königsberg ", which disappeared after her coup at Zanzibar, commanded the local waters, the nearest British ships of war being 1,800 miles away.

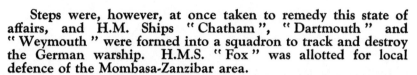

Steps were, however, at once taken to remedy this state of affairs, and H.M. Ships "Chatham", "Dartmouth" and "Weymouth" were formed into a squadron to track and destroy the German warship. H.M.S. "Fox" was allotted for local defence of the Mombasa-Zanzibar area.

On October 30 the "Königsberg" was located up the river Rufiji near Salale. Two days later, as a result of H.M.S. "Chatham" opening fire, the German ship moved two miles up the river. Finally, after the consideration of different methods of dealing with her, the "Königsberg" was shut in by a blockade of the river mouth, a blockship being sunk in one of the channels.

It was suggested that a combined naval and military expedition should deal with the trapped warship, but the difficulty of the undertaking and the recent experience of Tanga, which will be referred to, combined with the lack of sufficient military strength, prevented the co-operation proposed.

In the end, an air reconnaissance having revealed the exact situation of the "Königsberg" on March 25, 1915, the latter was attacked on July 6 by two monitors ("Severn" and "Mersey"), which steamed four miles up the Rufiji, aided by observation from aeroplanes.

The destruction of the "Königsberg" was finally encompassed on July 11 when her magazine blew up and she was set ablaze. Though the ship was destroyed, however, her loss in the words of General von Lettow, "had at least this advantage for the campaign on land, that the whole crew and valuable stores were now at the disposal of the Protective Force".

By the energy and skill of Lieutenant-Commander Schoenfeld the ten guns of the warship were salved and used thenceforward in the land operations.

Another stroke of good fortune enheartened the German forces about this time.

On April 4, 1915, H.M.S. "Hyacinth" sighted a vessel steaming westwards towards the mainland north of Zanzibar.

This was assumed to be a coal ship for the "Königsberg" and was chased into Mansa Bay where the "Hyacinth" shelled her, set her on fire, and left her sunk. No examination was made of her, it being assumed that her cargo was coal and therefore no coal from her would reach the "Königsberg".

The vessel, the "Rubens", was in point of fact a store ship with rifles and other warlike stores. 1,800 rifles, 4½ million rounds of small arm ammunition, and a couple of light field guns and 4 machine guns were among the stores.

The cartridges were considerably damaged by sea water and permanently affected to a considerable extent, but much remained of extreme value and the moral effect of the episode was substantial. " The arrival of the store ship aroused tremendous enthusiasm ", says von Lettow, " since it proved that communication between ourselves and home still existed ".

The venture was repeated later with greater effect, as will be seen.

(ii) THE SECOND REINFORCEMENTS FROM INDIA.

To return to the situation on land.

At the end of October, 1914, despite the seizure of Taveta and Kwijwi on Lake Kivu, no real change had taken place.

British territory was intact, except for the small area round Taveta, efforts against the railway had been resisted, though it was difficult to prevent damage by small enemy parties, and nothing decisive had taken place.

It was clear that the magnitude of an advance into German territory had been much underestimated in all its bearings.

Early in the war the despatch of an expeditionary force from India, additional to that under General Stewart already mentioned, had been considered.

As has been stated, a force of 8,000 all told was judged to be strong enough for the reduction of German East Africa.

The information available about the possible theatre of operations was most scanty, and in some respects, e.g. the attitude of the natives towards German rule and the willingness of the Askaris to fight, incorrect.

Steps were taken to prepare a force for the purpose indicated and its commander, Brigadier-General Aitken, was selected.

The apparently imminent entry of Turkey into the war as an enemy of the allied Powers, however, caused the indefinite postponement of the venture.

Enemy cruisers were sailing the Pacific and South Atlantic and constituted a serious menace, and the importance of denying to them bases on the east coast of Africa was apparent.

Raids in the Indian Ocean by the cruiser " Emden " lent additional urgency to the situation.

The despatch of the expeditionary force (I.E.F. " B ") was again decided upon and the capture of Tanga was assigned to it as its first task.

This task accomplished, an advance along the Usambara, in co-operation with a force moving southwards from the Kilimanjaro region, was to follow.

The operations were all to be carried out under the authority of the India Office and the General Staff in India.

The force was composed of two Brigades, the (27th) " Bangalore Brigade " and an " Imperial Service Brigade ".

The former was under Brigadier-General Wapshare, the latter was commanded by Brigadier-General Tighe.

The period of uncertainty between the original selection of the force for the expedition and its despatch had resulted in the employment of some of its component units on other tasks, and many of the regiments which eventually sailed for East Africa were strangers to each other and unknown to their commanders.

Two of General Wapshare's battalions saw their Brigadier for the first time the day before they embarked.

General Tighe met none of the units of the formation under his command until six days before he sailed.

The Commander of the Force did not see any of the troops under his command any earlier than did his second Brigadier.

The quality of some of the Indian troops was open to doubt.

Experience was to show that only the very best troops can be relied upon in severe bush fighting, and that mutual knowledge of each other, acquaintance with a common method of fighting, and confidence throughout the whole force are indispensable in the type of fighting which this force was to encounter.

Any critic of what occurred at Tanga should, before passing judgment, give full weight to the grave disadvantage which was faced by the General in command of a force in which mutual knowledge, uniform training and experience of working were largely lacking.

Other factors which were adverse to complete efficiency may be gathered from a perusal of official accounts.

All these drawbacks combined to add greatly to the difficulties of the force commander and were entirely beyond his control.

The issue of a new pattern rifle, to which the units were unaccustomed, just before embarkation, and the improvisation of machine gun detachments, some of which had no opportunity of practising with their guns before sailing, made matters no easier.

The total force, about 8,000 strong, sailed from India on October 16, 1914.

The convoy with the force arrived opposite Mombasa, keeping out of sight of the coast, on October 30.

A consultation at Mombasa resulted in a unanimous decision that the original plan to land at Tanga and move along the Usambara railway towards Kilimanjaro should be followed.

Information as to the situation at Tanga was very indifferent.

The German concentration in the Kilimanjaro area was known, and it was considered that any defence of Tanga was most improbable.

Some hastily prepared sketch maps (incidentally inaccurate in some important details) and the knowledge of someone who had visited the place, represented the data upon which the plans were evolved.

Little appeared to be wanting to make success as unlikely as it well could be.

General Aitken learned that a truce, concluded with the German Governor to safeguard Tanga and Dar-es-Salaam, would compel him to give notice of an attack and thus forego the great advantage of surprising the enemy.

(iii) THE ATTACK ON TANGA.

As has been stated, it was regarded as improbable that any resistance would be offered to a landing in force at Tanga, and, before proceeding to a brief account of the venture, it may be well to consider the situation from the enemy point of view.

General von Lettow had been aware of the despatch of reinforcements for the second time from India for some weeks before the latter were directed on their objective, and had made the natural deduction that an offensive would follow. He had " from general considerations always expected a hostile attack on a large scale" near Tanga, and in October personally reconnoitred all the country adjacent to that port.

Information that "fourteen hostile transports and two cruisers" had appeared off Tanga received on November 2, caused the immediate operation of the German plan of defence, and on the same day troops left Moschi and the posts along the railway line for the threatened point.

By the evening of November 3, German G.H.Q. were established at Korogwe, and at 4 a.m., von Lettow, with his headquarters, was on the railway 4 miles west of Tanga, his troops were on the move to the scene of action, and he was ready for the attack.

This he proposed to await in positions of his own selection after allowing the British landing to take place.

The total force at his diposal eventually would seem to have been 1,200 rifles with 3 small field guns and 8 machine guns.

The convoy from Mombasa with H.M.S. "Fox" reached a rendezvous 15 miles east of Tanga just before dawn on November 2, and the warship entered Tanga harbour at 7 a.m., where its commander gave the German District Commissioner the option of surrender or bombardment. The latter said it was incumbent upon him to refer the decision to superior authority and left the warship for the shore, ostensibly to refer the matter for settlement.

The necessity for reference by the naval commander to the General in command 15 miles out at sea, sweeping operations which the naval commander considered necessary in view of possible mines in the harbour and its entrance, and other circumstances combined to produce considerable delay, and it was not until late on the night of November 2 that the leading elements of the attacking force landed on the beach at Tanga. The delay was of course of the utmost value to the enemy.

Tighe's Brigade was first set on shore as a covering force, and by dawn on November 3 had taken up a position and its advanced troops had moved towards the town and about 6 a.m. received the first fire from the German troops in position. Other units of the Brigade advanced, and before long the Brigade reserve was in action.

A counter attack by enemy troops which had shortly before been detrained, drove the whole British force then in action, back in retreat. A British unit took up a defensive position covering the beach, and it was not until dawn on November 4 that General Aitken's force stood complete on land.

At 12 noon on that day the force moved forward in attack.

It is interesting to note that no reconnoitring patrols were sent out to any appreciable distance and that the bush was dense. *Runners only were of use for the maintenance of lateral communication.* The force advanced on a broad front.

At 2.30 p.m. touch with enemy patrols was established.

Landing straight from the ships in which they had been confined since leaving their own country, and tired out before they began the advance in consequence of want of rest, the rank and file of an Indian regiment could not face the rifle and machine gun which now met them and crowded back in disorderly retreat.

Their action left a gap in the attack and the closing of another unit to the right to fill it gave a wrong direction to the advance.

A second Indian unit, already shaken by the failure of the first, was dispersed by the attack of swarms of wild bees disturbed by the bullets through the trees.

The right of the advancing force, however, formed by the 101st (Indian) Grenadiers, advanced steadily, but, in spite of plucky attempts, failed to gain the enemy trenches.

A second German counter-attack caused the retreat and final disintegration of the Grenadiers in the dense bush.

Other troops remained fighting in the streets but without touch with the rest of the force.

A retirement was effected by the units which remained collected to a defensive position on a railway cutting where a third counter-attack was repulsed.

Meanwhile stragglers and followers had collected in a disorderly rabble on the beach.

With darkness the enemy retired; a bugle call intended to rally a portion of the force had been taken to convey a signal for retirement, a meaning attached to such a call in the German peace training.

Tanga, on the night of November 4-5, therefore, was in the possession of neither side.

General Aitken's first intention was to renew the attack again on the night of the 4th—it was bright moonlight—with the bayonet.

Assuming that the German forces were still in position, and realising that he had only two units which were not badly shaken by the day's experience and that these two regiments had sustained heavy casualties, the British Commander gave up the intention of a night attack, and eventually on the following day decided on the abandonment of the venture and re-embarkation.

By 4 p.m. on November 5 the evacuation was complete without any real attempt at interference by the enemy, and on the 8th the convoy left for Mombasa.

It is without the scope of this book to describe in detail any operations in East Africa before the assumption of command there by General Smuts, nor is it proposed to offer any criticism on such operations except of a very general nature.

There are one or two points upon which comment may be made, however, as this reverse was instructive in several respects.

It is of interest to observe that, as a consequence of the difficulty of communication and acquiring information in bush country, after the fighting on November 4, each commander thought that his opponent had remained in the position occupied at the end of the fighting.

The British General considered that his opponent was still in position and held Tanga, a patrol encounter had led to this assumption, and, it was not until the arrival of a British officer under the white flag, with a request for a truce to remove the wounded, that General von Lettow countermanded orders for the occupation of a fresh position considering that the defence of Tanga against such a strong force as that opposed to him would be a matter of difficulty.

The decision of General Aitken to abandon the attempt after his reverse was apparently sound in view of the condition of his troops, and one is forced to speculate on the consequences of a further attack by the German forces, had their commander been fully aware of his opponent's plight.

Two points emerge as worth attention, for they were to be emphasised over and over again in the next three years.

First, the extreme difficulty of communication in the bush, and

Second, the tremendous advantage resting with a properly conducted defence in bush country.

In conclusion, in fairness to the British Commander, there may be noted several conditions quite beyond his control which imposed a very severe handicap upon him.

    (i) His own ignorance—due to the short time placed at his disposal to become acquainted with them—of the character and capacity of many of the individuals and units hastily collected for his force.

   (ii) Similar unavoidable ignorance on the part of his Brigadiers.

  (iii) The eleventh hour issue of new pattern rifles and machine guns with which units were unfamiliar.

  (iv) The lack of cohesion and mutual knowledge of units.

   (v) Their indifferent fighting value in some instances.

  (vi) Practical ignorance of the local situation at the point of attack.

 (vii) Misleading and hastily prepared sketch maps.

(viii) The enforced abandonment of surprise as a factor in the attack.

Whatever opinion may be formed of the actual conduct of the operation, much blame must surely attach to the superior authorities who failed so signally to appreciate what fighting in such a country as German East Africa entailed in the way of preparation, if success were to be looked for.

What one is compelled to regard as the careless manner in which the authorities concerned with the conduct of operations generally entered into this particular campaign must be held to be the cause of endless waste and delay.

The British casualties at Tanga were:—

Killed:	Officers	31
	Other ranks	328
Wounded:	Officers	32
	Other ranks	278
Missing:	Officers	5
	Other ranks	143

A total of 817.

The German losses were 84 killed (5 officers) and 80 wounded (9 officers) and 1 missing. They captured from their opponents 10 machine guns, a large quantity of ammunition and many rifles.

Not the least advantage, however, to the German forces was the establishment of their Commander's high prestige and a great increase in the *moral* of his Askaris.

41

(iv) SITUATION AFTER THE REVERSE AT TANGA.

After a careful review of the situation it was decided that a renewal of offensive action was at the time out of the question.

In the circumstances just described an overestimate of the enemy's numbers was perhaps natural.

General Aitken's troops were landed at Mombasa.

On November 22 the War Office took over control of the operations in East Africa from the India Office.

One intelligible consequence of the episode at Tanga was a general nervousness on the part of different adjoining British territories.

On November 28 British warships disabled the engines of some German merchant vessels lying at Dar-es-Salaam to prevent stores reaching the " Königsberg " then blockaded in the Rufiji delta.

At the end of the month, Karungu, on the eastern shore of Lake Victoria, in British territory, was developed as a base. Some activity took place in the shape of operations by armed steamers on the Lake.

In Uganda, on the western shore of Lake Victoria, where the British forces had established a line of posts in German territory along the Kagera river, German troops advanced on November 20 and engaged British posts on the river.

The attacks were all repulsed, but at Fort Kyaka a withdrawal was effected in order to draw the enemy northwards into a counter-attack, but the movements ended in a slight withdrawal by the British post. All forces remained in German territory.

Reinforcements from the Indian forces now came up and the situation became more satisfactory.

In early December the enemy was again pushed back.

Fever, however, attacked all but the local units, and for some months activity on either side was confined to patrols.

The occupation of the Kigezi frontier by the Belgians to the west of the Kagera eased the situation greatly.

In the Voi-Tsavo area, Mzima, 30 miles west of Tsavo, and Maktau, about the same distance west of Voi, were now held by British detachments which faced the enemy on the Lumi river where the latter held a strong position on Salaita Hill and others on the foothills of Kilimanjaro.

Other small British posts were at Kasigau, some 20 miles south of the Uganda railway, and Loosoito, 35 miles north-west of Mzima.

Many patrol actions took place as the consequence of enemy activity against the railway.

(v) REORGANISATION OF BRITISH FORCES.

The British forces were reorganised into two commands, a " Mombasa area " which included Voi and Tsavo and a " Nairobi area " which included the Magadi line and Uganda.

General Aitken was recalled to England and Major-General Wapshare assumed command in his place on December 17.

Subject to the adoption of a generally defensive attitude, minor offensive undertakings which might seem feasible were agreed to.

Reinforcements on a scale which would allow of offensive operations against enemy territory were at this time, the end of 1914, unprocurable.

A redistribution of the forces best calculated to meet the policy decided upon was carried out and ensured the occupation of the following areas:—

Uganda, the East Lake Area (Kisii and Karungu), Nairobi, Magadi, Voi-Tsavo, Coastal, Mombasa, Giriama and Zanzibar.

Shortly afterwards a squadron of the 17th (Indian) Cavalry and the 130th Baluchis were sent from India, and reached Mombasa on February 8, 1915.

At the same time improvements were effected in staff organisation.

(vi) OPERATIONS IN COASTAL AREA SOUTH OF MOMBASA.

Attention was now directed to the coastal area south of Mombasa, where the enemy was active in British territory, and on December 17 a force of 1,800 with 6 machine guns and 5,500 porters (the area was infested with testse and very unhealthy) under General Tighe moved southwards from Msambweni near the coast.

Opposition to the advance was slight, in consequence of naval co-operation along the coast line, and on December 25 General Tighe occupied Jasin, in enemy territory, on the coast, just over the border, after a surprise attack on the place.

The main force was now placed at the mouth of the Umba river on its northern bank with outposts at Jasin and other places. The strength of the force was largely affected by sickness.

The enterprise at once attracted the attention of General von Lettow, who, following his custom, proceeded without delay to make a personal reconnaissance on the spot and decided to attack the British force holding Jasin.

By the evening of January 17 he had collected 9 companies and two guns 7 miles south of Jasin and issued his orders for an attack on the following morning.

A previous attack delivered before the German concentration was completed had been repulsed on January 12, and the detachment at Jasin had been reinforced in consequence.

Eventually a heavy attack developed at dawn on January 18.

Holding off attempts to relieve the garrison by the main body and other detachments, the enemy compelled the surrender of the post on the morning of January 19 after a fine defence. To quote General von Lettow: " Both friend and foe had been in an unpleasant situation and were near the end of their nervous strength ".

In view of the unhealthy climate, and in agreement with instructions from London to " give up risky expeditions ", all the troops remaining of the original force were withdrawn from the south, and on February 9 were at their starting point.

Another unpleasant reverse—though on this occasion a gallant resistance had been offered—was to be recorded.

100 killed, 130 wounded and 276 prisoners represented the British casualties.

The enemy losses were also severe: 88 (9 officers) killed, 186 wounded. Among the latter was General von Lettow.

(vii) DEFENSIVE POLICY ORDERED.

Once more the War Office ordered " a definitely defensive attitude from the Lake to the Sea ", and the remaining three months of good weather could not be employed in forward movements.

Such preparations for an eventual forward movement as could be made, however, were taken in hand, and perhaps the most important was the construction of a railway from Voi towards Taveta. The War Office sanctioned the proposal and by March arrangements were well forward.

Again activity was confined to small ventures and patrol work.

Sickness, the consequence of endemic tropical disease, now took heavy toll of all troops except those locally recruited.

(viii) SHORTAGE OF TROOPS.

At this juncture the question of man power came to the front and various measures were suggested and investigated with but little result locally. It was now realised that " the fighting (in East Africa) requires troops not only brave *but very highly trained* ".

There was *some* help available, and if it was small in bulk, it was admirable in quality.

400 Rhodesians—the 2nd Rhodesian Regiment—reached Mombasa on March 14, 1915. These were followed on May 6 by the Legion of Frontiersmen of whom 1,166 arrived in the 25th (Service) Battalion Royal Fusiliers.

These additions, however, though valuable, were a small proportion of what were needed.

The Belgians were approached and the seeds of future co-operation were planted, and 500 Belgian soldiers, as has been stated, prolonged the British Kagera line.

The reverse at Jasin caused the withdrawal of the British post at Shirati, in German territory, on the eastern shore of Lake Victoria, and the border here was quiet except for the work of patrols.

Among the questions which came up for consideration in any scheme for an advance in force was the matter of transport, at once of paramount importance and extreme difficulty.

An interesting feature of transport organization at this time was the concurrence of the local civil authorities in the application of compulsory service for filling the establishments of porter units.

Transport difficulties, which would be enormously augmented by the imminent rainy season, in the Magadi area decided the withdrawal of the forward posts on Longido mountain to Besil where an entrenched camp was established.

(ix) MINOR ENTERPRISES.

One result of the withdrawal was an immediately increased boldness of action on the part of enemy patrols.

Among minor enterprises at this time (March, 1915) was an attack on Salaita Hill made from Maktau to divert the attention of the enemy from a post at Loosoito which was threatened. Salaita was to be the scene of several events, and upon this occasion the British force was accompanied by what was then a unit of a novel kind in African warfare, a volunteer mechanical transport company. Heavy rain gave a foretaste of what was to be experienced in the use of this form of transport in the months to come. As a consequence of panic on the part of the native carriers the two machine guns of the force were abandoned. This experience also was to be repeated often later on in the case of porters.

On April 15, General Wapshare, on transfer to another sphere of employment, handed over the local command to Brigadier-General Tighe who was to retain it until he, in turn, handed it over to General Smuts some 10 months later.

General Tighe suggested certain forward movements, but the general position was such that the War Office could not accede to his proposals. No reinforcements were available and General Tighe was instructed to protect British Territory and to undertake nothing more.

In the light of after events, there can be no doubt that this decision was eminently sound.

On May 1 Brigadier-General Malleson was appointed to command the Voi area.

Enemy enterprise against the railway became so frequent and effective that reinforcements for the Voi area were sent.

In the minor operations at this time a force was provided with donkeys for transport purposes. The experiment was not repeated, as the braying of the donkeys revealed to the enemy the position of the force which would otherwise have remained concealed.

A useful innovation was introduced by the commanding officer of the Rhodesian Regiment while in command at Mzima. He divided his patrols into " fighting patrols " not less than 100 strong with machine guns, and " reconnoitring patrols " with one white officer or N.C.O. with two of the K.A.R. Askaris. The first able to fight, the second able to avoid being detected.

Increasing sickness among the ranks of the non-African units and the steady diminution of strength which ensued added to the enemy activity, and the task of protecting the railway became more difficult.

(x) OPERATIONS IN LAKE AREA.

On Lake Victoria the armed steamers had been organised as a naval force, and on March 11 the German steamer " Muansa " was attacked and driven ashore but afterwards refloated and repaired.

On June 23 an expedition against Bukoba, on the western shore of Lake Victoria, an administrative centre with a powerful wireless installation, undertaken by the British flotilla and a force of 1,700 rifles with 2 guns and 12 machine guns under Brigadier-General Stewart, resulted in the destruction of the wireless station and the fort.

(xi) FURTHER REVERSES.

On June 25 the railway from Voi was completed to Maktau, the advanced British post.

In the first week of the month the enemy had established himself, some 400 strong, at Mbuyuni, 10 miles west of Maktau towards Salaita Hill, and thence constantly harassed the railway working parties by means of patrols.

General Malleson accordingly resolved to drive off the enemy force from Mbuyuni. On the afternoon of July 13 he moved from his entrenched camp at Maktau with two columns; one 762 rifles with 3 guns and 8 machine guns and the other 461 rifles with 3 machine guns.

The force which was his objective was estimated at 600 rifles.

The venture was unsuccessful and a retirement to Maktau ensued.

The casualties of the two columns were 33 killed and 165 wounded with 13 missing.

After this reverse the Maktau force remained on the defensive and the enemy continued his raiding.

In the following month, on August 13, the post at Kasigau was captured by a surprise attack and 38 prisoners were taken, the remainder of the garrison making their way back to the British lines.

The subsequent success of a British ambush of a German patrol of 60 rifles which lost 32 of their number killed was something of an offset to the constant success of the enemy.

At the end of August an offensive operation was attempted against the German post which had been established on Longido after the British withdrawal to Besil.

Some 450 rifles, of which perhaps half were of mounted units, and machine guns left Besil on September 16 and, halting at Westerok for two days, reached the foot of Longido mountain at dawn on September 20.

The German force was on the look out and well entrenched, and repulsed the attack which sustained a total casualty list of 56.

In the coastal area the British forces had been reduced in consequence of slight activity on the part of the enemy.

On August 27 a patrol of 70 Indian Infantry was driven back with heavy loss, 15 being killed, and though small reinforcements—being all that could be spared—were sent to this region, where in its unhealthy swamps disease was lending effective aid to the enemy, little was possible except bare defence of the posts.

Raids on the railway increased and became of daily occurrence, and with the continuous shrinking of the British force, even defence threatened to become problematical.

Both the Naval and the Military Commander reported the situation as " very serious ".

(xii) OPERATIONS IN THE SOUTH.

German attacks on Abercorn and Karonga were repulsed in September, 1914.

The enemy controlled Lake Tanganyika and on November 17 two armed German steamers appeared at Kituta and a party of the enemy landed and effected some destruction, including that of the British steamer " Cecil Rhodes " which they found beached on the shore.

Re-embarking, the same party repeated their action 2 days later at Kasalakawe, but was attacked by a British detachment aided by a Belgian battalion returning to their own territory after coming to the aid of the local forces.

The latter were further strengthened by units raised from the white population of Northern Rhodesia and Nyasaland.

A period of inactivity followed until May, 1915, when it was reported that the enemy was endeavouring to repair the steamer " Hermann von Wissman " which had been disabled at Sphinxhaven on Lake Nyasa. A force of 180 rifles and 2 machine guns left Fort Johnston in two steamers and reached Sphinx-haven on the night of May 29-30, and the column landed about a mile south of Sphinxhaven in the early morning of May 30.

The enemy steamer was then destroyed beyond possibility of repair and the column re-embarked.

On the Rhodesian frontier a fortified post at Saisi was held by a mixed British-Belgian force, in all some 400 rifles with 2 small guns and 3 machine guns, under Lieutenant-Colonel Hodson.

Information was received of an impending attack which materialised on June 28, and was repulsed.

Major O'Sullivan relieved Lieutenant-Colonel Hodson and on July 25 a stronger enemy force returned to Saisi and on July 31 summoned the force, which was suffering very consider-ably from hunger and thirst, to surrender. On its refusal an atttempt was made to assault its position and on the night of August 2-3 the enemy retired.

The post was evacuated, after being destroyed to render its fortifications useless, at the end of October.

Some further reinforcements arrived from the Union of South Africa and in December 1915 Brigadier-General E. Northey was appointed to the command of all the forces in this area.

The forces from Southern Rhodesia which had been watching the Caprivi Zipfel co-operated with Union troops in that area, and, on the final surrender of German South-West Africa, this particular portion of the theatre of operations ceased to be a cause for anxiety.

(xiii) THE ENTRY OF THE UNION OF SOUTH AFRICA INTO THE CAMPAIGN.

The arrival of some reinforcements from South Africa has been mentioned. They were the forerunners of far greater strength from that source which had become a possible means of supplying a large number of troops on the successful conclusion of the campaign in German South-West Africa.

Conversations were started with the Union Government and, as a first result, it was decided that two Staff Officers should proceed from South Africa to British East Africa to become acquainted with the position there and to report as to how best the Union might aid the local forces.

These two officers returned to the Union in November, 1915, and it became clear that strong reinforcements would be made available.

The various stages of the formation of the contingent from the Union need not be described in detail, and it is enough here to record that at the end of March, 1916, 1 Mounted Brigade (3 regiments), 1 unbrigaded mounted regiment, 2 Infantry Brigades (4 battalions each), 5 Batteries of Field Artillery and a Field Ambulance and a General Hospital representing a total strength of some 18,700 had been despatched to the scene of operations in the north. Between 1,000 and 2,000 had also gone to the Nyasaland side.

The resumption of the offensive thus became possible.

On February 9, 1916, command of Lake Tanganyika on the water was secured, and arrangements for active co-operation by the Belgian forces became the subject of negotiation about the same time.

In October, 1915, the authorities decided that " 10,000 men " would be required to readjust matters, and a month later that no general offensive should be attempted without " substantial reinforcements ".

(xiv) GENERAL SIR H. SMITH-DORRIEN APPOINTED TO CHIEF COMMAND.

It was further decided that an adequate staff should be furnished from Great Britain, and the command of all the forces was offered to General Sir Horace Smith-Dorrien who accepted the charge.

Lord Kitchener was strongly against any forward action, and expressed the opinion, truly enough, that the strength which was contemplated, would prove inadequate.

The local forces were further strengthened by the addition of 2 Indian battalions which had become available on the withdrawal of the Indian Corps from France.

General Smith-Dorrien had decided upon a general plan to advance from Maktau and from the Magadi line on the Kilimanjaro enemy concentration and to endeavour, by landing a force on the coast—Dar-es-Salaam was the point he suggested for the landing—to encircle the main enemy body. The remaining British forces on the frontiers together with the Belgians would deal with the remainder of the German forces.

He proposed to wait until after the rainy season before taking any forward action.

(xv) REORGANISATION.

Meanwhile General Tighe made all possible preparations for the execution of the plan described above, and in these preparations a reorganisation of the forces occupied an important place.

The troops on the Magadi line became the 1st Division, those in the Voi-Tsavo area forming the 2nd Division, and a separate command was made of the troops in the Lake area.

On December 6 the position at Kasigau, which was unpleasantly near the railway and had been re-occupied after its capture by the Germans in August, was overwhelmed and captured by the enemy.

The German detachment there held 5,000 British rifles to their different posts which were occupied for the protection of the Uganda railway.

51

CHAPTER IV

(i) GENERAL SMITH-DORRIEN COMPELLED TO RESIGN OWING TO ILL-HEALTH IS SUCCEEDED BY GENERAL SMUTS.

GENERAL Smith-Dorrien became very seriously ill on his way to Africa and on arrival at Capetown was compelled to return to England. On February 6, 1916, his vacant post was offered to, and accepted by General J. C. Smuts, who left Pretoria on the 11th and arrived at Mombasa on February 19.

At this time the 1st Mounted Brigade (van Deventer), the 2nd Infantry Brigade (Beves) and 5 field batteries of the S.A. Field Artillery had reached the scene of operations, and, while the new Commander-in-Chief was on the water, an action of a severe nature had taken place at Salaita.

(ii) MOVEMENTS BEFORE THE ACTION AT SALAITA.

As the chief participants were the 2nd S.A. Infantry Brigade, this affair may be described in some detail, though it actually took place before the arrival of General Smuts.

Before the venture was undertaken, Mbuyuni, the scene of the British repulse on July 13 in the previous year, was found to be evacuated and was occupied, with the result that the enemy abandoned Kasigau and the detachment there rejoined the German main force.

In the first week of February the railway from Voi had been carried up to the Njoro Nullah, 3 miles from Salaita, where an entrenched enemy force was reported to be in position.

A reconnaissance in force on February 3 established the truth of the report as to the presence at Salaita of an enemy force, and the latter threatened a turning flank movement upon which the British column retired.

The recently arrived 26th (South African) Squadron of the Royal Flying Corps carried out reconnaissances, but could observe no trace of the German forces, an experience with which they were to become daily familiar over the thick bush.

On February 4 General Smith-Dorrien, then still actually in chief command, cabled asking General Tighe when the capture of Salaita might be expected.

The latter replied that he hoped to advance against the enemy at Salaita between the 12th and 14th and that the rail-head, then at Serengeti, would be at the former place 3 or 4 days later.

(iii) THE ACTION OF SALAITA.

The conduct of the operations against Salaita was entrusted to Brigadier-General Malleson, the Commander of the 2nd Division.

He had at his disposal the—

1st East African Brigade
2/Loyal North Lancashire Regiment,
2nd Rhodesia Regiment,
130th Baluchis,
2nd South African Infantry Brigade
the 5th, 6th and 7th S.A. Infantry,
Divisional Troops
Mounted Infantry Company,
Belfield's (Mounted) Scouts,
4th Indian Mountain Artillery Brigade (less one Battery),
No. 28 Mountain Battery (six 10-pdrs.),
No. 1 Light Battery (two 12-pdrs.),
Calcutta Volunteer Battery (six 12-pdrs.),
No. 3 Heavy Battery (two Naval 4-in. guns),
No. 4 Heavy Battery (two 5-in. hows.),
4 Armoured Cars,
Volunteer Machine Gun Battery,
61st Pioneers,

in all 6,000 rifles, 41 machine guns and 18 guns.

The enemy force was estimated at 300 rifles with machine guns and no artillery.

In point of fact it amounted to between 1,300 and 1,400 rifles, 12 machine guns and 2 small guns.

An interesting comment on the difficulty of aerial reconnaissance in this terrain!

The German local commander was Major Kraut.

6 more Field Companies, say 1,000 rifles, were distributed between Taveta and Salaita.

The total German force was, however, much inferior in strength to the attacking force.

The reconnaissance on the 3rd had established nothing beyond the fact that the hill was well entrenched, with some clearance of bush on the east and south-east approaches.

On the night of February 11-12 the Division bivouacked at Serengeti, having left Mbuyuni during the previous day.

Before leaving Mbuyuni, Lieutenant-Colonel Byron, commanding the 5th S.A. Infantry, with the C.O.'s of the two other regiments of Beves' brigade, the 6th and 7th, interviewed the Brigade Commander and sought information as to the nature and scope of the advance of which they had been advised as about to take place, and were told that, as far as was then known, the object of the advance was to eject the enemy from his position but nothing further, but that no doubt detailed orders would be given.

Map number two should be referred to.

On receiving Divisional Orders the same evening at Serengeti to the effect that his brigade would attack the enemy position from the north-east, General Beves, accompanied by his Brigade Major, interviewed the Divisional Commander, General Malleson.

Beves was an officer of long service. He had served in the Anglo-Boer War as a Captain in a regular British infantry regiment, had remained in South Africa and held the command of the Transvaal Volunteer Force until 1912 when he became Commandant of Cadets in the Union Defence Forces. He had commanded an Infantry Brigade under General McKenzie in German South-West Africa, and was brought up to the north to command the Infantry Brigade which accompanied General Botha's forces in the final operations in the campaign in that country.

He was an officer of regimental experience, careful, and attentive to the comfort and needs of those whom he commanded, a fact which contributed largely to the outstanding marching performance which his infantry achieved on the occasion last referred to.

He sought from his Divisional Commander an indication of his proposed action subsequent to his occupation of the enemy position, should he be successful.

54

It seems that he was told that no discussion on the Commander-in-Chief's orders would be permitted and he then pointed out that—

   (i) no element of surprise in the attack would be possible, as his brigade would be in full view from Salaita while still several miles distant;

  (ii) enemy reinforcements from Taveta—7 miles from the enemy position—and possible counter attack from that direction would have to be taken into account;

 (iii) as he was a battalion short, the 8th Infantry not having arrived, he asked for another battalion in view of the danger which might threaten his exposed flank; and

 (iv) intensive artillery preparation, and artillery co-operation during the attack were absolutely essential to make success possible, and that in the event of counter attack and an engagement in the bush, artillery co-operation would be almost impossible.

He was told that there would be adequate support from artillery, *that the assault would be over before any forces could reach the scene of action from Taveta,* and that, in any case, Belfield's Scouts would be thrown out well in advance towards Taveta to give timely warning of any move from that direction.

Beves' Brigade moved out independently from Serengeti in a north-westerly direction at 5 a.m. and did not rendezvous at Njoro drift with the other units of the force, nor did Beves receive any orders beyond those which had been given to him overnight.

As he had a wide detour to make, only the East African Brigade and Divisional Troops moved to Njoro where the drift was reached at 6.45 a.m.

The plan (see map number two) contemplated an attack on Salaita Hill (called by the Germans Oldorobo) from the north, the direction of the attack being selected because from the same quarter the enemy had upon two occasions delivered effective counter-attacks. *Counter-attack again might therefore be looked for.*

This attack from the north was to be delivered by the (2nd) South African Infantry Brigade to which were added Belfield's (Mounted) Scouts and two armoured cars to cover Beves' outer flank and a mountain battery and the Volunteer Machine Gun unit.

The rest of the artillery was to come into action behind the 1st East African Brigade which was kept as a general reserve at Njoro.

Aeroplanes reported some newly dug trenches extending to the north from the base of Salaita.

Beves' force moved from Serengeti in column of route at 5 a.m., and at 7 a.m., 3,000 yards north of Salaita (A), moved on in mass for another 1,000 yards.

Here (B), the Brigade adopted a looser formation and came under fire from light field guns which, however, was not serious.

Deployment was, therefore, deferred until 8 a.m., when at a distance of 1,000 yards from the foot of the hill (C), and to the north-east of it, the 7th S.A. Battalion was sent forward with the 5th (less two companies in Brigade reserve) in echelon on its left. The ground here sloped gently southward and was covered with thick bush of varying density.

At the same time the 6th S.A. Battalion was sent forward on the right of the 7th, being ordered to extend the line of the latter but to refuse its own right. This presumably with the danger of counter-attack from the north in mind.

The effect of these movements was to establish an attacking line moving against the enemy position from the north and north-east with its right thrown back facing towards Taveta.

With the exception of the two companies in reserve, the whole brigade was in the attacking line. The mountain battery was in rear of the extreme right of the advance.

At 9 a.m. the 7th S.A.I., when 300 yards from the hill, came under heavy rifle fire from the enemy entrenchments at its base over a partially cleared field of fire.

The 6th S.A.I. meanwhile had crossed the line of trenches which had been reported by the air reconnaissance and found them unoccupied. The view that these were " dummies " and sited with a view to confusing the advance was probably correct, and might hold good with regard to the entrenchments on the face of the hill as well. Only those at the bottom of the hill were occupied.

The Artillery shelled the slopes but, as von Lettow writes: " the numerous English howitzer shells did very little damage ", and the action of the artillery had no appreciable effect upon the enemy rifle and machine gun fire.

At 11 a.m., General Beves, after consultation with Lieutenant-Colonels Byron and Freeth, commanding the 5th and 7th S.A.I., respectively, ordered these two battalions to withdraw in a north-easterly direction, with the 6th S.A.I. covering the movement.

Just about this time information was received from Belfield's Scouts—which had so far been out of touch in the bush on the northern flank—that an enemy force was moving on Salaita from Taveta.

This was Schulz's Detachment advancing by order of Major Kraut " to make a decisive attack on the enemy's right or northern wing " (The South African Brigade).

It reached its objective about 11.30 a.m. while the withdrawal was in process and in view of the short notice of its approach came as a surprise.

Delivered by 600 rifles, the attack caught the brigade at a disadvantage in the bush and caused it to give way in considerable confusion.

While the onset was held long enough to allow the 6th S.A.I. and Mountain Battery to get away to the north-east, contact between these units and the remainder of Beves' force was lost and not re-established until the point of the deployment for attack had been reached.

Several platoons of the 7th S.A.I. on the left of the Brigade lost touch and retired in disorder on the East African Brigade.

While it is clear that the retirement after the shock of the counter-attack was far from orderly, it would seem that no panic set in.

The ultimate extrication of the force was covered by a finely fought action by the 130th Baluchis who resisted a bayonet attack delivered by the enemy on the portion of the line between the Indian Regiments and the Loyal North Lancashire Regiment which stampeded the baggage and ammunition mule train.

The East African Brigade was held back until 10.45 a.m. and came into action against the eastern face of the hill. This advance was held up at the edge of thick bush about 1,000 yards from the enemy trenches by a heavy fire.

The losses were not severe, 138 all told in the South African Brigade and slight in the remainder of the force, but the moral effect of the reverse following previous defeats was considerable and added further to the spirit of the German Askaris.

That such a plan as that which has been described could succeed was almost impossible, and quite so in face of an enemy of the calibre of General von Lettow.

There seems to have been little co-ordination of the efforts of the two brigades, and it is not easy to understand why move-ment on the part of the East African Brigade should have been postponed until a quarter of an hour before General Beves decided to retire after having been in action for four hours.

The enemy was occupying positions which he had held for months, and the action was fought over ground which he had thoroughly reconnoitred and was unknown to his attacker. His troops were hidden in bush, and, as has been seen, the estimate of his strength, made by the British staff, was purest guess work and quite incorrect. That no effective estimate was, in the circumstances, possible seems to have been overlooked.

The preconceived notion, already referred to, that no inter-ference by the enemy could take place before the capture of Salaita had been effected, argues an unwarrantable confidence in such a doubtful situation.

If it is also realised that the German commander, though his own troops were completely concealed, was able to watch every movement of the force advancing to attack him, and that to counter-attack on the first appearance of a good chance to do so had already been shown as the invariable practice of the enemy commanders, the whole scheme bears evidence of lack of prepara-tion and a too ready acceptance of success as assured.

This lack of appreciation of what such an attack might involve seems to have been shared with the higher command by numbers of the South Africans.

The following comments, made by an experienced South African officer well able to form an opinion, who was present in a responsible position with the Brigade, may be quoted with advantage:—

" With the exception of the Brigadier and a few of the senior officers, the South African Brigade entered light-heartedly into the Salaita operation, and with totally inadequate appreciation of the seriousness of the task which had been set them.

' The enemy, after all, were for the most part only native troops '—an attitude on the part of South African troops which is readily understandable. The lesson of Tanga

had failed to penetrate, for, again, was not the attacking force
' only Indian troops '. To this attitude of arrogance, due to
ignorance, Salaita came as a rude shock, and the first step in
the South African's education in a type of warfare new to
him was that the well led native Askari soldier was an
opponent to be reckoned with.

That the South African troops were not highly trained—
either in a general or specialised sense—goes without saying,
as the period between the recruitment of the Brigade and its
first action with the enemy (including sea transportation)
was only a matter of weeks, but they were by no means
wholly untrained troops, for both in the commissioned and
non-commissioned ranks was to be found a high proportion
of individuals with previous A.C.F. (Active Citizen Force)
training and even previous war service. Want of steadiness
or other shortcomings in the Salaita action could be more
accurately attributed therefore to lack of experience rather
than to lack of training.

This experience, however, was quickly gained* and
Salaita expedited its acquisition. Soon the South African
infantrymen realised that mutual safety—either in attack or
defence—lay in keeping in touch with the rest of the platoon
and in reliance on his entrenching tool, rather than in
individual attempts to seek cover—generally somewhere to
the rear."

The lesson was taken to heart by the fighting soldiers in the
ranks and with commendable rapidity and was turned to
advantage in their next encounter.

The price paid for this object lesson, in the way of casualties,
was light, if all the possibilities of a reverse in such circumstances
are realised.

There were defects in the staff arrangements of the Division.

The establishment of stretcher bearers was inadequate and
unnecessary wastage occurred in the firing line, as it took four
men instead of two to get the wounded out.

No signal and field telegraph section accompanied the South
African Brigade, and during the action there was no communica-
tion with Divisional Headquarters or with the East African
Brigade and it was impossible to direct the covering artillery fire.

---

* General von Lettow writes about the South Africans "many of
whom", he says, "were very young". "After the action of Oldorobo,
however, we observed that the enemy sought very thoroughly to make good
the deficiencies in his training."

No Field Ambulance section was attached to the South African Brigade and hence there was no means of rapidly evacuating wounded.

The nearest dressing station was two miles away through the bush at Njoro Drift.

A decreased accuracy in the fire of the enemy when advancing in the counter attack reduced the casualties of the South Africans considerably.

(iv) GENERAL SMUTS REACHES EAST AFRICA.

General Smuts reached Mombasa on February 19 and was met by Major-General Tighe whose first report was of the reverse at Salaita a week earlier. The two Generals left for the Voi-Maktau railway at 8 p.m. on the same day, reaching Mbuyuni on the following morning where the Officer Commanding the 2nd Division, Brigadier-General Malleson was in command.

The new Commander-in-Chief went forward and viewed Salaita—still held by the enemy—at a distance of 1½ to 2 miles.

He then proceeded to Kadjiado and thence to Longido West from where good view of Meru and Kampfontein, Engare Nanjuki and Ngare Nairobi was obtained.

On February 23 he arrived by motor at Nairobi where G.H.Q. was situated and where he formally assumed the chief command.

General Smuts' first step, after acquainting himself with the situation at G.H.Q., was to divide the latter into two parts—Advanced G.H.Q. and Base G.H.Q.—a plan which held good throughout his period of command.

Advanced G.H.Q. comprised the Chief of the General Staff with some General Staff officers and representatives of all the administrative services. All heads of the latter, however, remained at Base G.H.Q., under the control of the D.A. and Q.M.G. A portion of the General Staff also remained behind.

Advanced G.H.Q. accompanied the Commander-in-Chief and remained with him.

On February 29 the Commander-in-Chief, with advanced G.H.Q., returned to Mbuyuni to make preparations for an early advance.

The general situation was at this time as follows:—

In the south Brigadier-General E. Northey had reached the scene of his command about the same time as General Smuts arrived at Mombasa, and found his force, about 2,500 rifles, scattered from Karonga on Lake Nyasa to Abercorn on Lake Tanganyika, a front of 250 miles.

The units which made up the strength mentioned were the 1st K.A.R. (six companies) a small regiment from the Union of South Africa, a contingent of white volunteers from the Rhodesias and the Northern Rhodesia Police, an African unit recruited from the local natives of that territory.

About 1,500 rifles of the enemy, also disposed along the frontier at defensive posts, faced him.

General Northey at once started the reorganisation of his troops.

To the north and west in February, 1916, the Germans occupied the island of Kwijwi, Belgian territory on Lake Kivu.

On the Uganda frontier the British held the line of the Kagera river which, with the high mountains of the Kigezi district, Lake Kivu and the river Russisi flowing from that lake into Lake Tanganyika, formed a strong German defensive line.

In the same month command of the waters of Tanganyika had been finally secured by the British steamers and a Belgian offensive was in contemplation.

CHAPTER V

(i) GENERAL SMUTS UNDERTAKES THE OCCUPATION OF THE KILIMANJARO AREA.

ON February 23 General Smuts cabled to the War Office stating his readiness to effect the occupation of the Kilimanjaro area before the rainy season. Approval of this course was received two days later.

Eventually the operations undertaken before the advent of the heavy rain broadened out to include an extensive flank movement by van Deventer as far west and south as Kondoa Irangi, but nothing so ambitious was contemplated in the first instance.

(ii) THE SCENE OF OPERATIONS.

The following is a general description of the country which was the scene of the ensuing operations.

The dominant physical feature was the huge mountain of Kilimanjaro which completely barred all movement except on the lower extremities of its foot hills.

The country through which movement was possible— though at a varying rate of advance and throughout most of it with much difficulty—lay between Kilimanjaro and the Pare mountains to the south. Along these mountains ran the Ruwu river which emerged from Lake Jipe, which lies on the eastern side of the Pare and is ten miles long by two miles wide. This river was, as were all considerable rivers in German East Africa, unfordable and infested by crocodile, and running westward towards the larger Pangani which it ultimately joined, combined with the mountain range and fever-laden swamps and dense bush to produce as formidable an obstacle to movement on the south of the theatre of operations as did Kilimanjaro on its north.

Between the two hostile forces flowed to the south the Lumi river which was crossed by the only road which existed and which led to Taveta. The river was an appreciable obstacle lending itself to a strong defence and covered the enemy front from Kilimanjaro to Lake Jipe.

To the west of Taveta lay two hills, Latema and Reata, also a very strong natural position. A high spur of Kilimanjaro,

Chala, overlooked the stage of the operations to be described, which was about five miles from east to west and of which the boundaries were, on the north and south, Kilimanjaro and the Pare, and on the east and west the Lumi and Latema and Reata, respectively.

An enormous advantage accrued to the German Commander in that his troops entirely concealed—for air reconnaissance revealed no sign whatever of their presence in the bush—and holding every height which rose from the dense vegetation, on ground which they had previously reconnoitred thoroughly, could observe each movement of any importance made by the forces advancing against them. The latter were almost as ignorant of the terrain as the former were well posted in its features.

For the most part the country was covered with dense bush, though the latter occasionally thinned out here and there, and comparatively open ground appeared.

Map number four may assist to a better understanding of the position.

An advance from the direction of Longido was less complicated by the physical features of the country as aids to defensive action than by difficulties of water and supply which imposed a definite limit on the numbers of troops which could be subsisted.

(iii) THE BRITISH FORCE.

The forces at the disposal of General Smuts for the Kilimanjaro operations were as follows:—

Under his immediate command:

2nd Division.

Major-General Tighe.

Mounted Troops.

4th S.A. Horse.
Belfield's Scouts.
M.I. Company (L. N. Lancs.).
No. 10 (R.N.) Armoured Car Battery.

1st E.A. Brigade (Infantry).

Brigadier-General Malleson.

2/L. North Lancs. Regiment.
2/Rhodesia Regiment.
130th Baluchis.
3/K.A.R.

63

Kashmir Rifles.
Volunteer M.G. Company.
Artillery.
No. 2 Group, R.A.
4th Ind. Artillery Bde.
No. 6 Field Battery.
No. 8 Field Battery.
No. 9 Field Battery.
No. 10 Heavy Battery.
134th Howitzer Battery.
2nd Div.: Ammunition Column.
Div. Signal Company.
½ Coy. Faridkot Sappers and Miners.
Section E.A. Pioneers.
2nd Division approximate total rifles: 4,700.
19 guns.
34 machine guns.
Detached Force.
Brigadier-General van Deventer.
S.A. Mounted Brigade (van Deventer's own brigade).
1st S.A. Horse.
2nd S.A. Horse.
3rd S.A. Horse.
3rd S.A. Infantry Brigade.
Brigadier-General Berrangé.
9th S.A. Infantry.
10th S.A. Infantry.
11th S.A. Infantry.
12th S.A. Infantry.
Artillery.
2nd S.A. Field Brigade (Nos. 2 and 4 Batteries).
28th Mountain Battery.
S.A. Div. Ammunition Column.
Detached Force approximate total rifles: 5,900.
14 guns.
28 machine guns.
Force Reserve
Brigadier-General Beves.
2nd S.A. Infantry Brigade (Beves' Brigade).
5th S.A. Infantry.
6th S.A. Infantry.
7th S.A. Infantry.
8th S.A. Infantry.

Artillery.
No. 5 S.A. Field Battery.
No. 12 Howitzer Battery.
Force Reserve approximate total rifles: 3,800.
6 guns.
16 machine guns.
Under G.H.Q.
No. 26 Squadron, R.F.C.
61st Pioneers.

The detached force which moved by the west of Kilimanjaro was the 1st Division and was composed as follows:—
1st Division.
Major-General Stewart.
Mounted Troops.
E.A. Mounted Rifles.
1 Squadron 17th (Indian) Cavalry.
K.A.R. M.I. Company.
Infantry.
25/Royal Fusiliers.
29th Punjabis.
129th Baluchis.
Cape Corps Battalion.
1/K.A.R. (4 companies).
E.A. Machine Gun Company.
Artillery.
No. 1 Group R.A.
1st S.A. Field-Battery (Nos. 1 and 3 Batteries).
No. 7 Field Battery.
27th Mountain Battery.
1st Div. Ammunition Column.
Div. Signal Company.
¼ Company Faridkot Sappers and Miners.
No. 1 Division approximate total rifles: 4,000.
18 guns.
22 machine guns.

(iv) THE GERMAN FORCES.

Of the total strength of the German forces which was given on page 22, the proportion which faced General Smuts in the Kilimanjaro area in March, 1916, was approximately 5,200 rifles, of which force 700 were Europeans. With each company were enlisted porters in addition, as well as some irregulars.

3

The force was furnished with 49 machine guns and two field artillery batteries with 7 guns, while 11 other guns were in various defensive positions.

The company was the administrative unit and companies were allotted to different detachment (abteilung) commanders, each detachment being known by its commander's name.

The following were the detachments in the Kilimanjaro area at this time:—

Fischer:	7 companies, 1,200 rifles, 10 machine guns.
Schulz:	5 companies, 1,000 rifles, 10 machine guns.
*Kraut:	5 companies, 900 rifles, 8 machine guns.
Stemmermann:	4 companies, 700 rifles, 6 machine guns.
Adler:	3 companies, 600 rifles, 9 machine guns.

Near Meru (Aruscha District) were 400 rifles and 2 machine guns (1 company and a small detachment) and a company, 200 rifles with 2 machine guns each, was at either end, north and south, of Lake Jipe.

The whole of the forces which operated against General Smuts in March, 1916, at Latema-Reata and the subsequent engagements down to Kahe were under the personal command of General von Lettow Vorbeck.

(v) AN APPRECIATION OF THE SITUATION.

In estimating the value of the criticism which will be offered on the operations in the Kilimanjaro area it must be borne in mind that, when the first movements were started, General Smuts had only been in East Africa for fourteen days which he had occupied in a hurried tour of his immediate command, and had visited G.H.Q. at Nairobi, as well as Kadjiado and Longido to the west of Kilimanjaro.

He knew *nothing* of the officers of the British and Indian armies who held commands and staff appointments, and had barely taken over chief command from Major-General Tighe who had a complete knowledge of the local situation.

Beves' S.A. Infantry (2nd) Brigade had taken part in the engagement at Salaita under Brigadier-General Malleson, but van Deventer's S.A. Mounted and Berrange's 3rd S.A. Infantry Brigades joined the Field Force only just before the operations began.

---

* Major Kraut was second in command to General von Lettow.

Staff work at G.H.Q., where South African officers had arrived with the new Commander-in-Chief, was bound to be unusually difficult.

The expected advent of the rainy season, however, made it imperative that an advance should be made at the earliest possible moment, and the risks and difficulties inherent in the process of " swapping horses while crossing the stream " had to be taken.

In these circumstances it would be merely reasonable on grounds of prudence that the recently arrived Commander-in-Chief of the British forces should refrain, as far as possible, from intervening in matters of detail, administrative or tactical, until the operations should have concluded and better opportunity of judging the characteristics and capacity of his subordinates should have been afforded to him.

As early as December, 1914, Major-General Aitken had expressed the opinion that " carefully organised operations against the Moschi area would produce the best immediate results ".

Major-General Tighe, with the approval of the War Office and the concurrence of General Sir H. Smith-Dorrien after his appointment to the chief command in East Africa, had made preparations for such operations before the arrival of General Smuts, and the plan included simultaneous advances on the west and east of Kilimanjaro on the Aruscha-Moschi-Taveta line.

General Smuts accepted the plan in its broad form, and, eventually, after such changes in detail as he considered necessary, put it into effect.

The situation which confronted him was as follows:—

The enemy occupied as his main position roughly the area Salaita-Taveta-Muyoni with a detachment watching towards Longido.

He held Salaita (recently strengthened), useful as a pivot of manoeuvre or to cover a withdrawal of his forces to the south.

His troops were concealed in thick bush, here abundant, and the area in his possession was well reconnoitred and entrenched and prepared with avenues and clearings which could be covered by machine gun and rifle fire.

He had already, at Salaita on February 12, scored heavily against the British force at Mbuyuni, largely in consequence of a faulty plan of attack by the latter which was carried out piece-meal, and of isolated offensives and of the omission to hold reserves in hand.

The German Commander's dispositions were unknown to the other side and he was lying very close and gave no indication of showing his hand.

His information was far better than that of his opponent.

It was reasonable to assume that General von Lettow was aware of the change in the command of the British forces, and of the nature of the tactics which the latter would adopt. General Botha's campaign in German South-West Africa had recently been brought to a successful issue, and wide and, as far as possible, rapid turning movements might be expected. To use von Lettow's own words: " One was bound to hit on the idea that the enemy encamped east of Oldorobo did not intend to get his head broken a second time on that mountain ".

That the enemy would stand if an enveloping movement became a serious threat was highly improbable. As in German South-West Africa, so here would his strategy be dominated by the need for keeping his relatively small force as strong as possible for as long as he could do so. To maintain the high *moral* of his askaris would naturally too be his concern, and he would probably only fight when conditions precluded any serious chance of envelopment.

The fall of Salaita, combined with the appearance of a mounted force, free to move westward from the foothills of Kilimanjaro, would probably decide him to retreat.

(vi) GENERAL SMUTS' SCHEME.

On March 4 General Smuts' troops were disposed as follows:—
     1st Division (Stewart): Longido.
     2nd Division (Malleson) (less detachments): Mbuyuni and Serengeti.
     1st S.A. Mounted Brigade (van Deventer): Mbuyuni.

The 2nd S.A. Infantry Brigade (Beves) with one field and one howitzer battery was kept under the hand of the Commander-in-Chief as a " Force Reserve ", and he also retained van Deventer's Mounted Brigade at his own disposal.

It is now possible, having von Lettow's full and careful account of the campaign, to give the dispositions of the enemy and sketch map number three shows generally the dispositions of the forces engaged.

The arrival of the 3rd S.A. Infantry Brigade (Berrangé) completed all the preliminary movements which had been carried out by March 5.

General Smuts' general scheme was as follows:—

The 1st Division (Stewart) to cross the country (bush and waterless for 35 miles) between Longido and Engare Nanjuki, and thence to advance between Meru and Kilimanjaro to Boma Jangombe with the ultimate object of cutting the enemy retreat by the Usambara railway.

To Stewart von Lettow opposed a force (Fischer) of 1,000 rifles.

Stewart was to move on March 5, two days before the main advance on Taveta would begin.

(vii) OPERATIONS BEGIN.

On March 7 van Deventer with his own (1st S.A.) Mounted Brigade and the 3rd S.A. Infantry Brigade (Berrangé) was to leave Mbuyuni and Serengeti in the evening, and, after a night march to the Lumi river, seize the high ground round Lake Chala and move against Taveta.

The 2nd Division (Malleson) was ordered to advance against Salaita and, supported by the army artillery, entrench a line facing the hill on the morning of March 8.

The Force Reserve was to move to the Lumi on the night of March 7-8 behind van Deventer and remain there disposable as events might suggest.

General Smuts accompanied the Force Reserve.

On March 8 the movement by the north was revealed by clouds of dust to von Lettow who had looked for activity in that quarter as " the direction of the enemy's airmen showed his evident interest in the country one or two hours north of Taveta ". He adds " this enveloping movement rendered the Oldorobo position, to which we owed many successful engagements during the course of the year, untenable ".

The German commander then decided to deploy his troops for a fresh stand on " the mountains which close the gap between the North Pare mountains and Kilimanjaro to the westward of Taveta ". Latema and Reata, mountains which command a nek over which the road to Kahe passes, were selected as the positions for defence, and thither on the night of March 8-9 was ordered Major Kraut with his detachment. The movement was covered by Schulz who remained holding the mountain of North Kitovo which commanded the Taveta-New Moschi road.

The extreme left of the German position was held by Stemmermann who occupied the south-eastern slopes of Kilimanjaro and secured the Rombo-Himo-Moschi road.

Leaving Mbuyuni at 3 a.m. on March 8, General Smuts reached the Lumi at 8 a.m.

Here he found the Force Reserve with one regiment of the Mounted and two of the 3rd Infantry Brigades. These troops were now disposed on the right and left banks of the river and in the afternoon were attacked suddenly, the attack being repulsed with small loss to the brigades. Desultory firing was kept up by the enemy during the night.

Salaita—as a matter of fact unoccupied—was heavily bombarded all day.

On March 9 van Deventer had reached Chala where the mounted brigade occupied the south-western and the infantry the south-eastern end of the lake.

The bombardment of Salaita was sustained until 2 p.m. when the position was occupied by troops of the 2nd Division.

Stewart had reached Engare-Nanjuki on March 7 and was continuing his advance on the following day.

During the 9th van Deventer's mounted troops and the 12th South African Infantry were engaged in desultory fashion over a considerable area with the enemy who eventually retired to the Reata-Kitovo position.

Lumi bridge, Taveta and Massowoni were occupied at the end of a day of general skirmishing.

Two important points had been recognised so far.

The first that G.H.Q. must be established in a central spot to maintain touch with the different detachments, receive reports and convey orders. While the actual distances were not great, the nature of the country made movement slow and inter-communication extremely difficult. The fact that it took two staff officers some 5 or 6 hours to cover rather more than the same number of miles illustrates the conditions clearly.

A second, and somewhat ominous, reflection was that Berrangé's infantry on the slopes of Chala, though they were scarcely out of sight of supply depots, suffered badly throughout March 10 from want of food.

The remainder of the forces had been engaged over a large area of difficult bush country for three days. There had been casualties, not heavy but all over the terrain which had been traversed. Though they were a comparatively short distance from railhead (it was the nature of the country more than the distances involved which caused the difficulties) Berrangé's infantry men were lacking essential supplies—ammunition had been expended and needed replacing. The enemy had withdrawn into a very strong position of his own selection a few miles beyond Taveta. As is known *now*, the natural strength of the position had been added to by preparation " for a stubborn defence ". An action, and it seemed imminent, would mean substantial casualties.

The present temporary discomfort of the South Africans was negligible compared with the constant hardship and scanty rations which they were fated to endure later, but it gave ample food for thought.

The shortage was to some extent due to the difficulty of communication throughout the forces and this could be remedied, but even at this early stage of the campaign the difficulties of transport and supply obtruded themselves.

Early on March 11 G.H.Q. reached Taveta, was settled in some large bandas (native huts) in Taveta early in the morning and by afternoon had located and established touch with almost all portions of the force.

From here it was possible to convey information upon which the administrative staff could base its action, present and future, for the supply and comfort, as far as possible, of the fighting formations.

Map number four will give an idea of the position of the forces on this day and may perhaps afford a rough indication of the nature of the country and the varying density of bush and forest.

On March 11 van Deventer had reached Massowoni and Mamba and was making for the Himo towards Moschi.

Beves with his brigade—the Force Reserve—was on the march from the Lumi to Taveta and was nearing his destination.

(viii) THE ACTION AT REATA.

The 2nd Division from Salaita had reached Taveta, and its commander, to whom the direction of the venture was assigned, was ordered to attack the position on Latema-Reata to which the enemy, turned out of Taveta on the 10th by the 2nd S.A. Horse from van Deventer, had retired. This enemy party was presumably Stemmermann, as Kraut had been entrenched there since the night of March 8-9.

One month earlier, on February 12, the South African Infantry (Beves' 2nd Brigade) had moved to the attack on Salaita.

Except that on the second occasion the enemy held two hills instead of one, the problems were extraordinarily similar.

In each case the German forces were on ground that they had held for the greater part of two years—and, it may be taken, had reconnoitered almost to the last bush.

In each case the defender's knowledge of the ground was as thorough as that of the attacker was defective.

In each case the German Commander of his deliberate choice held very high ground which afforded him an extensive view of his opponent's approach and movements, and, by reason of its being covered with dense bush, gave his own troops complete concealment.

The action was undertaken—see General Smuts' despatch of April 30, 1916—to determine whether the enemy was a " covering force or in such force as to threaten a counter-attack ".

Within such limits as the above condition might impose, the method of the attack and its conduct were left entirely to its commander, at first General Malleson, and, later, as will be seen, General Tighe.

The scheme adopted by General Malleson was simplicity itself, and took the form of a frontal attack unrelieved by any local movement on either flank.

At Salaita the advance on the west and north and north-east simultaneously made it difficult to decide at once which was the real attack, but at Reata, to give the action the name used by von Lettow, the intention was obvious from the start and that the attack failed is not to be wondered at.

The extreme difficulty of the country to the south, dense bush and swamp, probably precluded any flank attack from that

72

direction, and, in any case, exhaustive reconnaissance and preparation would have revealed an intention of the kind very early to the enemy, but van Deventer was close at hand to the north.

The most favourable result which could ensue as the consequence of a successful frontal attack pushed home was that the enemy would be ousted from the position but on to his line of retreat to Kahe which he could, and did, reach more or less at his ease.

The two hills Latema and Reata barred the way from Taveta to Kahe by the road to the latter place which passed over a nek between them and which was completely commanded from their heights. They rose 700 feet above the level of the plain which intervened between them and Taveta and were covered with dense bush which concealed every movement on the hills except here and there on the sky-line. The plain between the nek and Taveta was open except for scattered bush, and concealment of any movement by day from a watcher on Latema or Reata was impossible. The bush gradually became thicker as it approached the nek.

The attack began just before noon on March 11 directed on Latema on the spur which commanded the nek.

The 130th Baluchis were on the right and the 3rd K.A.R. on the left of the firing line with the 2nd Rhodesians in support—in all about 1,500 rifles.

The small strength of mounted troops, Belfield's Scouts (local East African Europeans) and a mounted infantry company, watched the flanks, and the artillery came into action at a range of some 3,500 yards.

On reaching the foot of the slopes of Latema, machine gun and rifle fire met the extended line of the attack inflicting many casualties and checking any further forward movement. The support from the artillery was of little, if any, value, as no estimate of the effect of its fire was possible.

At 4 p.m., Brigadier-General Malleson, who had initiated the attack and had been ill all day asked to be relieved of his command, his condition had become worse and he was incapable of further effort, and Major-General Tighe took his place.

General Tighe put the reserve, the 2nd Rhodesian Regiment, into the fight, but at 6 p.m. they were repulsed and compelled to retire, in consequence of a German counter-attack from Reata delivered on their left flank.

The only ascertainable damage caused by the British artillery so far was a certain number of casualties inflicted, in consequence of short ranging, upon the Baluchis and K.A.R.

The task of the Rhodesians was rendered no easier by the setting sun which shone into their eyes and threw them into sharp relief to their watching enemies in the dark bush.

At about 5 p.m. the Force Reserve were reaching Taveta, and the 5th S.A. Infantry (Byron) were ordered on to the scene of fighting.

General Tighe now ordered another frontal attack supporting the Baluchis with the freshly arrived South Africans.

This assault was also beaten back without reaching its objective—the Latema ridge near the nek—and the troops engaged in it were ordered to make good such ground as they had gained by entrenching.

It seemed now that the enemy—evidently quite comfortable despite the attacks which he had repulsed—was from such a position well able to " threaten a counter-attack ".

The Commander-in-Chief returned to G.H.Q. at dusk and ordered the 7th S.A. Infantry to be placed at the disposal of General Tighe whom they reached at 8 p.m.

At 9.15 p.m. General Tighe reported that the two battalions of S.A. Infantry with him " were just going in with the bayonet " and asked for another battalion.

This bayonet attack, well and gallantly led by Lieut.-Colonel Byron, advanced through the unreconnoitered bush " which proved to be much thicker than was anticipated ", up a steep slope, at night, in the face of machine guns, here, as always, admirably served in a position deliberately selected and prepared by the enemy.

That it failed is not surprising. That it reached the crest, and, as will be shown, two parties attained the two heights of Latema and Reata and stayed there, is a tribute alike to the leading of the actual advance and the grit of the men in the ranks.

Byron, slightly wounded, reached the nek with 20 men, but was forced to retire. He had ordered Lieut.-Colonel Freeth and Major Thompson of the 7th S.A. Infantry with portions of that regiment to make good the slopes of Latema and Reata, respectively, where they commanded the nek. An instance of sound tactical judgment.

74

Among others who, cut off in the bush, had found their way back to Taveta after these attacks, was a young officer of the K.A.R. who brought a report of an enemy force making its way round General Tighe's left flank. Making allowance for the fact that this young officer had just been through a very unpleasant experience which had temporarily left its mark on him, there was nothing in the least improbable in his report. If a way round existed, the possibility of a counter-attack on the reserve at Taveta, a few miles to the rear of Tighe's troops, would have to be taken into calculation.

There were now only two battalions—the 6th and 8th S.A. Infantry—at Taveta, and no more were available locally, and General Tighe's request for reinforcements, which presumably were to be used in further attacks, was refused by the Commander-in-Chief.

It had been impossible to prevent the abortive bayonet attack by the two South African battalions, as they were well committed to the task when General Tighe communicated his intention to G.H.Q.

Heavy and continuous firing continued through the night, but requests from G.H.Q. for a clear statement of the position produced nothing at all definite until 3.30 a.m. on March 12 when Tighe's chief staff officer reported that all attacks had failed and that the General was trying to collect the troops and restore order in a situation which seemed to be very confused.

The staff officer added that " Major Thompson and 200 of the 7th S.A. Infantry were cut off in the bush and that all attempts to establish communication with them had failed ".

All efforts to dislodge the enemy had failed also and the attack was completely disorganised. The General again asked for reinforcements.

These were again refused, and it seemed imperative, in view of the situation forward and the possibility of counter-attack at which the enemy had shown himself adept in the bush where his troops were in their element, to get the attacking force out of the bush and beyond reach of the enemy and to reduce the distance between it and the reserve at Taveta.

General Tighe was therefore ordered to retire to more open ground below the enemy position, dig in, and await daylight. He was also instructed to regard Major Thompson's detachment as a casualty.

By daybreak Tighe's force had been disengaged from the position without any interference by the enemy.

As will be seen, the latter had withdrawn. If this had not been the case, the temporary retirement of Tighe's forces would undoubtedly have been compromised, as a retirement in the bush before von Lettow's troops invariably induced the latter to counter-attack.

At dawn, before General Smuts had received information to guide him in his next movements, troops were observed on the sky line building schanzes on Latema. These were obviously British troops, as the enemy had, days before, completed all his defensive arrangements, and, in any case, would not show himself so obviously with purpose.

Accordingly all available motor vehicles at Taveta were emptied of their contents and filled with Beves' infantrymen and rushed to the hill where Lieut.-Colonel Freeth was found with 18 men while Thompson was occupying Reata with 170. Freeth had been joined by odd men from the Rhodesians and King's African Rifles who had hung on during the night.

The ridges were now made good and fighting was not renewed.

Kraut had withdrawn to the south-western slopes of Reata on the Taveta-Kahe road, where von Lettow joined him at six o'clock on the morning of March 12 and ordered a general retirement along the Kahe road towards New Steglitz where he installed his G.H.Q.

On a report from Kraut at about 11 p.m. on March 11 to the effect that the enemy had attacked and " penetrated the Reata position in great force " General von Lettow cancelled his instructions that van Deventer's mounted men, who had reached Marangu, were to be attacked next morning, and withdrew from Reata and Himo, leaving Stemmermann at the latter place to cover the movement.

Immediately after Kraut's report Byron, ignorant of the whereabouts of Thompson, was forced to retire leaving behind him Thompson and his 170 men, who constituted " the great force " on Reata.

This much exaggerated statement serves to illustrate the uncertainty and confusion which arises in night operations and which the dense bush aggravated.

Here the wrong information served one side well, for it achieved what all the gallantry of Tighe's troops had failed to do by compelling the German commander to evacuate his strong position. As von Lettow writes: " this report made it appear that a strong hostile force would now press forward from Reata in the direction of Kahe and cut us off from our communications. I therefore ordered all the troops to fall back ".

Later on, in the light of the actual facts, he expresses his regret that he " had ordered the troops forming his left wing (i.e. between Kitovo and Himo) to withdraw to the Kahe-Reata road ".

In other words, had the report not been much exaggerated, he would have hung on.

The British forces had sustained some 300 casualties (heavy, for a few hours fighting in Africa) with a high percentage of killed. At one point Major Mainprise, Brigade Major of the East African Brigade, with a number of men was killed by machine gun fire to which all through the campaign a large proportion of battle casualties were due. The enemy's machine gun work was as thorough and effective as the rifle fire of the Askari was, as a rule, poor. The machine gun in the skilful hands of resolute German European soldiers was often deadly in the bush.

The German losses were given as 17 killed (5 Europeans), 67 wounded (10 Europeans) and 39 missing (2 Europeans).

After the occupation of the position on the morning of March 12, the artillery shelled the retiring enemy. As von Lettow puts it: " the enemy occupied Reata mountain and for a while fired into the blue ", a by no means unusual target for artillery in this country so well adapted for complete concealment and offering often no facility whatever for the observation of fire.

(ix) COMMENTS ON THE ACTION AT REATA.

We may now consider this action of Latema-Reata with a view to recording any lessons which it may afford.

The fighting took place in dense bush, though preparatory movements on the British side were carried out over ground where little or no cover from view was available.

What was the situation as known on the morning of March 11 at Taveta and in the surrounding country which was the scene of operations?

A small brigade of *British troops—comprising three weak infantry units—faced the enemy at Taveta. The latter had retired voluntarily into a position, obviously of great natural strength, where his numbers and dispositions were totally concealed by dense bush, and from the heights of which a full view of his opponents' movements was to be obtained.

General Malleson's force was preponderantly strong in artillery, but it was here, as so often in East Africa, useless, for it was impossible to pick up a definite target in the dense bush which also rendered the observation of fire out of the question.

The German commander had already shown at Salaita that, if the slightest chance of counter-attack were to present itself to him, he would promptly avail himself of it. From his own account we learn that two companies under Captain Koehl were intended to deliver such an attack " which would have suited the situation and proved decisive ", but in the unknown and dense bush it could not be undertaken.

As to its decisive effect, had it been delivered, there can be small doubt.

The whole trend of the action from the time when contact with the enemy was established after noon indicated the presence of a very considerable enemy force which apparently had no intention of retiring, unless it should be turned out of its position. A force, in fact, comfortably holding its attackers and well able to deliver a counter-attack in circumstances ideal for its employment.

To decide whether this was the case or not was the object of the attack (see despatch already quoted).

Van Deventer's advance was bound to force the abandonment of the Reata position on the following day, though his movement was originally strategic and not planned for tactical co-operation with the force before Reata. General Smuts gave instructions for such co-operation when he ordered van Deventer to turn south against the enemy's left flank.

The attempts to gain the position by frontal attacks *after daylight failed* and " when there was no opportunity of adequately reconnoitring the ground over which the attack must be made nor was it certain that the enemy was not present in large numbers " (see despatch quoted above) must, it would seem, be regarded as an error of judgment.

---

* " British " is used to denote the forces as distinct from the enemy and the term includes Indian and African native troops.

Night operations of any kind, even in country far less difficult than that at Latema and Reata, are undertakings which always entail much risk and call for most careful preparation. We read in Field Service Regulations that the special responsibility of commanders and staffs in connection with night operations is to ensure that:—

(i) The plan is simple.

(ii) Thorough reconnaissance by day, and, if practicable, by night is carried out. All arrangements . . . must be worked out with the utmost care.

(iii) Every step to secure surprise is taken, special attention being given to concealment from air (and of course from any other point of observation) of preliminary movements and preparations.

While, as has been stated, the plan was simplicity itself, *no previous reconnaissance* except from the air to some extent which revealed nothing, was undertaken, or indeed was possible. The preliminary movements and preparations were necessarily undertaken in full view of the enemy.

General Smuts attached the greatest importance to van Deventer's movement on his right and on March 10 had gone over to van Deventer and throughout that day taken every precaution personally to see that the advance of the latter did not proceed too rapidly and so get too far ahead.

Only if General Smuts had personally ordered, or done so through his staff, that continued attacks should be pushed—and he gave no such order—would it seem permissible that the local commander should dispense with the precaution of a reference to the Commander-in-Chief who was within a few minutes' call by telephone.

In view of the declared object of the attack (v. ante), *the night attack up a steep mountain through dense unreconnoitered bush and against a prepared position* must be regarded as unwise. It is possible, authoritatively to state that it was contrary to the original intention of the Commander-in-Chief.

The soldierly boldness of General Tighe's action and the gallantry of those whom he led must not obscure the judgment in considering the episode which was only one—if a highly important one—of several movements which depended for their joint effect upon a co-ordination of the plans of the Commander-in-Chief.

Prior reconnaissance, careful advance, the *gradual* committal of troops to action are elementary principles for the proper tactical employment of troops in any mobile warfare. The action of Latema-Reata strikingly emphasised the extreme importance of these principles in bush fighting.

There was an interesting sequel later in the campaign as a consequence of the opinion formed by von Lettow of the tactics employed against him on this occasion, i.e. *locally* at Reata.

In October, 1917, at Mahiwa, far to the south, he heavily defeated a British force, and he says in connection with the event: " I had learned in the engagement at Reata (11th March, 1916) that General . . . (incidentally, he is mistaken as to the identity of the general, as the one whom he mentions was not in action at Reata), threw his men into action regardless of loss of life and did not hesitate to try for a success, not by skilful handling and small losses, but rather by repeated frontal attacks which, if the defence held its ground and had anything like adequate forces, led to severe losses for the attack. I guessed that here at Mahiwa he was carrying out the same tactics. *I think it was by taking advantage of mistaken tactics in this way that we were able to win this splendid victory* ".

The exaggerated report which led von Lettow, quite rightly, had it been true, to order a retirement, compelled him to evacuate his position. Had the confusion and difficulty of observation, which was due to the thickness of the bush and the darkness, not caused the strength of Thompson's party to be greatly over-estimated, it is most probable that, far from evacuating his position, Major Kraut would have been able to destroy or capture the whole detachment.

The same conditions made the employment of Koehl's force in counter-attack impracticable. Correct timing is the essence of successful counter-attack, and the Germans in East Africa were too well versed in this manoeuvre to attempt it without the information needed for its proper use.

The employment of their reserves in counter-attack by von Lettow and his subordinates is well worth attention and will be referred to again later.

In circumstances such as those attending the events of the night of March 11-12, 1916, near Taveta all reports should be carefully investigated and checked. The demeanour of the informant often helps to a correct estimate of the value of his information.

The fact remains, however, that the collection of information and the maintenance of touch and communication, and therefore of control, are extremely difficult to achieve in bush operations.

Recognition of the fact, however, and constant attention to the problem in training will tend to reduce the difficulty.

The value and effect of the machine gun, and, now-a-days, the light automatic gun, were clearly shown at Reata. The Germans were particularly skilful in the handling of these weapons, and their crews were picked white men at the outset, though casualties compelled the employment of chosen native soldiers later. Physical fitness, bodily activity, good tactical sense and an eye for ground are specially needed qualifications for machine gunners in bush country.

Great use was made by the Germans of avenues and clearings cut in the bush for the employment of their machine guns.

An open space in the bush should, if possible, be avoided in action especially in attack. If the clearing is extensive and *must* be crossed, its further side should be made good and all the vicinity *on the flanks and to the rear* of the advance well searched before any considerable body of troops is committed to the open ground.

Attention to this in training will be well repaid and may be easily given in suitable country.

The action of Reata has been dealt with at length as it furnishes such valuable information in connection with bush fighting.

(x) THE IMPORTANCE OF THE LUMI RIVER.

It is now necessary to touch upon the operations round Chala which, like the action at Reata, were part of General Smuts' general plan.

The line from Chala to Jipe, with the serious obstacle of the Lumi river, was an unusually strong defensive position. For its preparation the enemy had had 18 months of uninterrupted opportunity.

General Smuts had been on the spot for only a few days before undertaking his advance in the execution of which speed was essential in view of the approaching rainy season.

He decided that the weak spot in the formidable line which faced him lay near Chala where, from such information as he could gather in the time at his disposal, General von Lettow had omitted to guard his left flank, at any rate with forces adequate for the purpose.

In the event, the strength of the enemy on this flank was not enough to cause any real inconvenience, and the barrier of the Lumi, which was crossed without opposition, was ignored in von Lettow's scheme of defence. The fact that much pioneering work, which was allowed to proceed unchecked, had to be undertaken, made the absence of interference all the more welcome.

While the positions round Taveta were of such natural strength that comparatively small forces could have secured them as points upon which to retire, the defence of the Lumi line would have called for as strong forces as could be made available for the purpose.

The enemy Commander-in-Chief, however, possessed intimate knowledge of the terrain (as did all the members of his forces) and had forces strong enough to hold up the advance against his left by the river for some time without jeopardising a retirement into his prepared positions further back.

That he did not resist the threat to his left would seem to argue want of appreciation of—

(i) the importance of the Lumi; and
(ii) the possibilities of a stout defence of the river line.

It must be remembered that von Lettow, on interior lines and in familiar country, could move his forces in ample time to forestall any change in the direction of the lines of advance adopted by his opponent.

The rapidity with which he succeeded in turning von Lettow out of the Taveta area, when time was of the utmost importance for the completion of the occupation of the whole Kilimanjaro district, materially assisted General Smuts.

A defence of the Lumi might well have caused the postponement of this success for several months for the whole area was only just secured before the rain came in earnest and put an end to all movement in this quarter. *Days* were thus of importance.

The passive abandonment of the Lumi as a defensive aid would seem in the circumstances to have been an unwise act on the part of General von Lettow.

(xi) THE ADMINISTRATIVE ARRANGEMENTS.

The arrangements for the administrative services during these operations were as follows:—

The lines of communication for the force on the Voi-Maktau side of Kilimanjaro ran from Serengeti by the railway to Voi and thence to Nairobi or Mombasa, as occasion should demand, by the Uganda railway. Taveta was only about 10 miles from Serengeti.

*To the 2nd Division were allotted for medical services Nos. 2, 3 and 4 South African Field Ambulances with a section of No. 120 Field Ambulance.

These units were *all* deficient in transport.

For the evacuation of casualties which was controlled by the D.D.M.S. L. of C. " B " and " D " Sections of No. 22 Indian Clearing Hospital formed a casualty clearing station at Maktau where all sick and wounded were to be received.

To the 1st Division on the Longido-Magadi line were allotted " A " and " C " Sections of No. 22 Indian Clearing Hospital which formed a clearing station at Longido West whither No. 33 British Stationary Hospital was also moved.

The L. of C. of the 1st Division ran from Longido to rail head at Magadi and thence by rail to Nairobi.

The removal of the sick and wounded of the 1st Division which only suffered 13 casualties was effected by motor ambulance to Longido. Ambulance wagons drawn by 8 mules proved the most satisfactory.

Casualties at Latema-Reata were collected at Taveta in a house which the Germans had used as a hospital. A large number of bandas (Native grass huts) were also erected there.

From Taveta casualties were evacuated by empty supply wagons to railhead and thence via Voi to Nairobi.

As has been stated, though a few miles separated the forces on this side from the head of their railway, lack of communication between the different detachments interfered greatly with the forwarding of supplies.

* These include the arrangements for van Deventer's force and the Force Reserve.

CHAPTER VI

(i) OPERATIONS OF THE 1ST DIVISION.

THE task allotted to the 1st Division under Major-General Stewart was broadly described on page 69, and was designed to conclude with an effort to cut the enemy retreat by the Usambara railway to the south of Kahe.

Stewart was opposed by Major Fischer (1,000 rifles).

The 1st Division was allowed "two clear days' start before the advance on Taveta should begin" (see despatch of April 30, 1916), and on March 5 began its advance from Longido West. During the day it reached Sheep Hills—8 miles—and resumed the advance on the night of March 5-6.

The main body of the force was directed on the Engare-Nanjuki, while a mounted detachment moved to the south and, turning eastwards, on Ngasseni, two double companies and a section of mountain artillery moving to attack a German detachment at Ngasserai.

Each of these forces had reached their objectives by 8 a.m. on March 6 and the German detachment had been turned out of Ngasserai. Ngasseni Hill was occupied at 3 p.m.

On the evening of March 7 the Division had reached Geraragua on the Sanja river.

Ahead were thick bush and forests and local information indicated preparations for a strong defence. Rain had swamped the tracks back to the starting point and the supply situation had become difficult, necessitating pioneer work on the roads.

Meanwhile Stewart, on the 8th, had sent his mounted troops to reconnoitre a line of advance to the Mbiriri, and it was not until late on the 11th that touch was regained with them, when it was learnt that the column had returned to its starting point after two days in the bush where it had sustained a few casualties.

The main body remained at Geraragua until noon on March 10, when, in response to a message from General Smuts impressing upon the divisional commander the need for haste, the Division moved on 9 miles to the vicinity of Mbiriri stream where it remained for the night of March 10-11.

General Smuts had now decided to attack the Reata position on the 11th and again requested haste on the part of the 1st Division. In response to this incentive the Division made another advance of 12 miles and reached a bridge (left intact) over Sanja river, 3 miles west of Boma Ngombe, on the night of March 11-12.

During this night the action at Latema-Reata was fought, and the 1st Division, with its mounted troops a day's march in its rear, ceased to be a factor in the situation, so far as the planned interception of the enemy was concerned.

General Stewart remained at the Sanja bridge until March 13 when a third order from G.H.Q. to push on with all speed resulted in the despatch of Lieut.-Colonel Laverton with the mounted troops to the south-east, with a view to operating against the Usambara railway, and the advance of the greater part of Stewart's infantry as a mobile column under Brigadier-General Sheppard, the commander of the 2nd E.A. Infantry Brigade.

This last force (1,500) was ordered in the direction of Moschi as far as the Kikafu river whence it was to move on Masai Kraal.

Sheppard reached a point 3 miles beyond the East Kware river when, at 1.30 a.m. on March 14, he halted in consequence of heavy rain. Headquarters of the Division remained near Boma Ngombe where a motor cyclist from van Deventer at Moschi established direct touch between the Division and the main force.

(ii) THE ADVANCE RESUMED.

General Smuts, after the fight at Latema-Reata, decided to resume his advance and General Beves with his 2nd S.A. Infantry Brigade was ordered to march at 10 a.m. on March 13, the 2nd Division remaining at Taveta and relieving the 8th S.A. Infantry on the captured position.

The Commander-in-Chief left Taveta early the same morning in the wake of van Deventer.

Climbing Massowoni, General Smuts got into communication with van Deventer just after the latter had left Mue, and he gave a report that the enemy were leaving for Mombo (100 miles to the south) mostly by train. The truth of this obviously inspired native information was early disproved, but van

Deventer was ordered to abandon the southward movement which he had been instructed to set in train and to occupy Moschi which he proceeded to do and General Smuts joined him there in the course of the morning.

Von Lettow had no intention of immediate retirement as may be gathered from his account of events, the value of which is occasionally affected by a curious omission of dates. This may be accounted for by the loss of his " own records for the most part ".

He writes: " I could not accede to the requests of my company commanders that we should attack ", and, " all we could do was to let the enemy run up against us on suitable ground ", a policy which had served him well so far.

The country between Himo and the Ruwu, viewed from the former place, was densely bushed and difficult to a degree which precluded any rapid advance.

At Moschi General Smuts ordered the following movements and dispositions:—

1st Division to occupy Aruscha—leaving a battalion and some mounted men at Boma-Ngombe. After occupation Van Deventer was to hold Aruscha with his mounted troops.

Major-General Stewart—whose difficulties had not been lessened by the involuntary delivery of one of his reports by a captured Indian despatch rider to von Lettow—after reconnoitring the Aruscha-Kampfontein road to the west of Meru was to withdraw with the rest of his command to Longido and there await instructions.

General Smuts had already decided upon complete re-organisation and some changes in higher appointments after the immediate operations, which had given him an opportunity for judgment of methods and individuals, should have been concluded.

The 4th S.A. Horse to remain at Mue attached to Berrangé whose 3rd S.A. Infantry Brigade was placed on the right bank of the Himo, while Beves held the left bank.

General Smuts then returned to G.H.Q. in Beves' camp.

(iii) MOVEMENT TOWARDS THE RUWU RIVER.

On March 14 patrols were sent out towards the Ruwu and Kahe, van Deventer being told to push his patrols as far as possible towards the latter place in order to clear up the doubtful situation.

The endurance of the troops had been well tested in the demands which a week's continuous marching and fighting had made upon them, and it was necessary to decide upon a clear objective before committing them to a further advance.

It was now arranged that Generals Tighe, Stewart and Malleson should return to India.

The authorities in India had more than once asked that General Tighe should be returned to them, as soon as he could be spared. He had borne the burden of command during the trying period of comparative inactivity forced upon him by lack of men and resources, an experience which must have been especially galling to a man of his temperament. He was a courageous man and possessed all the fighting instinct of his race, he was an Irishman, as witness his conduct of the attack at Reata.

Brigadier-General Hoskins, on his way by sea to assume the appointment of Brigadier-General, General Staff, was promoted to Major-General and assigned to the command of one of the three new divisions to be formed in place of the two which had hitherto existed.

Heavy rain—the forerunner of the rainy season—fell from time to time occasionally preventing movements and aerial reconnaissance which was now resorted to more freely.

So far as the enemy troops were concerned, aerial action did little damage and produced trifling information now or later in the campaign. As von Lettow writes: " Owing to the dense bush and high forest in which our camps were hidden aerial reconnaissance can hardly have been any use to the enemy. The bombs dropped by the enemy caused only a few casualties at Kahe and did not interfere with us in getting away our stores ". It may here be observed that the ground at Kahe was comparatively open.

For the next few days the forces remained in their camps. On March 18 on a report from Belfield's Scouts, a small local mounted unit, that they had occupied Rasthaus, south of Himo towards Kahe, and that they had been ejected by enemy askaris, an advance was ordered to be made by two battalions from each of the two South African Infantry Brigades towards Rasthaus Hill.

Accordingly, two battalions under Beves were directed on Unterer Himo and two under Berrangé on Euphorbien Hill.

Two battalions from the 1st E.A. Brigade were instructed to move at the same time from Latema in the same general direction while the E.A. Mounted Rifles and a Squadron of 17th (Indian) Cavalry took the Moschi-Kahe road. See map number five.

Later on the mounted troops were supported by the 2nd E.A. Infantry Brigade (from Stewart's division) under Brig.-General Sheppard, late Chief of Staff to General Tighe.

Van Deventer with the 1st S.A. Mounted Brigade and Stewart (still at Moschi) were warned to hold their commands ready to move at once.

By the evening Unterer Himo and Euphorbien Hill were in possession of Beves and Berrangé respectively, and all the detachments engaged in the forward movement were ordered to entrench for the night, send out patrols at daybreak and to abstain from any forward movement without orders from G.H.Q.

The mounted troops under Lieut.-Colonel Laverton, occupied Masai Kraal on the Kahe Road, but reported that they were faced by one company and one machine gun with two companies in reserve (Stemmermann) and, as Laverton had barely 100 rifles, he was ordered to withdraw to Mue for the night and return to Masai Kraal at dawn.

On the following day, March 19, Beves, under whom the two battalions from Latema had been temporarily placed, was told to move against Rasthaus from the east while Berrangé co-operated with him from the west with the aid of Laverton's mounted troops.

At noon, however, Laverton reported that he was held by the enemy force, which, on information from a captured Askari, he had reported overnight, in bush which was impossible for mounted troops and difficult for infantry.

On this Sheppard was instructed to send the 129th Baluchis to support Laverton and push the enemy back. Should their attempt fail, he was to go himself with the balance of his brigade and carry out the task.

In the evening, in consequence of reports from all detachments of increasing density of bush, their commanders were ordered to re-occupy their positions of the night before and at once to withdraw to them.

Sheppard was ordered to entrench himself at Masai Kraal, and any movement on the following morning except by patrols, was, as before, only to be instituted on orders from G.H.Q. It was not proposed to " run up against the enemy on suitable ground ", if it could be avoided.

General Sheppard assumed temporary command of the 1st Division on the departure of General Stewart.

Telephonic reports now succeeded each other at G.H.Q.

Berrangé reported that one of his battalions had halted on the edge of the bush in its withdrawal towards its bivouac when it was at once attacked by the enemy—once more showing how unwise it was to become exposed halted in any clearing—but was retiring and had not asked for assistance. In the end it got into camp with 30 casualties among whom was its commander, Lieut.-Colonel Breytenbach who was severely wounded in the leg.

The enemy had adopted the now familiar device of advancing machine guns on the flanks. This, however, had been anticipated and guarded against. The South African infantryman was adapting himself to bush fighting.

Immediately after this, Sheppard reported that he had reached Store, some 3 miles beyond Masai Kraal, and as it was " a good place ", proposed to remain there for the night. He asked if he was to hand over and take over the division, but in view of the risk of a change of command in touch with the enemy, was ordered to remain.

Beves was the next to report and said the bush was so dense as to make " control and cohesion almost impossible ". He also added that the bombs from the aeroplanes were " very effective "; an optimistic view.

On the following morning, 20th, it was clear from the reports that an attack on the enemy in the bush along the Himo and thence to Kahe was impossible without loss of cohesion and control and that co-ordination would be out of the question. This meant that Kahe was the only possible objective, and that a flank attack from the west was the means by which it should be reached.

Accordingly, early on the morning of March 20 the following dispositions were ordered:—.

The brigade from Latema to take over Unterer Himo when Beves was to return to Himo and send 3 of his battalions round to Sheppard under whom an advance was to be made from Store on the following day, 21st; van Deventer to move south in the afternoon (20th) with his mounted brigade and the 4th S.A. Horse and endeavour to outflank the enemy, engaged with, Sheppard, at Kahe the next day.

All other detachments were ordered to remain in their positions " feeling " the enemy, but refraining from any serious attack.

These orders were altered later to the following extent in view of the need for more rapid movement. Beves was ordered to send on his freshest battalions, without waiting relief by the detachments from the 1st E.A. Brigade, leaving his most used up battalion to hold the position for the time.

In all these dispositions artillery was allotted to the different forces, but the country was wholly unfavourable to its effective employment and its action had little, if any, effect upon the results of the operations.

It is at least open to argument, bearing in mind the great difficulties of transport and supply and the small amount of artillery possessed by the enemy, if any artillery, except moutain batteries and perhaps some howitzers, should have accompanied the Expeditionary Force.

On the only occasion when the enemy artillery did any damage—at the standing camp at Msiha later—it achieved this result because it had the advantage of observation from the Nguru mountains, whereas the British guns were without this facility and were impotent, as in fact they almost always were, lacking the power of observation.

General Beves reached Himo about 4 p.m. on March 20 and three of his battalions, the 6th, 5th and 8th S.A. Infantry left for Sheppard in the order given, the first unit reaching Acacia on the Kahe road at 6 p.m.

All detachments were now ordered to be ready to march on the next day immediately on receipt of orders from G.H.Q. which they were advised would not be given until van Deventer should have indicated his whereabouts. He had communicated his intention of trying to outflank the enemy " from direction between Kahe and Baumann Hill ", i.e. from the north-west.

(iv) ACTION AT STORE.

General von Lettow, however, had also been giving orders, and at 10 p.m. heavy firing was heard at G.H.Q. from the south-west and Berrangé from Euphorbien Hill reported it as " from direction Masai Kraal ".

At 11 p.m. Sheppard telephoned to G.H.Q. and stated that the enemy had charged his outposts; that he happened to be reinforcing them at the time and the charge had proved abortive. A heavy attack had then developed upon him at Store but he was " all comfortable ", and he asked for biscuits and 50,000 or 60,000 rounds of small arm ammunition.

The attack continued until 1 a.m. on the 21st.

According to von Lettow, Stemmermann was holding a fortified position on the road facing north. He says the British patrols had " with considerable skill " worked up close to his detachment and concealed Sheppard's movements. When he himself arrived in the afternoon, he writes, " it was not at all clear what was really going on in front ". He thought the movement might be a feint to cover an attack in force at some other " more dangerous " spot, and that, if such were the case, the manoeuvre would have been very menacing as the dense bush would prevent the detection of an attack until " probably too late ".

Pushing back Sheppard's screen, he came upon the main body, and the action which he describes as " very severe " ensued. He mentions his casualties as " not inconsiderable ", and including three company commanders.

Sheppard's casualties amounted to 20.

On March 21 an air reconnaissance reported the presence of van Deventer's mounted troops at 6.30 a.m. just west of Pangani bridge near Kahe moving east.

(v) MOVEMENT AGAINST KAHE.

Sheppard was now ordered to attack Ruwu and Kahe road bridge on receipt of the Commander-in-Chief's order from G.H.Q., but, if he heard firing to the south-west, to attack without orders, reporting to G.H.Q. to allow of Berrangé being warned.

The latter was told to be ready to attack Rasthaus and the line of the Himo. On receiving orders to that effect, each was warned of a gap between them and to look to their flanks.

The 2nd Division at Taveta was advised of the position and instructed to send a battalion to Kingarungu where a footbridge crossed the Ruwu some 20 miles east of Kahe.

At 12.30 p.m. Sheppard reported his movement on Ruwu Bridge and asked that Berrangé should advance at the same time parallel with him.

This was not agreed to, as Berrangé, collected at Euphorbien Hill, threatened any force which might debouch against Sheppard's flank which it protected far more than it would by an advance against Rasthaus where the situation was obscure.

At 11 a.m. an aeroplane gave the Mounted Brigade as partly over the Pangani at the bridge with the remainder crossing.

At 1 p.m. Sheppard was advancing against Ruwu bridge from the direction of Store, Berrangé was in position at Euphorbien Hill, the detachment from 1st E.A. Brigade at Unterer Himo, and van Deventer approaching Kahe from the south-west.

At 1.50 p.m. dust pointing to the retirement of the enemy, orders to advance were given to the detachments at Euphorbien and Unterer Himo. Two and a half hours later these forces were warned not to become engaged to an extent which would compromise a withdrawal to their original positions which at 5 p.m. they were told to carry out.

(vi) ACTION AT SOKO NASAI.

Sheppard, asked to state his opinion as to the practicability of a flank movement by infantry, reported that his advance was held up by dense bush and the enemy, with whom he was heavily engaged on all his front, and that he had arranged to entrench and maintain his position.

Sheppard's force, which began its advance about 11.30 a.m., after moving forward a mile or more, became the target for one of the Königsberg guns. Incidentally von Lettow overestimates considerably the effect of this artillery fire. As a result of faulty information as to the actual course of the Soko Nasai, a strong resistance by the enemy about 1 p.m. came in the nature of a surprise and the leading units, emerging into an open area, encountered heavy rifle and machine gun fire from thick bush on the far side of the opening. The flanks of the enemy position, sited in the dense bush south of the open ground, rested on the Soko Nasai and Defu rivers, respectively.

Efforts to advance across the 500 yards of comparatively open ground failed, and an attempt was made against the enemy right flank which was, however, prepared for the movement and checked it, inflicting substantial casualties on the attackers.

At 4 p.m. Sheppard had sustained considerable losses all along his front, and three quarters of an hour later, on the receipt of the order from G.H.Q. to stand fast on the ground he occupied, entrenched for the night.

The artillery had done its best to assist the attack, but dense bush and the impossibility of discovering a target or observing fire again made their efforts of small use.

We learn from von Lettow that once more Schulz was entrusted with a counter-attack along " previously reconnoitred and determined tracks ". While this attack reached its objective —the British flank—it failed of full effect.

The German commander, mindful of the threat from van Deventer, whose dust had revealed his advance, had eight companies in reserve at Kahe station, but, as he thought it necessary to remain near Stemmermann—heavily engaged—was unable " to exercise rapid and direct control " over them.

(vii) ENEMY RETIREMENT.

Consequently, when he received a report that " strong forces of the enemy were advancing in our rear towards the railway at Kissangire ", General von Lettow was forced to issue orders for an immediate withdrawal towards that place. He says he hoped to defeat van Deventer there by throwing all his forces rapidly against him. Included in these forces was Schulz's detachment which was called off from its counter-attack.

Von Lettow goes on to say that he arrived at Kissangire station and discovered " to my very great astonishment that all the reports about strong hostile forces moving on that place were erroneous and that our withdrawal had therefore been un-necessary ", he adds, " in the African bush it is particularly important, whenever possible, to supplement the reports one receives by personal observation ".

Allowing that the wrong report may have accelerated the enemy's retirement, van Deventer's movement rendered the German position at Kahe untenable. It might have been possible for General von Lettow rapidly to have concentrated a consider-ably superior force to give van Deventer at least an anxious time, at a point so far south as Kissangire, but Sheppard was too near van Deventer in point of fact to have allowed any serious venture by the enemy against the latter.

Within ten days the German commander had been twice compelled to act upon false information, for at Reata he explains his sudden retirement by a misleading report that the enemy had " penetrated the position in great force ". As General von Lettow was well acquainted with the country in each instance, the episodes emphasise the extraordinary difficulty in obtaining correct information and maintaining control and touch in extensive operations in bush.

(viii) VAN DEVENTER'S MOVEMENT ON KAHE.

It will be remembered that van Deventer with his mounted brigade and the 4th S.A. Horse had been ordered to move on the afternoon of March 20 from New Moschi to outflank the enemy engaged with Sheppard. In compliance with this instruction van Deventer left New Moschi at 4.30 p.m. on the 20th. Leaving the southern road to Boma Ngombe some three miles from New Moschi in the light of a full moon he struck south, and by 4 a.m. on March 21 had arrived at a spot three miles to the west of Baumann Hill and there waited for day to break.

Reconnaissance failing to reveal any crossings, the brigade moved northwards (this movement, as already recorded, was communicated at 6.30 a.m. to G.H.Q. as the result of an air reconnaissance) towards Kahe Hill and came into contact with the enemy. With much difficulty two squadrons attained the opposite (left) bank of the Pangani drawing fire from a heavy enemy gun. At the same time (7.30 a.m.) enemy forces moved from Kahe station against van Deventer's main body and an action ensued without result for some hours.

The two squadrons which had crossed the Pangani seized Kahe Hill towards noon, and for the next three hours defended it against many counter-attacks. Van Deventer sent the bulk of the 3rd S.A. Horse over the river to reinforce the first two squadrons, passing them over a bridge near Kahe Hill. This movement had also been reported to G.H.Q. by an air reconnaissance. The defence of the hill was effectively supported by artillery fire from the 2nd S.A. Field Battery from which a F.O.O. had swum across the river to the position. One of the rare occasions upon which observation and consequent effective fire were possible.

By 2.30 p.m. Kahe station and the northern bank of the river were in the hands of van Deventer, and at about 8 p.m. the latter reported that he " held Kahe, Kahe Hill and the railway to Baumann's Hill ".

Sheppard was at once advised of this and van Deventer was ordered, if the enemy were still in his positions on the following morning, to operate on his line of retreat.

Signal fires in the enemy's lines were interpreted by local natives to indicate retirement.

The 1st Division (Sheppard) sustained 261 casualties on March 21st; 37 killed, 221 wounded, and 3 missing while van Deventer's loss was 1 killed, 12 wounded and 4 missing.

The losses of the German forces (on the defence except at Masai Kraal) were 30 killed, 90 wounded and 51 missing, a total casualty list of 171.

(ix) OCCUPATION OF KAHE.

At daybreak on March 22 patrols discovered the evacuation of the enemy positions. The reserve of the 1st Division, the 1st K.A.R., was sent forward and reached the Ruwu river finding the bridge (which was, however, quickly repaired) burning and a 4.1" gun from the Königsberg destroyed and abandoned.

The German force had retired south along the Usambara railway and touch with them was lost. It was found after patrol action during the next day or two that von Lettow had occupied a strong position at Lembeni.

(x) SOME LESSONS OF THE OPERATIONS.

The operations which have just been described were of much interest as showing some of the difficulties which attend the co-ordination and direction of separated detachments of all arms and considerable strength in thick bush country.

It was found that all movements proceeded extremely slowly and that it was essential, if ground gained were to be retained, that forward movements should be ordered to begin as soon after dawn as possible. The severely oppressive heat too makes this course advisable.

It will have been noticed that on several occasions detachments were ordered back to their starting points by nightfall. This was for security, and because a late movement prevented proper reconnaissance of ground for a night camp, a very necessary precaution in face of an enemy such as General von Lettow who turned the knowledge of the ground possessed by himself and his subordinates, as the result of previous thorough reconnaissance, to full account over and over again.

Very small extension was possible without loss of control and loss of control in the bush often means chaos. Any extension should therefore be carefully watched.

The flanks were especially vulnerable. The enemy throughout the campaign lost no opportunity of slipping round the flanks and enfilading or taking in reverse an advancing force by means of machine gun fire. This practice was almost invariably resorted to to deal with a retirement.

The experience gained between Himo and the Ruwu emphasised the lesson given elsewhere that every commander should keep reserves under his own hand. Such a reserve properly used is the only means of dealing with the sudden emergencies which arise in bush warfare. The employment, actual or contemplated, of von Lettow's reserves in all his actions is most instructive.

Counter-attack in defence which, as a rule, argues previous reconnaissance, is a powerful aid to the defender.

Individual fire trenches can be sited to better advantage in the bush than larger ones.

Picquets should not be placed too far out, they can be circumvented in bush and are apt to come in with a rush and mask fire on the enemy.

Lateral communication between forces a few miles apart was often impossible. This might be improved by the maintenance of parties of natives—who are expert bush cutters—under special control and direction for opening up paths between forces in close proximity to each other. At Tanga, see page 39, lateral communication was only possible by means of runners.

These were some of the lessons which the operations seemed to afford and the South African soldier was not slow to grasp those of a tactical nature.

(xi) FORCES DISTRIBUTED FOR RAINY SEASON.

On March 23 General Smuts saw van Deventer and Sheppard at Kahe and Ruwu and, as he writes in his despatch, " I accordingly established my headquarters at Moschi, placed a chain of outposts along the line of the Ruwu and set to work to reorganise my force ".

" The conquest of the Kilimanjaro-Meru area, probably the richest and most desirable district of German East Africa was satisfactorily completed."

It remained to distribute the forces in the most suitable positions in view of the imminent heavy rains. A reorganisation on the following lines was also effected and the troops were disposed as follows:—

General Headquarters   Moschi.
   1st Division
      Major-General Hoskins   Moschi.
      E.A. Mounted Troops
      1st E.A. Infantry Brigade   Mbuyuni.
      Brig.-General Hannyngton
      2nd E.A. Infantry Brigade
      Brig.-General Sheppard   New Moschi.
         with *one battalion* at Kahe
      Divisional Troops   Mbuyuni.
   2nd Division
      Major-General van Deventer   Aruscha.
      1st S.A. Mounted Brigade
      * Brig.-General H. Botha
      3rd S.A. Infantry Brigade   Aruscha.
      Brig.-General Berrangé
      Divisional Troops
   3rd Division
      Major-General Brits (on his way
         from South Africa).
      2nd S.A. Mounted Brigade
      Brig.-General Enslin (to arrive
         from South Africa).
      2nd S.A. Infantry Brigade
      Brig.-General Beves   Himo.
      Divisional Troops

Army Troops.

Belfield's Scouts - - - - Moschi.
Army Artillery - - - - - Himo.
Royal Engineers - - - on line Taveta-Moschi.
Air Services - - - - - Mbuyuni for Moschi.

* Later Brig.-General Nussey.

Map number six gives the above dispositions.

Opposite General Smuts General von Lettow disposed of his forces as follows:—

A few companies were placed on the high ground at Kissangire " to observe the seven and a half miles of waterless thorn desert extending to the Pangani ". Major von Boehmken was in command here. East of von Boehmken was Otto's detachment on the North Pare mountains.

Major Kraut " took up a position on Ngulu Pass between the North and Middle Pare mountains, while the main body settled down in several fortified camps in the fertile Lembeni country ". Map number six indicates these arrangements.

General von Lettow's record states: " In spite of the various withdrawals we had recently carried out, the spirit of the troops was good, and the Askari were imbued with a justifiable pride in their achievements against an enemy so superior ".

CHAPTER VII

(i) AN APPRECIATION OF THE SITUATION AT THE END OF MARCH, 1916.

ON March 28 the movements to the camps for the rainy season began, and the Commander-in-Chief, with G.H.Q., struck camp early and left for Old Moschi.

Rain had fallen during the preceding week, and, though movement had not been interferred with to any great extent, the change of weather had proved troublesome to many who were unused to the climate, and malaria and dysentery began to appear.

General Smuts now decided to make one more highly important movement before the rainy season should set in in earnest.

In his despatch of the 27th October, 1916, he reviews the situation as it presented itself to him in March of that year, and states three alternatives which he considered faced him at that time in his prosecution of the campaign.

The intelligence with which he was furnished " credited· the enemy with the two-fold intention of conducting an obstinate and prolonged campaign in the Pare and Usambara mountains and thereafter retiring to fight out the last phases of the campaign in the Tabora area from which much of his supplies and most of his recruits were drawn ".

In estimating the action of a military commander in war it is necessary to judge it *in the light of information which was at his disposal at the time of the action* and, according to the information which was supplied to General Smuts at this time, he drew the conclusion that General von Lettow would " fight out the last phases of the campaign in the Tabora area ".*

This forecast of the enemy's probable action was accepted for some time, and it was not until May 2, when intercepted messages made it clear that a western enemy command had been formed under General Wahle, that a general retirement to the north-west could be ruled out, as, at all events, a clear possibility.

---

* It should be noted that information was to the effect that the country to the south of the Central Railway was worthless to the enemy as a direction for retirement. This was of course quite incorrect.

At the time of van Deventer's move south it was to be inferred, from the information furnished to General Smuts, that a west-ward retirement would take place.

It cannot be gathered from von Lettow's own account whether a move to the north-west was contemplated by him or not, as the first indication of any definite line of retirement given by him is that of withdrawal to the Mahenge country. This decision he apparently came to at the end of June, 1916.

(ii) THREE ALTERNATIVE LINES OF ACTION.

GENERAL SMUTS' CHOICE.

The three alternatives which the British Commander now considered, and which are given in the despatch already mentioned, were—

(i) An advance inland from the coast along the existing railway lines (*a*) from Tanga or (*b*) from Dar-es-Salaam.

General Smuts rejected (*a*) because Tanga had ceased to be of importance after his seizure of the Usambara railway to the north and considered that, while much was to be said for (*b*), its adoption was unadvisable, partly because during the S.E. monsoon the landing of a large force on the coast was " an operation of great difficulty and even danger ", and partly because the deadly climate at that season would cause the disappearance of a large portion of his army from disease.

(ii) An advance on Tabora by way of Lake Victoria now controlled by British armed steamers.

The adoption of this plan would entail the transfer of strong reinforcements to the north-west and the consequent weakening of the force opposite the enemy who remained within striking distance of the Uganda railway. Besides, little would be accomplished which could not be achieved by the employment of the British and Belgian forces already in the north-west as part of a general concentric advance.

General Smuts therefore rejected this plan also and turned to

(iii) Striking at the enemy forces either along the Pangani and Usambara railway or by means of an advance into the interior from Aruscha.

100

Information was to the effect that " the violence of the coming rainy season would be mostly confined to the Kilimanjaro-Aruscha area " and that " further west and south the rainy season was milder and would not markedly interfere with military operations ".

This information, in the light of experience, was incorrect in so far as it gave ground for a supposition that the rain would exercise no " marked " interference with military operations. As will be seen, it was a very serious obstacle both as regards its effect on the communications and the health of the troops.

The statement, however, came from shrewd judges of such matters as the movement of mounted men and transport, as those who vouchsafed it were friendly Afrikaners who had settled in the Aruscha district. Indeed it was not often that information came from a source so well able to provide sound intelligence.

General Smuts was assured that the rains were not likely to affect his advance or his consequent transport arrangements. He was also told that it was high ground all the way *with no special risk of malaria or animal diseases.*

The information received by General Smuts was confirmed by the result of independent enquiries made by van Deventer at Aruscha.

If then the Commander-in-Chief decided that an immediate move on Kondoa Irangi was worth while and would give adequate return, taking into consideration any risk which it might entail, there was evidently reason to suppose that the advance might be carried out without entailing the dangers and difficulties which would attend similar movements in districts in which the rain would cause far greater trouble than in the Kondoa Irangi area.

Whether those who gave information were not fully acquainted with the country to the south of that in which they had settled, or whether the rainy season of 1916 was much wetter than was usually the case, the sickness among the troops and mortality among the animals proved to be very severe, and the transport question difficult to the last degree.

General Smuts, aware that opposition by the enemy to an advance on Kondoa Irangi would be slight (von Lettow, writing of van Deventer's advance says: " The road to Kondoa Irangi and the interior of the Colony was now hardly closed "), considered that if he were to occupy that place quickly the enemy retreat to Tabora would be cut off, the Central Railway would be in sight, and von Lettow would have to relax his hold on the Usambaras to meet van Deventer who could be maintained and supported at Kondoa Irangi.

The Usambaras, as soon as his own advance were resumed after the rain, could be quickly cleared against weakened opposition, and, moving his own force in co-operation with that of van Deventer to the Central Railway, he might have a chance of finishing the campaign on that objective.

From the account of the scene of operations along the Pangani—see p. 125—its suitability for an obstinate defence may be gauged, and it is now known from von Lettow's own account that he had viewed several portions of the ground along the Pangani route which he thought might become of importance in his future operations and had left Major Kraut and Captain Schoenfeld to make more detailed personal reconnaissances. There is no doubt that the withdrawal of von Lettow's companies from the Pangani region to face van Deventer accounted for the slight opposition offered to General Smuts as far as Buiko and greatly accelerated his advance.

In the event, though the enemy did not stand and fight for the Central Railway, General Smuts' forces—that under his personal command and that of van Deventer in co-operation—reached the Central Railway, according to his plan, at the end of August, 1916.

(iii) GENERAL SMUTS DECIDES ON THE KONDOA-IRANGI MOVE.

General Smuts accordingly decided to send van Deventer with his (2nd) Division to seize and hold Kondoa Irangi, making use of his mounted troops (the 1st S.A. Mounted Brigade) to ensure a rapid advance.

He gives his reasons for his resolve which have just been stated more fully in his despatch. He writes: " I decided to push the whole of the 2nd Division into the interior under van Deventer, and for the present to keep the other two divisions with me in rain quarters. In this way it would be possible to occupy a valuable portion of the country within the next two months; and if, as I expected, this move would and must have the effect of compelling the enemy to withdraw large forces from

the Pares and Usambaras to stem the tide of invasion into the
interior, I could, if necessary, strengthen van Deventer still
further and yet have sufficient troops left to make a comparatively
easy conquest of these mountains against the enemy's weakened
defence. *These anticipations were fully realised* ".

(iv) THE COMMANDER OF THE 2ND DIVISION: MAJOR-GENERAL VAN DEVENTER.

The Commander whom General Smuts selected to carry out
the advance from Aruscha was Major-General J. L. (Jaap) van
Deventer.

Van Deventer was a splendid physical specimen of his race.
He spoke with a husky voice, the consequence of a severe throat
wound received in the Anglo-Boer War of 1899-1902.

If he had been an older man, he would have made a reputation for himself in that struggle. As it was, he came to the front
towards the end of that campaign as the right-hand of General
Smuts in the expedition led by the latter into the Cape Colony
in September, 1901. He was responsible for several tactical
successes—of which the capture of a squadron of the 17th Lancers
at Modderfontein was a notable instance—in the course of the
venture.

Like most of the Boer generals, he had only led small bodies
of men and had never controlled a formation stronger than, at
the outside, a small regiment, nor had he any experience at all
of the innumerable details of staff work incidental to the manage-
ment of any unit comprising several arms.

He had one great advantage over some of his comrades, for
he had been under discipline in the Transvaal Staats Artillerie
in the days of the Republic and fully appreciated the need for its
application to *all* ranks.

When he commanded his division, and, later, the whole
expeditionary force in East Africa, his early training and
recognition of the need of order stood him in good stead.

While many commando leaders were even enthusiastic about
the value of discipline, its application to themselves was not
always as readily accepted by them as were their right and duty
to apply it to those under their command.

Van Deventer was energetic, courageous and competent, and
a loyal adherent to General Smuts, and made a good detachment
commander who could be left to himself if necessary.

103

A tribute has been paid to him by Brigadier-General Fendall, an officer of the Administrative Staff belonging to the British regular army, who, in his book " The East African Force, 1915-1919 ", writes of van Deventer: " He was a big man morally as well as physically, extraordinarily clear-headed, he always saw the point of an argument at once, and could and did look at all sides of every question. He had a very high standard by which he judged the conduct of all men.

His plans were always logical, always based on his idea of what he would do if in the position of the enemy commander ".

This is high praise and gains weight from the fact that the author, as may be ascertained from his book, occasionally saw little good in any person or thing that came from the Union of South Africa.

General van Deventer's sudden death a few years after the war deprived the South African Forces of a soldier with a capacity for command of an unusual quality.

(v) VAN DEVENTER'S ADVANCE—ACTION AT LOLKISSALE.

Before moving, the Commander of the 2nd Division had been apprised by his patrols of the presence of an enemy force at Lolkissale, a high rocky hill in the Masai steppe 35 miles south-west of Aruscha. The position commanded the only water springs anywhere in the vicinity and its capture was an essential feature in any forward movement.

Accordingly, the 1st Mounted Brigade was ordered to attack the position, and to this end marched from Aruscha at noon on April 3. The force amounted to 1,200 rifles accompanied by two field batteries. The latter with two regiments were directed on the position from the north, the third regiment (2nd S.A. Horse) was sent to move round Lolkissale and place itself on the following morning so as to intercept an enemy retirement. One squadron of the 1st S.A. Horse was despatched to the west towards Mbulu.

By 9 a.m. the main force was within 3,000 yards of the northern face of the mountain which was covered with large boulders and bush.

The regiment, which had moved independently, after marching nearly 50 miles, joined in an attack which began at 9.30 a.m.

At nightfall the enemy were ringed in by the regiments of the Brigade, but were maintaining their position under disadvantageous conditions, among which was the fact that the German Askaris were firing black powder in old pattern rifles.

The attacking force and their horses were suffering badly from thirst, as the enemy held the water.

The attack was resumed at daybreak on the following day, and at 4 p.m. an enemy flank detachment retired on their main position, uncovering a water spring which was at once taken.

Before darkness set in, a detachment of the 2nd S.A. Horse had reached a point 30 yards from the enemy trenches, but the main German position was still intact.

The attacking force was in a very difficult position, for heavy rain had fallen, it was without food, and the horses, which were beginning to die from horse-sickness, were still without water.

There was no choice beyond abandonment of the venture or immediate capture of the position.

During the night of April 5-6 the ring was drawn closer round the German force, and at daybreak a heavy close range fire was delivered as a prelude to a general assault by the South African troops when the white flag was hoisted by the enemy commander.

The German force was captured, and consisted of the 28th Field Company and other details, in all some 400 rifles with many porters. Two machine guns and ammunition and stores fell into van Deventer's hands.

The enterprise was a good example of the use of mounted riflemen and their mobility.

Signs, however, were not wanting already of the heavy wastage which was very gravely to affect the fighting power of the Division, for 250 of the horses of the Brigade were already dead and large numbers were sick.

Captain Rothert was in command of the enemy force and was severely wounded on the second day of the attack, a circumstance to which General von Lettow attributes the surrender. He says: " our people were in possession of the water and could well sustain the fight against the enemy who had none ". He evidently knew Rothert as a good soldier and considered that he would have held on long enough, had he not been put out of action, to get his force away.

" Some of the Askaris gave evidence of sound military education ", writes von Lettow, " by refusing to join in the surrender " and together with the wounded rejoined the German forces near Ufiome.

(vi) VAN DEVENTER ADVANCES FURTHER SOUTH.

Such information as reached British G.H.Q. at this time revealed no enemy withdrawal from the Pare region, but, after the capture of Lolkissale, evidence of the German Commander's intention to strengthen his forces on the Kondoa Irangi side was to hand and the advance of van Deventer was pushed on and he was ordered to occupy Ufiome, Mbulu and Kondoa Irangi.

The 3rd S.A. Infantry Brigade* with a Howitzer battery and a machine gun company was ordered south in the wake of the 1st Mounted Brigade and marched in torrents of rain.

After some patrol encounters on the way, the mounted troops occupied Ufiome on April 13, and reached Salanga—roughly midway between Ufiome and Kondoa Irangi—on the night of April 13-14, driving an enemy detachment before them.

Here a halt was called to allow some rations to come up, and on April 16 the Mounted Brigade, now only 650 rifles, again advanced towards Kondoa Irangi where, from a distance of 7 miles, the enemy was observed holding positions on the hills to the north of the village.

Establishing touch with the enemy on the following day, van Deventer attacked the German forces on the 18th. On April 19 the latter retired and evacuated the village which van Deventer occupied after pursuing the enemy (about 400 rifles) some miles to the south.

Heavy and continuous rain had now saturated the country. The infantry were endeavouring to make their way south through seas of mud, the wireless instruments broke down and communication was only possible by means of mounted orderlies.

Horses and mules died by the hundred, mechanical transport became embedded in the mud, and, though cattle were found at Kondoa Irangi—it was a rich cattle district—van Deventer's mounted men were compelled to supplement a meagre meat ration with fruit and nuts.

---

* Less one Battalion, the 10th S.A. Infantry.

In the face of every kind of obstacle Kondoa Irangi had been occupied, but van Deventer's entire force had been reduced to immobility.

Unfortunately the information about the rains and their effect had proved incorrect, as also was the statement that the country south of the railway was unsuited to the subsistence of the German Forces.

Von Deventer's immobility was perhaps of no special importance at this juncture, as General Smuts obviously could not allow him to go futher until his own coming advance should have reached a point in the direction of the Central Railway where the enemy would have to take the movements of the two forces into serious account. The main consequences of the unforeseen magnitude of the rainfall were the heavy incidence of disease upon the personnel and the great wastage of animals, and, consequently, the difficulty of getting supplies forward to van Deventer during his enforced stay at Kondoa Irangi.

Later, on June 19, van Deventer reported 1,200 sick and wholesale loss of horses and mules. On June 20 he stated that 1,600 horses and 1,800 mules in addition to large numbers then en route to Kondoa Irangi were essential " to make his division effective ".

As always in this campaign, loss of animals meant loss of lift in supplies, and scarcity of supplies entailed a swollen sick list.

(vii) GENERAL VON LETTOW ACTS AGAINST VAN DEVENTER.

General von Lettow now decided that " the enemy was evidently directing his principal effort towards Kondo Irangi " and resolved to " occupy " (i.e. contain) the enemy station in the Kilimanjaro country (General Smuts) and " direct (his) main force against the hostile group which had meanwhile pushed forward to near Kondoa Irangi ". He accordingly moved fifteen field companies and two mounted companies across to the west, and concentrated a force near Kondoa Irangi which at one time, in consequence of the heavy casualties van Deventer had incurred, outnumbered the latter in rifle power, and, in view of the extended perimeter necessarily occupied by the 2nd Division, made the position of the latter at one time unpleasantly doubtful.

General von Lettow, before leaving personally for Kondoa Irangi, handed over command of all the troops opposite General Smuts to Major Kraut and organised a separate administrative service for them.

Until the rains should have ceased, the forces under General Smuts were weather bound and could undertake no forward movement.

(viii) THE SECOND BLOCKADE RUNNER.

Information was now received that there was a defended base at Ssudi Bay (on the extreme south coast below Lindi) and that vessels entering harbour had been fired upon by a 4″ gun, machine guns, and rifles, and that a cargo steamer was beached inside.

Incidentally, the Naval authorities reported that, as a result of their attention, the cargo vessel had been put out of action and rendered quite unseaworthy. In point of fact, no trace whatever of the vessel was found when the advance reached Ssudi, and it eventually turned up at Batavia! Arms, ammunition—including several thousand rounds for the Königsberg 4″ guns—and other warlike stores were part of the cargo.

The immediate result of this was a remarkable increase in the volume of the enemy fire and the campaign was probably prolonged by this stroke of luck. Von Lettow records that: " we were quickly able to bring up the four field howitzers and two mountain guns which had come in the ship ", while less essential, but cheering, were " one Iron Cross of the First Class for the Captain of the Königsberg and enough of the Second Class to enable half her company to have one each ".

The General himself received a well-earned Iron Cross of the First and Second Class, while there were a number of decorations for the Askaris.

(ix) EVENTS SUCCEEDING THE OCCUPATION OF KONDOA IRANGI.

It was on April 21 that news reached G.H.Q. from van Deventer of his occupation of Kondoa Irangi.

The time between his departure from Lolkissale and the attainment of his objective had been one of confusion, congestion on the sodden roads, and efforts in all directions on the part of the staff to deal with the abnormal situation.

Transport and supplies were annexed all along the rain-sodden tracks between Moschi and all units forward in the direction of Aruscha and Kondoa Irangi by the first formation fortunate enough to get its hand upon them, and the pacification of irate responsible officers, used to regulation methods and shocked by the complete absence of them in the action of the commando brigade, was not the least difficult work which at this time fell to the lot of the senior officers of the staff.

The following was a typical instance. The B.G., R.A., some of whose transport and ammunition columns had disappeared into the " blue ", if the grey, impenetrable curtain which covered everything from view may be so called, made daily spirited efforts to obtain, if not his missing vehicles, at all events some tidings of them. The following entry in the diary of the writer, prompted by a considerable experience of " commando " mentality, gives the solution: " suspect van Deventer has collared everything he can lay his hands on for supply purposes ".

On April 21, van Deventer reported that six field companies of the enemy were opposite him, of which three had faced the attack on Latema-Reata, while the remaining three came from Nyasa, Ujiji and the Congo border. Half of these forces had reached his neighbourhood three days before his message and further reinforcements were expected. A concentration against him was clearly in process of arrangement.

He reported heavy and continuous rain and that his operations were hampered by weak horses.

It may give some idea of the wastage involved if it is stated that at this time the Union offered 1,000 horses a month for the two mounted brigades and was asked to send *at least* twice that number.

The loss of two shiploads of horses and mules at this time from glanders and anthrax was an additional trouble.

The closer co-operation of the Belgians was being arranged at this time, but was hindered by want of transport which they could not supply. Their minimum demand of 300 carts made matters no less difficult.

In his report of the occupation of Kondoa Irangi van Deventer stated that the dense vegetation and bush made an exact computation of the enemy losses impossible, but that 20 dead had been left and he had captured 3 Europeans and 30

Askaris. The enemy had destroyed large quantities of supplies and the wireless installation. He was in pursuit of the enemy force which was retiring by the Dodoma and Kilimatinde roads " wholly demoralised ".

This encouraging estimate of his adversaries' state of mind was corrected to some extent by subsequent events.

He added that enemy reinforcements had again been sent to his front and that his " mobile " force was reduced to 600 and would not be able to move without remounts.

(x) THE PARE-USAMBARA AREA.

Opposite General Smuts, in consequence of continuous heavy rain, the Pangani river, the line of the coming advance, and its tributaries were in flood and forming large swamps.

Wapare scouts reported an evacuation of the Pare mountains and, in order to arrive at a correct estimate of its extent, General Smuts instructed Pretorius, a scout, to investigate.

(xi) PRETORIUS.

Pretorius was a most remarkable man. Leaving South Africa after the Anglo-Boer War of 1899-1902, he betook himself to German East Africa where he had settled, if his life included anything so hum-drum as settlement, on the Rufiji river.

Here he had an extensive garden along the river bank. He was, however, far less interested in productive return from the garden than in its value as an inducement to elephants to trespass. On one of the extremely rare occasions when he could be induced to utter a word about himself, he explained that only when elephant were actually damaging cultivated land was it permissible to shoot one without paying a very heavy fine. It was understood that no inconsiderable damage was done to the garden with fatal consequences to the marauders, for he was a dead shot.

He had tremendous influence with natives. The Germans for obvious reasons, not the least compelling of which were this influence and his intimate knowledge of the country, took steps to secure him as soon as war broke out, and, in the course of the activities incidental to the effort to capture him, Pretorius sustained a severe wound. The disability was great enough to

110

make any movement on his part impossible unless he were carried. Transported by natives, he eluded capture and, crossing the Rovuma river, alone, except for his native allies who carried him, reached Portuguese territory. Arrived at Pretoria he offered his services and unique knowledge to the authorities.

Brave, resolute, and calmly self-confident, Pretorius was invaluable.

Alone, except for a carefully chosen band of natives, he used to camp practically alongside the enemy whose movements he immediately conveyed to General Smuts, usually by a native messenger. He rarely came in himself and remained invisible except when he became too ill from malaria to carry on without medical assistance. At the earliest possible moment after having been patched up he would return to his watch.

The enemy was under no illusion as to the danger of the constant surveillance and it is said that one German scout, irritated by constant failures to entrap Pretorius, set out to do so himself vowing not to return until he should have been successful. In one detail he carried out his promise for he did not return, but was captured by the object of his attention, with his entire safari, within 24 hours.

(xii) FURTHER EVENTS AT KONDOA IRANGI.

Pretorius returned a week after his departure and confirmed the Wapares' report of enemy movement from the Pare district. He also gave valuable information gathered in the course of a week's activity in the enemy lines.

Railhead from Voi reached New Moschi on April 25.

On this date the Belgians began their advance on Kigali, the capital of Ruanda, in the north-west of the Protectorate. This territory, where the dominant race was the Watussi, had been carefully and tactfully administered by the Germans to whom the local Sultan was very favourably disposed.

German prisoners captured by van Deventer stated that the rapidity of the latter's advance had come as a great surprise.

Van Deventer reported that he had three of his mounted regiments and two batteries at Kondoa Irangi and that his remaining mounted regiment and infantry were moving on the last-named place from Lolkissale.

111

Incidentally he asked that he might be supplied with " a large sum of money " to pay native porters, guides and scouts whom he was engaging. Money was the easiest of the sinews of war that it was possible to give him at this time, but no amount of it could produce the common necessaries of life at Kondoa Irangi or along his communications, and his men now began to experience the shortage of rations which was to become their daily lot. Quarter rations, half that amount, and often no rations at all had to be supplemented by mealies, pawpaw and bananas, and van Deventer's hospitals began to fill.

He now asked that he should be allowed to concentrate all troops between Lolkissale and Kondoa Irangi at the latter place, as he foresaw the likelihood of a strong concentration against him.

At this date, mid-April, the main force of the enemy, according to all information, remained along the Tanga railway, and there was nothing to support a view that any actual transfer from the north-east to the west had taken place. Such enemy reinforcements as van Deventer had reported as opposite him had come from the Lakes region.

Added to this, the growing difficulties of transport and supply to Kondoa Irangi and the medical situation made anything but the very slowest movement impossible.

He was accordingly ordered to remain for the time being without a further concentration of his force.

In fact, the initiative, wrested from von Lettow at Taveta, was once more with him and so remained until General Smuts, again able to advance on the cessation of the rains, resumed it and moved from the Ruwu at the end of May.

The next move was to come from the enemy and, early in May, it came.

(xiii) THE ENEMY ACTIVE AT KONDOA IRANGI.

Though information for some time tended to indicate that no substantial transfer of strength had taken place from the Usambara region, it is clear from his own account that von Lettow had been preparing for action against van Deventer, and at the end of April news of companies passing to the south through Handeni came to hand.

Pretorius on his return had reported the Pare deserted.

The movement against Mbulu set in train from Lolkissale by the despatch of a mounted regiment was reinforced and van Deventer was ordered to clear the place which he did on May 11 when his detachment occupied it without opposition, the enemy withdrawing southwards.

An intercepted wireless message on May 2 contained instructions for the formation of detachments in Tabora, Mwansa and Bukoba districts into a western command with headquarters at Tabora. Control of the railway and supplies, however, remained with the Chief Command. A division of the enemy forces was therefore foreseen and provided for.

Major-General Wahle " a retired officer who happened to arrive on the 2nd August (1914) on a visit to his son " was appointed to the north-western command.

The dispositions of the German Commander-in-Chief—two companies at Lembeni opposite General Smuts and a force opposite van Deventer—who reported it as " in great strength " —at Chambalo, 20 miles south-east of Kondoa Irangi and about 10 miles west of the Kondoa-Handeni road were well arranged so as to give timely warning of any movement. Patrols operated freely from each centre.

On May 3 van Deventer reported that captured enemy porters advised him of Askari companies constantly passing through Handeni to Morogoro and stated his conviction that the enemy intended " a big stand " on his front. He added that his infantry were 50 per cent. below full strength and mounted men were waiting along the road for remounts. He had expected the 11th Infantry on April 29 and the 9th and 12th were on the march to him with his howitzers.

He was obviously worried about his loss in strength and for the second time asked that two battalions from Beves (2nd S.A. Infantry Brigade) waiting at Kumbulun, a short distance from Aruscha, should be sent to him.

From now onward it became a question from time to time whether detachments should be made to strengthen him.

He was told not to move forward and that the battalions he mentioned could not, for the present at all events, be sent to him.

The troops on the way to him were in bad case, sickness becoming rife, clothes and boots wearing out, supplies very short, and, generally, they found themselves in circumstances which demanded from them fortitude and endurance to an unusual degree and their response to the demand was now, as always in this abnormal campaign, to their eternal credit.

The Belgian movements in the north-west were much hampered also by the heavy rains and were accompanied by episodes taxing the tact and diplomacy of all concerned.

On May 4 van Deventer reported " Patrol Saranda road waylaid 1 man wounded 2 missing ". This is obviously the episode described by von Lettow as an occasion upon which " an old Effendi (native officer) acted with great skill; he lay in ambush at a water place and fired at the English, who came there for water, with good effect; according to his observation six were killed ". It is highly improbable that any patrol would give a single opponent the chance of killing six of them, and allowing " Yuman Marsal " full credit, he appears to have been well endowed with the usual gift of exaggeration possessed by the native.

On May 7 van Deventer advised G.H.Q. of the advance of the enemy from Chambalo and Kwa Mtoro on the Saranda road. His own patrols were retiring.

Van Deventer was by this time naturally enough pre-occupied with his own situation and could not be expected to think of much else—he again reported that the enemy was advancing against him in force by the Dodoma and Saranda roads—but his suggestion that the time was now ripe for an advance against the Tanga railway, which was completely protected by huge swamps, in all directions, though serious enough so far as he was concerned, did not lack an element of humour.

In addition to his men's boots which were worn out, his horses' shoes were going the same way.

Bearing in mind that the German Commander was mainly concerned to continue the campaign as long as he could, it was not possible to resist the idea that his activity at Kondoa Irangi might be due to a desire to induce the British Commander-in-Chief to detach as freely as possible more troops in support of van Deventer.

It must be remembered too that as any British force advanced, its strength diminished with astounding rapidity in this country of fever, dysentery and tsetse fly.

If, therefore, von Lettow could induce his opponent to strengthen van Deventer and, by so doing, weaken himself, the advance down the Pangani with reduced numbers might, with the aid of the climate, quite possibly be delayed from time to time and held up for weeks.

This view could not be put aside, and van Deventer was advised of it and told that while every effort was being, and would be, made to forward supplies and remounts and reinforcements belonging to his own units, General Smuts expressed his confidence in his lieutenant's ability to hold his own with his own division.

Von Lettow's account gives no indication of any clear policy behind his action at this time.

Though he asks his "reader to imagine himself in the position of a Commander with insufficient means, exposed to attack by superior numbers who has continually to ask himself what must I do in order to retain freedom of movement and hope?"; it is possible that he had an answer to his question and that, had General Smuts detached further troops to Kondoa Irangi, which he declined to do, his opponent would have taken full advantage of what would have been a mistake.

Intelligence at this time indicated eighteen companies as opposite the 2nd Division and from a native source came the first intimation—which proved to be correct—that an enemy retirement would be to Morogoro.

Lines of communication troops were now pushed out—as weather conditions would allow—to relieve van Deventer's troops from Aruscha southwards and allow them to rejoin him.

He had started to prepare an aerodrome at Kondoa Irangi but was much inconvenienced by "baobab trees and lack of tools". The baobab is, of course, of immense girth and proportions.

On May 7 van Deventer had reported his withdrawal from his advanced positions and on May 9 von Lettow—whose transfer of forces was now complete—"decided to take possession of the low hills now held by the enemy".

He had brought into action two naval guns (3.5" and 4") and at about 8 p.m. an attack was launched on the 11th S.A. Infantry which was supported by the 12th Battalion.

115

These two units (1,000 rifles) were holding a large hill to the south of Kondoa Irangi included in van Deventer's 5 mile perimeter for the whole of which he had about 3,000 rifles, 18 machine guns and 12 guns.

Von Lettow, as a result of his concentration, disposed of some 4,000 rifles, 20 machine guns (manned by Europeans and splendidly served) 3 heavy guns and some lighter artillery.

The advantage of the defence, whose riflemen were incomparably better marksmen than the Askaris opposed to them, was discounted considerably by the extent of the perimeter and the comparatively weak strength available for its protection. A third of this strength was in the position now selected by the enemy for attack.

The operation was maintained until 3 a.m. on May 10 being pressed with much determination and gallantry, the Askaris, well led, charging repeatedly home.

The defence, however, was never seriously strained, and in the early morning, in von Lettow's words: " Captain Lincke, who had assumed command, after Lieut.-Colonel von Bock had been seriously wounded, and Captain von Kornatzki killed, came to the conclusion that, although he could remain where he was, he would after daybreak be obliged to abandon all hope of being able to move on account of the dominating fire of the enemy ". He therefore " cautiously broke off the action while it was still dark and fell back on the position he had started from ".

Von Lettow adds that " considering the small number of rifles that actually took part in the fight—about 400—our casualties, amounting to about 50 killed and wounded, must be considered heavy ".

3 German and 58 Askari dead were counted at daybreak in front of the defender's position, and signs of further considerable casualties were evident.

A later German account admits a total casualty list of 147, of which 55 were killed, and it would seem that the 61 dead left behind were not counted or that the Napoleonic device of not making too much of losses was adopted.

The British losses were two officers and four other ranks killed and one officer and seventeen other ranks wounded.

The German casualties on this occasion, taking them as 147 and including the 61 found dead, omitting any dead who may have been removed, gave nearly 15 per cent. of the attacking force killed with a total loss of about 35 per cent. which is more than " considerable ".

Such an experience as this could not fail of effect, and the severe defeat of this detachment may have had something to do with the reluctance of the enemy to try conclusions again at close quarters here.

The attitude of the enemy before van Deventer at Kondoa Irangi was throughout curiously supine.

Van Deventer's extended perimeter afforded endless opportunity for attack by such mobile troops as von Lettow commanded to say nothing of his communications.

Supplies were reaching Kondoa Irangi in small quantities and at irregular intervals along a rain-soaked route where transport was held up everywhere, and the loss of any supplies in the circumstances would have been most serious, and small enemy parties well led could have caused much inconvenience and serious loss.

Yet the enemy ignored the possibilities of ventures against van Deventer's lines of communication, and confined serious effort against his positions to one unsupported attack apparently undertaken by a small detachment (" 400 rifles ", cf. von Lettow ante) entirely on the initiative of its local commander.

The delivery of such an isolated attack on a strong position by 400 rifles, unsupported by any of the 4,000 available and unrelieved by any kind of diversion elsewhere was not what his opponents had come to look for by this time from General von Lettow who was in chief command on the spot.

It would seem that three objects might reasonably be assigned as the task of the German forces before Kondoa Irangi.

(1) The capture of van Deventer's positions and perhaps his force in whole or part.

(2) The delivery of frequent attacks ostensibly dangerous enough to induce the enemy commander-in-chief to detach freely in van Deventer's support and thus weaken himself and compromise his own eventual advance.

(3) The observation of van Deventer with a view to holding him to his positions.

(3) may be disregarded, for such an object would not call for so strong a concentration as von Lettow effected at Kondoa Irangi. The German Commander-in-Chief was aware that van Deventer could not move for many weeks, and a far smaller force could have observed the latter and given ample warning of any impending movement on his part, for von Lettow must have been well served by the number of spies who were available.

If at first the recapture of Kondoa Irangi see (1), was contemplated it would seem that the idea was soon abandoned and it is hardly probable that its abandonment would have been influenced by the repulse of a small detachment.

The second of the objects—and it almost seems to be the most likely of the three—enumerated above could not be attained without far more apparent intention of serious attack than was afforded by the single venture of the detachment already mentioned.

Further experiments of the nature of that of the night of May 9-10 would seriously reduce the numbers of his Askaris and could not but detrimentally affect their *moral.*

The lack of venturesomeness which characterised the action of the German Commander-in-Chief before van Deventer is difficult to account for, and one is forced to the conclusion that the experience of von Kornatzky's detachment on the night of May 9-10 and it heavy defeat was the cause of it.

Von Lettow writes that after the incident " *the enemy did not seem to be in great strength as yet;* but, even if successful, our attack would have to be made over open ground against defences which with our few guns, we could not sufficiently neutralise. The certainty of suffering considerable and irreplaceable losses decided me to refrain from a general attack and instead to damage the enemy by continuing the minor enterprise which had hitherto proved so advantageous ".

It is not clear what " damage " he succeeded in doing to van Deventer whose losses and difficulties were due to the climate and to no action by his enemy in circumstances which were favourable to effective action by the latter in several directions.

The German concentration induced by General Smuts moving van Deventer to Kondoa Irangi was singularly barren of any kind of result, except that of weakening the enemy forces in the Usambara area for which purpose the British Commander-in-Chief had devised the advance of his 2nd Division and which the action of his opponent had assisted him to achieve.

While the necessity for conserving the strength of his forces was always the proper concern of General von Lettow, in the circumstances in which he found himself, it would seem that a good deal more could have been done by the large concentration which his opponent's strategy had compelled him to effect before van Deventer.

It was the climate, and not any action by the enemy, which produced the embarrassments of the Commander of the 2nd Division who had reason to be thankful that the enemy failed to add to them when such a course seemed to be quite possible.

There is one more possible explanation of General von Lettow's tardy concentration before van Deventer and evidence is not wanting which tends to show that it may be the right one.

The German Commander-in-Chief attached much importance to the occupation of Kondoa Irangi, see his observation quoted on p. 101 and regraded the capture of Lolkissale as opening " the interior of the colony to the enemy coming from Aruscha ".

He was apprised on April 5 of van Deventer's success at Lolkissale and was then compelled hurriedly to move troops across from Lembeni which arrived too late to prevent the capture of Kondoa Irangi.

It is not intelligible why, seeing that he regarded Kondoa Irangi as of such importance and was right in this view, he did not take measures to ensure its safety by the provision of an adequate garrison. Had he done so, it is possible that van Deventer with his depleted mounted force would have found the capture of the place beyond his power.

There is reason to suppose that, according to advice which he received and relied upon, he drew the conclusion that a move by General Smuts against Kondoa Irangi in such weather as would attend the venture was impossible of success and did not take it into serious consideration.

If this be the case, his opponent succeeded in outwitting and forestalling him.

CHAPTER VIII

(i) VAN DEVENTER AGAIN ASKS FOR REINFORCEMENTS.

ON May 12 General Smuts acceded to the continued requests of van Deventer for reinforcements to the extent of sending the two battalions of Beves' (2nd S.A. Infantry) Brigade which were at Kumbulun to Kondoa Irangi, and they moved from the former place on that date under the command of Lieut.-Colonel Taylor, the senior battalion commander. These units were the 7th and 8th S.A. Infantry.

Van Deventer now telegraphed saying that the whole of Beves' Brigade should be sent to him and that there was " not the slightest doubt " in his mind that the enemy had concentrated all strength possible against him.

It was in all the circumstances natural perhaps that van Deventer should not give much thought to the campaign as a whole, but the country was beginning to dry up, and the rain was lessening, and a general forward movement was now engaging the attention of the Commander-in-Chief.

Though it is now apparent that the reverse sustained by the enemy at Kondoa Irangi was far more serious to him in a material sense than could possibly be known at G.H.Q. at the time, the moral effect of it was even more important, for it decided the German Commander-in-Chief to refrain from any wholehearted attempt against van Deventer again.

But even if von Lettow *were* credited with an intention to attack again, van Deventer was well able to take care of himself. What he was in need of was all kinds of supplies and the means of transporting them, not more mouths to eat the slender rations he had and more sick to encumber his hospitals. Another march to him even in the improved climatic conditions, would mean many casualties from disease. Such casualties were heavy in the regiments which now went forward.

5 miles was a large perimeter but within the remembrance of some was the siege of Wepener (Jammersberg Drift) in the Anglo-Boer War where less than half the number of rifles with van Deventer had 15 years before successfully defended a

perimeter of 7 miles against a far more formidable force of 6,000 of his own countrymen under the redoubtable General de Wet.

Nature which had kept the Eastern Force with General Smuts completely immobile during the rains had now reduced the 2nd Division under van Deventer to precisely the same condition in which it remained for the next two months.

Heavy casualties in men, horses and mules from death and disease, in consequence of the lack of food, drugs and material, had occurred in van Deventer's command as a result of its forward movement in the rainy season.

Von Lettow, freely served by native spies in and round Kondoa Irangi, was well aware of van Deventer's predicament and could in 10 days or so, if he desired and decided to do so, move any number of his troops across from the west to meet the advance along the Pangani.

This last movement might be seriously compromised by any further detachments in van Deventer's direction, for the forces moving along the river would be subject to the steady and inevitable loss of rifle power which had invariably to be taken into account in the case of European and Indian troops when estimating the strength which could eventually be deployed in action.

General Smuts now finally told the Commander of the 2nd Division that he could have no more troops.

(ii) AN APPRECIATION OF THE SITUATION WITH REFERENCE TO THE EMPLOYMENT OF ADDI-TIONAL MOUNTED TROOPS.

An important point now to be decided was the method of employing the second mounted brigade due to arrive shortly with General Brits.

Should it in the early stages be employed east or west of the Pares?

Its movement to the west of the mountains was decided upon for three main reasons:—

1. Touch with van Deventer at the earliest possible date was of importance. It could be best obtained by troops reaching out westward.

2. A retirement before van Deventer would give opportunity for far-reaching results if mounted men could be used to intercept it.

3. Only small patrols of the enemy—though numerous and very active—had been located east of the mountains.

(iii) AN APPRECIATION OF THE SITUATION GENERALLY.

On May 18 General Smuts was able to go to Kahe on the Ruwu, hitherto since its occupation cut off by the rains. Here he found Pretorius who had been ambushed at Marago Opuni where he had come upon a company of the enemy with a machine gun. With his usual resource he had extricated himself with a loss of 2 Europeans, one of his natives and 7 horses and mules. If it is stated that Marago Opuni was 40 miles in a straight line south of the furthest British outposts, some idea of this extraordinary man's activity may be formed.

General Smuts now advised the War Office of the outline of his coming campaign, asking that horses might be sent regularly (1,000 a month from sources other than the Union) and emphasizing the opportunity for an advance by Northey (Nyasaland) in the south-west, the Portuguese in the south and the Belgians in the north-west.

The latter were still on the move and on May 19 attacked and occupied Sebea.

Taylor with the 7th and 8th S.A. Infantry en route for Kondoa Irangi had reached Ufiome, but reported his men to be footsore and badly in need of boots, and van Deventer was helping him on by means of motor lorries.

The latter reported the great majority of his remaining horses without shoes and that his mules were in the same condition.

His position, so far as his animals were concerned, had not been improved by the loss of a number of mules in consequence of a stampede by lions. These were some of the complications which beset a military commander in this country.

The enemy's probable action now became an interesting subject of speculation in connection with the coming movements.

The problem which seemed to face him was how to retain his hold on the Central Railway, or at all events on some portion of it, which would serve him from depots and how he could prolong hostilities.

His opponent's advance would compel him to take steps to withdraw in due course—

(A) to the west towards Tabora;
(B) to the east towards Morogoro and Dar-es-Salaam;
(C) to south of the Central Railway;

or

(D) he could of course stand and fight north of the Central Railway.

Unless depots of ample dimensions had been arranged in places away from the railway, the latter would be important to him for supply purposes.

It seemed that (A) might be ruled out. Its adoption would, of course, ensure the concentration of all his forces under the hand of the Commander-in-Chief, but the intercepted messages had shown that a Western Command had been established and that the railway and supply would remain under the Chief Command.

(D) might be eliminated also, for it was obviously foolish to take the risk of encirclement if, as was the case, to keep his force intact, and effective for the duration of hostilities was von Lettow's chief concern. Many, however, disagreed with this view and expected a decisive engagement on or near the Central Railway.

Von Lettow's remarks on this point are interesting. He writes: " The enemy expected us to stand and fight a final decisive engagement near Morogoro. To me this idea was never altogether intelligible. Being so very much the weaker party it was surely madness to await at this place the junction of the hostile columns ".

There remained the courses described under (B) and (C) and in the end he took (B) except that his withdrawal to the south took place at Morogoro and he did not move further to the east.

In any case the contemplated movements of the two forces under Generals Smuts and van Deventer together with the situations of those forces were best calculated to meet any of the several movements open to the enemy. See map number seven.

Several plans were, as usual, suggested, and one was that a small force should move down the Usambara railway and the balance of Beves' Brigade as well as the new Mounted Brigade should be sent round to Kondoa Irangi to get between the enemy and Tabora and push him eastwards.

For the success of such a plan it had to be assumed that there were very few troops in the Usambara area, an assumption for which the intelligence available gave no ground. It also entailed acceptance of the enemy's intention to go towards Tabora, whereas information indicated a contrary purpose.

It also meant at least six weeks' delay, for clearly no small force could move down the Usambara railway until the concentration at Kondoa Irangi should have taken place.

Finally it involved staking everything on a situation which was only one of several which might arise.

The plan was not accepted but is mentioned as an instance of how plans are framed on insufficient data and preconceived ideas.

Van Deventer at this time mentioned that it was " very difficult to get information from behind the enemy ", that is as a result of his own efforts.

Deserters and prisoners were the normal source of information, and over and over again their statements proved to be exactly contrary to fact. Misleading your opponent by false information is a time-honoured practice and was freely employed by the Germans in East Africa.

Later on van Deventer wired that prisoners on his front stated that the retirement of the enemy would be to Tabora as " Morogoro was too unhealthy to be held ". It was, however, known that Morogoro was an important European centre.

Northey communicated on May 19 his intention " to attack all along line Abercorn to Karonga " on the 25th.

To this General Smuts replied expressing his pleasure at Northey's intention and gave it as his opinion that, if the latter and the Portuguese were to move to the Central Railway from the south-west and south-east respectively, the campaign could be concluded there. This view contemplated a rate of progression by the Portuguese at any rate very far beyond what proved to be within their power.

Van Deventer made a final effort to obtain a minimum of 8,000 troops to take advantage of " an excellent opportunity to surround the enemy here ", and asked if that strength could be placed at his disposal immediately.

He was again of course solely considering his local position and showed the inability to think of movement except in terms of mounted troops which several of the best leaders among his countrymen shared.

As a matter of fact his mounted troops were at this time immobile and remained so for two months longer.

It would have taken nearly two months to meet his request which was once more and for the last time refused.

(iv) THE ADVANCE DOWN THE PANGANI.

On May 22, the weather being fine, General Smuts and G.H.Q. left Old Moschi and at noon reached Kahe where they were met by Major-General Hoskins, commanding the 1st Division and his Brigadiers, Brig.-Generals Hannyngton and Sheppard and Brig.-General Beves, and the method of the advance was explained.

The country over which this advance was to take place is described in General Smuts' despatch of October 27, 1916, as follows:—

" The nature of the country was such as almost to preclude all rapidity of movement. The Pares and Usambaras are huge blocks of mountains with fertile valleys; the southern slopes are precipitous, and immediately below runs the Tanga railway while further south dense bush extends for 15 or 20 miles to the Pangani, an impassable river flowing almost parallel to the railway and the mountains. The enemy held the mountains and the railway and had outposts along the Pangani river ".

Dense thorn bush covered the flat country, which was waterless, between the mountain ranges and river, but near the river open grass land lay between it and the bush referred to to a width of some hundreds of yards to a mile.

It was along this belt of easier ground that the main advance made its way.

125

The enemy had prepared strong defences round Lembeni and Ngulu Gap and to the south about Same. As we have seen, the German Commander had followed his usual custom of careful personal reconnaissance of all likely places where successful resistance might be offered to the advance against him.

(v) COMPOSITION OF THE EASTERN FORCE.

The composition of the force which now took the eastern line of advance to the Central Railway was as follows:—

The whole operation was under the personal direction of General Smuts who kept under his hand a "Force Reserve" which consisted of the undermentioned units under Brigadier-General Beves:—

Belfield's Scouts.
5th S.A. Infantry.
6th S.A. Infantry.
No. 8 Field Battery.
134th Howitzer Battery.

The remainder of the force was under the command of Major-General Hoskins, commander of the 1st Division, and was as follows, being organized in three columns:—

Western Column.
Brigadier-General Sheppard.

One squadron, 17th (Indian) Cavalry.
2nd Rhodesia Regiment.
130th Baluchis.
Battalion Kashmir Rifles.
No. 5 Battery, S.A. Field Artillery.
27th Mountain Battery (less 1 section).
One double company, 61st Pioneers.
One British Field Ambulance.
Two sections, Indian Field Ambulance.
Ammunition and Supply Columns.

Centre Column.
Brigadier-General Hannyngton.

E.A. Mounted Rifles (approximately 3 troops).
40th Pathans.
129th Baluchis.
Half battalion, Kashmir Rifles.
No. 6 Field Battery.

No. 7 Field Battery.
One section, E.A. Pioneers.
Two sections, Indian Field Ambulance.
Ammunition and Supply Columns.

Eastern Column.
Lieut.-Colonel Fitzgerald.

One Company, K.A.R., M.I.
3rd K.A.R.
One section, 27th Mountain Battery.
One section, Indian Field Ambulance.
Ammunition and Supply Columns.

Divisional Reserve.
Major-General Hoskins.

Divisional Headquarters.
Mounted Infantry Company.
E.A. Mounted Rifles (less detachment with
  Hannyngton).
25th Royal Fusiliers.
29th Punjabis.
L.N. Lancs Machine Gun Company.
No. 1 Armoured Car Battery.
One section, E.A. Pioneers.
One section, British Field Ambulance.
E.A. Field Ambulance.
Ammunition and Supply Columns.

(vi) THE ADVANCE BEGUN.

The plan of the advance was as follows:—

The main body, i.e. the western column (Sheppard), the Divisional Reserve and the Force Reserve to move along the Pangani. The Commander-in-Chief and G.H.Q. followed the same route.

The centre column (Hannyngton) was directed along the Tanga railway and had upon its left the Pare and Usambara mountains of which the height ranged from 4,000 to 7,500 feet. On the mountain slopes were thick bush and virgin forest.

The Pangani was also bordered with forest, mainly of raffia palm.

Between these two forces lay the waterless tract of bush country already mentioned.

A difficult terrain where all power of extended observation was with the enemy and which afforded ample opportunity for the use of von Lettow's personally selected " passages " and " fields of fire ".

East of the mountains marched the Eastern column (Fitzgerald).

The western and centre columns moved from the line of the Ruwu on the evening of May 22, the Force Reserve (Beves) coming on from Store and following the two columns at daybreak on May 23.

The Eastern Column (Fitzgerald) left Mbuyuni after nightfall on May 20, proceeding by a road fit for transport which had been constructed from Mbuyuni past the eastern shore of Lake Jipe in the direction of Ngulu Gap.

(vii) THE LINES OF COMMUNICATION OF THE EASTERN AND WESTERN FORCES.

The communications of these separate forces at the start lay for the main body back, along the way of its advance down the Pangani, to Kahe and thence to Moschi; for the centre column along the Tanga railway and road beside it to the same places; and for the eastern column, until it should, as it shortly did, join the centre, back along the road by which it came to Mbuyuni.

The railway from Voi, after almost superhuman efforts during the rainy season, had been connected with the Tanga railway, but some time was to elapse before it became of use beyond Kahe.

While the drier weather made actual progress along van Deventer's lines of communication easier, or perhaps the position may be made clearer if it is said that the improved conditions made some appreciable and more or less regular movement of transport possible, the fact that there were now two strong forces to be supplied instead of one made the replacement of van Deventer's losses a lengthy and difficult business.

Not only had deficiencies to be made good, but current needs, now more pressing than ever, had to be met, and the supply service could no longer concentrate on the supply of van Deventer, as it had been able to do when the rest of the forces remained immobile.

The lines of communication of the 2nd Division stretched for some 200 miles from Kondoa Irangi to Moschi via Ufiome, and Aruscha. They were over what in East Africa went by the name of roads and no railway served the force at Kondoa Irangi beyond Moschi. See map number seven.

On the eastern side lines of communication hospitals were established at Kahe, New Moschi, Taveta and Mbuyuni.

With van Deventer the various mobile medical units became immobile and acted as stationary hospitals. They were placed at Kondoa Irangi, Mbulu, and Aruscha, with sections at Lolkissale and other places.

(viii) PROGRESS OF THE EASTERN FORCE.

By May 25 the Eastern Column (Fitzgerald) had reached Njata, the Centre Column (Hannyngton) was 20 miles north of Same, and the main body (Hoskin's and Sheppard) about a mile north of Marago Opuni. No special incidents had marked their advances.

Ngulu and Kandoro on the east and Kissangire and Lembeni on the railway were found unoccupied. Same bridge had been blown up.

No sign of the enemy in strength was detected, but on May 26 an enemy patrol of 1 European, and 5 Askaris with porters, from Same was captured at the end of a footpath cut from Same to the spot where they were found. Their orders were to await the arrival of the advancing force, estimate its numbers, and return to Buiko, so that the enemy main body was evidently still to the south, an opinion which was confirmed by an air reconnaissance which reported a large fortified camp at Mikocheni close to Buiko.

The activity of the enemy patrols in the strip between the railway and the river was further realised when on the morning of May 27 General Smuts took an excursion into the plain on the left of the main advance. He was anxious to reach the hill of Old Le Sara from which he intended to make a personal reconnaissance of the country ahead. He first encountered two very diminutive natives with bows and arrows. These were Wandorobbo, slaves of the Masai, who wandered about the steppes following herds of game, hunting with poisoned arrows and throwing spears. They were not a formidable pair and disappeared in terror with great relief when told that they might go.

5　　　　　　　　　　129

Having reached and climbed Old Le Sara, however, two or three patrols, obviously of the enemy, were noticed by the few companions of the Commander-in-Chief approaching the hill from different directions and evidently keeping a rendezvous.

Slipping down to the cars under cover through the bush the party fortunately met a patrol of Belfield's Scouts at the foot of the hill and regained the main body.

Hannyngton was now ordered to join up with Fitzgerald, take command of the combined columns and follow the Same-Gonya road, sending patrols along the railway line.

The advance went steadily on without any incident of importance until May 29 when the mounted troops of the main body came in contact with the enemy a mile east of Mbirioni and the latter, after blowing up a bridge, withdrew by train towards Mikocheni. Here the enemy Commander took up a position on the slopes of the mountain where the flats were the narrowest and where road, mountain, railway and river met.

Fire was opened on the advancing columns and the transport strung out over the plain from a 4.1″ gun of the Königsberg's armament.

The possession of the heights and the target of the stretched out columns visible on the grassy plain below were two advantages rarely accorded to the artillery of either side in this country of dense bush.

The fire of the gun was very ineffective and resulted in one man being killed and one wounded in the Force Reserve.

The day was occupied in reconnaissances and in moving up the long line of troops and transport, and sunset found the force much dispersed and its units camped where they stopped when the light failed, without being able to make any proper arrangements for defence.

The situation lent itself admirably to the successful delivery of one of General von Lettow's counter-attacks, but was fortunately unknown to his representative on the spot who was also mainly concerned with his own safety.

Trains had been observed pointing southwards.

On the following day no opportunity was taken of a splendid target afforded by Sheppard's camp in full view from the German position as well as by the transport parked behind Mbirioni and it was concluded that the enemy had retired.

An attack made between 1 and 2 p.m. on the Rhodesians from the right bank of the Pangani and supported by some 7-pounders was not pressed and was evidently a diversion to cover a withdrawal.

The Rhodesians, reinforced by the 29th Punjabis, remained in possession of the German trenches which they had occupied in the morning.

Towards evening Sheppard's mountain battery opened on the enemy camp at Mikocheni from the Pare foothills and his column remained there.

The German position had now been located as from the Pangani to the foot of the Pare with trenches running across its lowest slopes.

Sheppard was ordered to send a section of his mountain guns and a double company up the mountain during the night and himself to push on against the enemy's right early the following morning while the Rhodesians and 29th acted similarly against the left.

A bridge, afterwards known as " German Bridge ", was found in an advanced state of construction across the river with most of the material needed for its completion (except wood which grew in abundance at hand) beside it. The Rapids south-west of Mbinioni were reported as easily to be bridged and preparations to this end had also been made by the enemy on the spot.

Major Kraut commanded a force estimated at from 1,500 to 2,000, but it included 200 Germans and machine guns which, in the hands of their European crews, often wrought havoc in their opponents' ranks advancing against prepared positions, and every additional mile of the advance meant casualties in every unit and among all ranks from disease.

The relative strength of the two opposing forces along the Pangani cannot therefore be stated in exact figures, and the longer the advance continued so did actual numbers tend to approximate.

The evacuation of Tanga was reported to have begun on May 21.

In the north-west two Belgian columns, commanded respectively by Captains Molitor and Olsen had effected a junction at Niansa, and the country between Rusisi and Kagera rivers and north of latitude 2.30 was clear of the enemy.

The weather since the movement from Kahe had been fine.

On May 31 the movements which had been ordered made it clear that the enemy had vacated all his positions up to Mkomazi where scouts came into touch with his rearguard at about 2 p.m.

General Smuts now moved to Buiko, where he took up his quarters at the railway station, his forces being suitably disposed in the neighbourhood.

In the evening the 4.1" gun opened at long range against the troops moving up to Buiko. It seemed obvious from the fact that it could not be traversed that the gun was on a truck on the railway, and an effort was made to locate it and bomb it from the air, but without result. It did slight damage.

The aeroplanes were ordered to reconnoitre the railway with a view to interfering with rolling stock and movement, and Korogwe and Mombo in search of indications of intended resistance.

General Smuts now decided to await the arrival of Hannyngton's force before moving on, and an expert estimate of the time that it would take to repair the railway from Kahe to the point reached by the advance was asked for.

Information as to his situation was also asked for from van Deventer from whom no recent reports had been received.

(ix) THE SUPPLY POSITION IMPOSES A HALT ON THE EAST.

The enemy in retiring had effected numerous demolitions of bridges on rail and road alike, and on May 31 the forces at Buiko were unable to move further as supply arrangements had broken down. The advance had been taken more than 100 miles from its starting point but a halt was now imperative. The troops were now on half rations as their normal allowance.

It was decided to change the line of supply from the river route to the Tanga railway and the road alongside it.

Before another forward movement could be undertaken it was necessary to build up some reserve at Buiko and to guarantee its maintenance. A switch such as that which now became necessary means delay and some confusion under the most favourable conditions; under those which existed at this time on the Pangani premature advance might well mean something far more serious. It was obviously sounder to wait now deliberately than to be held up later—in a few marches at most—by force of circumstances and perhaps in a place and situation far less satisfactory.

(x) GENERAL SMUTS VISITS VAN DEVENTER.

In view of the enforced inactivity which faced him, General Smuts decided to carry out an intention which he had formed of visiting van Deventer on the west.

Before starting, the Commander-in-Chief settled many details in connection with the resumption of the advance, foremost among which was the bridging of the Pangani, for the next movement to the south would be on the other side of the river.

By this time Hannyngton had reached Mkomazi.

A letter had been picked up from à German officer at Mauri to von Brandis (Chief of Staff of the Northern Troops) stating that von Kornatzki, one Battalion Commander, had been killed and another (this was von Bock) wounded and that 125 Askaris had lost their lives in the attack at Kondoa Irangi. This figure is much in excess of that given by General von Lettow—already quoted—(on page 116) but is more in accordance with a reasoned calculation and accounts for a reluctance to engage van Deventer on such terms again. The loss of over a hundred seasoned Askaris was a very serious matter in von Lettow's circumstances.

Having handed over local control for the time to Major-General Hoskins, General Smuts left on his 300 mile journey to van Deventer on June 2. He travelled by car accompanied by three staff officers.

Sleeping at Old Moschi, he reached Lolkissale, the scene of van Deventer's success on April 6, at 7.30 p.m. on the 3rd.

On June 4, after a very early start and many breakdowns, the consequence of water in the engine from a drift the day before, and driving some distance in the dark, the party bivouacked 24 miles from Kondoa Irangi, just off the track in the bush. A patrol of 8 mounted men of van Deventer's rode into the camp about 11 p.m. and, in view of the proximity of the enemy, were kept with the Commander-in-Chief.

Leaving camp at 6 a.m., General Smuts arrived at Kondoa Irangi at noon on June 5.

The first news of Portuguese activity came to hand about this time by way of Zanzibar.

The Portuguese had attempted a combined naval and military operation for the crossing of the Rovuma, but had been repulsed with a loss of 308 killed and missing and an unreported number of casualties from wounds. Their boats had grounded under fire. They were expecting reinforcements and proposed to await their arrival before renewing the attempt. British ships were standing by to assist, if necessary.

The afternoon of General Smuts' arrival at Kondoa Irangi was occupied by a visit to van Deventer's right flank and an examination of the ground held by the enemy from there.

It had become abundantly clear during the journey from Lolkissale that the supply and transport position of the 2nd Division was grave and the Inspector-General of the Lines of Communication was asked what he could do to ease the situation by taking over up to Ufiome. This step was arranged a few days later.

Hoskins reported the progress which had been made in bridge building and was instructed to move on as soon as he could do so without waiting for the Commander-in-Chief's return.

On June 6, General Smuts rode out about 9 miles to the east of Kondoa Irangi and viewed the country to the south and south-east.

Here General Manie Botha was found. His mounted men were engaged with the enemy who had placed a force on the extreme east of van Deventer's position almost covering the Handeni road and in any case denying it to him.

The fighting was of a very desultory and inconclusive nature and the enemy did not appear to be in strength, though they were using two 7 pounders and 2 or 3 machine guns.

It looked like a bluff to cover the road to Handeni for some purpose. Possibly a retirement in consequence of the Pangani advance or to secure the passage of reinforcements which native intelligence at this time indicated as on a large scale.

Returning to Kondoa Irangi at 8 p.m., General Smuts left on his return to the eastern force on the following morning, June 7.

His visit had been productive of good result.

It had made it possible to assist van Deventer with better effect as his needs were more correctly gauged, and he himself, better posted as to the general situation, was a good deal happier about his own.

Personal discussion between the Commander-in-Chief and his lieutenant had helped in a decision as to how best to co-operate in their future movements.

Lolkissale was reached at 4 p.m., 117 miles having been covered in less than 10 hours, which was rapid movement in such country.

General Smuts arrived at Moschi at noon the following day, and leaving 24 hours later, camped for the night of June 9-10 on the road by the Tanga railway, 4 miles south of Lembeni.

General Brits had been met at Moschi and he was told that the units of his (3rd) Division—the two infantry battalions under Taylor—would rejoin him on the Central Railway!

Van Deventer was ordered to retain command of the Handeni road.

Northey reported his advance as in progress and was warned to move cautiously towards Iringa with the possibility of the retirement of all the enemy forces in the north towards him in mind.

While at Moschi, General Smuts telegraphed to the War Office in connection with the proposed removal of German missions, and, as the telegram indicates his views on such a question, its purport is of interest.

He deprecated the wholesale removal of the missionaries and their families not only because it was an " odious task which would be resented by Christians everywhere ", but, also, and mainly, because the removal of white civilising influence would mean the break up of these small centres of civilisation and the reversion of the population to complete barbarism. This he regarded as much against the interests of the State as of the Church. If total removal should be ultimately decided upon on political grounds, other well-disposed missionary bodies should be ready at once to take over so that the good already achieved should not be totally lost.

At 4.30 p.m. on June 10, not June 7 as in the official despatch, General Smuts rejoined the eastern force at Mkalamo and resumed the direction of its operations.

135

CHAPTER IX

(i) THE ADVANCE ON THE EAST RESUMED.
(Map number eight should be referred to.)

GENERAL SMUTS, on his return to Mkalamo, found that that place had been occupied by Sheppard after an encounter—which cost him 25 casualties—on the previous evening and that on the same date, June 10, Hannyngton had reached, and held, Mombo.

A German district officer had come into Hannyngton's camp and reported the presence of 500 women and children together with settlers and missionaries, at Wilhelmstal in the hills above Mombo.

Hannyngton was now ordered to continue his advance to Korogwe while the main body moved on down the west bank of the Pangani.

The latter, after a brush with the enemy in which an officer was killed, reached Luchomo, and Hannyngton made Vuruni river without seeing any hostile forces.

A constant movement forward of lines of communication troops behind the advance was of course a matter for arrangement and in the case of Wilhelmstal, where the first enemy population was taken over " a firm and tactful officer " was called for.

General Smuts sent a telegram to van Deventer to be read on parade, congratulating the 11th S.A. Infantry on its conduct in repelling the attack on Kondoa Irangi.

All military documents had been destroyed at Wilhelmstal where no information was available.

Sheppard was ordered to push on southwards.

Van Deventer reported that the enemy opposite him had strongly reinforced his right and taken a large hill, so that the Handeni road was still the object of von Lettow's concern.

The Commander-in-Chief now placed Brig.-General Sir Charles Crewe, whom he had sent on a mission to the Belgians to arrange the administrative details connected with their co-operation, in command of the Lake Detachment. General Crewe assumed command in the north-west on June 15.

Water difficulties began to arise on leaving Luchomo, as the Pangani—hitherto a valuable ally of the main force—was perforce abandoned. Sheppard was compelled to send back all his animals and water carts from Funda to Luchomo. This particular complication was familiar to those who had served in the recently concluded campaign in German South-West Africa.

Preliminary arrangements were now made for the co-operation of the Navy in the occupation of the ports on the coast. These undertakings were designed to take place in timing with the advance of the eastern force inland.

General Smuts, following his custom, made personal reconnaissances of the country ahead of him from different high points.

(ii) DIFFICULTIES ON THE LINES OF COMMUNICATION.

The German trolley line, running from Mombo to Mkalamo, was repaired and efforts were made to get up some kind of light vehicles to work it with. It was used in the end as a hand pushed tramway and could convey some 30 tons of supplies a week.

Activity in the building and repairing of bridges and the railway line and cutting roads and generally improving the lines of communication was incessant, and search for water was continued in all directions.

The enemy had removed the sleepers from the railway over long stretches, the chains had disappeared, and the destruction of culverts and bridges was general. At Buiko, the main railway centre between New Moschi and Tanga workshops, tanks and all points had been blown up.

A week's halt had been made at Buiko when supplies were pushed forward by means of every device which suggested itself to the harassed supply staff, and numerous casualties to personnel and vehicles was one of the results.

The railway would have aided largely in solving the immediate difficulties but the railway was not available and the Commander-in-Chief decided to do without it for the time.

The advance went on.

137

(iii) THE OCCUPATION OF HANDENI.

Aircraft was ordered to bomb the enemy wherever there was a chance of doing so with effect, and to pay special attention to any enemy force at Nderema where, is was assumed, it would be covering the main water supply.

June 15 found Hannyngton in occupation of Korogwe, and the enemy opposing the main body in a strongly entrenched position from Handeni Hill to a low ridge just west of Diriba and covering the water at Handeni.

To deal with this situation Beves was directed by way of Gitu and Sheppard to Nguguini, the latter leaving a battalion at Kilimanjaro.

On the evening of June 16 Sheppard was some 4 miles west of Handeni, and Beves at Gitu, the latter having been sniped at just before camping.

On the following day Beves and G.H.Q. had reached Ssangeni on the Mssangassi river, where good water was found, and Sheppard a point 4 miles west of Handeni Hill. Hannyngton, having provided a garrison for Korogwe, was on the march from Mauri towards Handeni.

On June 9 the Lake Detachment captured Ukerewe island, on Lake Victoria, valuable for its rice supply.

Some Dutch women on a farm near Handeni stated that only two companies were at that place, the remainder of the enemy force having left for Morogoro or Tabora. They also repeated the obviously inspired statement that " a big stand would be made at Tabora ".

Natives who correctly stated the local position of the enemy also reported the existence of a good motor road to Morogoro, and gave valuable information as to the waters on that route.

On arrival at Ssangeni, General Smuts, accompanied by the bulk of the Headquarter staff and other officers of high rank, rode out into the bush and ascended a rocky kopje which reared itself prominetly from the sea of dense foliage which surrounded it for miles.

It soon became apparent that the party was several miles ahead of the nearest advanced elements of the force to which it belonged, and concerned staff officers, taking a hasty inventory of the weapons with which it was armed, made the discovery that a mauser pistol in the possession of the B.G.R.A. was the only means of defence available.

General Smuts—his companions were of relatively small importance—was in full view of anyone who might be hidden in the bush, and there was every probability that there were many so hidden.   Half a dozen resolute Askaris could have captured the Commander-in-Chief with ease and entire safety to themselves.   General Smuts completed a long survey of the surrounding country and then, to the relief of his staff, made his way down the kopje and back to his lines.   A double company was sent out to occupy the kopje in view of possible further excursions to it, and the episode is recorded to give an idea of how simply anyone can lose touch in the bush.   The kopje was named Fulton's Kop in connection with the ensuing operations from the name of the officer who commanded the post.

Brits, with his mounted brigade, had at this time reached Same on his march from Mbuyuni by way of Ngulu Gap to join the Commander-in-Chief.

Map number nine will give some idea of the plan of advance on Handeni and, perhaps, of some of the difficulties attending any attempt to outflank the enemy.

Since Reata the practice of marching up against prepared positions in full view of an enemy entrenched and hidden from sight, adopted by some of his predecessors, had been changed by General Smuts for constant efforts to outflank his agile opponents. As von Lettow remarks of these attempts " their effectiveness was greatly reduced by the difficulty of the country ".

On June 18 General Smuts returned early with G.H.Q. to Fulton's Kop to watch the result of the following movements which had been ordered.

Sheppard to move against Handeni at 5.30 a.m., sending a battalion against Mkonge and Bango hills.   Beves with the 6th S.A. Infantry to leave Ssangeni at 6 a.m. and move towards the Morogoro road, Byron (5th S.A. Infantry) to proceed at 6 a.m. to Fulton's Kop and there pick up his detached double company. Byron was to be used against Pongwe, should the development of the operations suggest the course.

Hannyngton had reached Msala the evening before and was moving at 4 a.m. on the 18th towards Handeni.

At 10.30 a.m. Sheppard occupied Handeni unopposed.

At 9.55 a.m. Beves reached the Morogoro road and an hour later the double company from Fulton's Kop occupied a bare rocky kopje due south of its former position.

At 11.15 a.m. rapid and sustained machine gun fire broke out to the south-east of Fulton's Kop combined with rifle and pom-pom fire, and, after dying down, was repeated shortly after noon. This proved to be the result of Beves becoming engaged.

A party of the enemy was surprised and attacked with machine gun fire, and, later, counter-attacked the 6th S.A. Infantry, renewing their efforts after midday and inflicting a loss of one non-commissioned officer killed and one man wounded. The counter-attacks were repulsed and the enemy retired with a loss of about 15 killed.

At 2 p.m. Byron was ordered to Pongwe. An hour later, heavy smoke over the latter place indicated its evacuation and the enemy retirement was placed beyond doubt.

At nightfall Sheppard was at Nderema, Beves on the Morogoro-Handeni road, Byron at Pongwe, and G.H.Q. with 1st Divisional Headquarters and the balance of the force back at Ssangeni. Hannyngton was pressing along the Korogwe road towards Handeni.

It is now clear that the main body under Kraut had left the German positions betimes by way of the motor road, a rear guard under Captain Freiherr von Bodecker being left to cover the retirement.

Once more General Smuts' objective had eluded him, aided by the densely bushed country and its features and a thorough knowledge of both, and by the usual skilful conduct of a rear guard action.

Von Bodecker took the Pongwe-Kangata path thus protecting the right rear of Kraut's main body.

Byron had become engaged with von Bodecker at Pongwe, the latter disengaging with some loss after having been surprised. Byron sustained no casualties.

On June 19 General Smuts visited Nderema, Handeni, and Beves' camp at Pongwe, returning in the evening to Ssangeni.

He ordered Beves to take the 6th S.A. Infantry and once more unite his force at Pongwe on the following day, G.H.Q. moving to the same place.

Brits and his mounted men had at this time reached German Bridge on his way down the Pangani route.

Handeni, an important road junction, contained several European houses and a well-built boma (fort and official quarters) and some farms were near at hand. The water was, however, bad in places and productive of dysentery, and the enemy left behind a considerable number of sick.

The advancing troops too had suffered badly and the numbers of General Smuts' force were now much diminished by disease aggravated by privation.

The enemy was reported to have shown "considerable demoralisation" in his retirement. This had been heard before, but, if it were true, the effect must have been fleeting as the events of the next twenty-four hours were to show.

A mixed force under Lieut.-Colonel Lyall, consisting of one battalion, a squadron of E.A.M.R. and a machine gun section from Sheppard's column, was ordered to move southwards along the Handeni-Morogoro motor road and to make good as much of it as possible.

Handeni will always be associated in the minds of some of those who now reached it with a peculiarly potent beverage which was found there. It was labelled " Witzki " and there was a considerable quantity of it. They have sometimes wondered if the omission on the part of the enemy to remove this stimulant was as involuntary as it appeared to be. Handeni " Witzki " mixed with Nderema water was calculated to reduce the strongest man to impotence.

(iv) GENERAL VON LETTOW REJOINS HIS EASTERN DETACHMENT.

Van Deventer now wired that a big gun which had been seen at Dodoma was being sent to the enemy position opposite, and, if this were the case, he anticipated another " big attack ". He added that he had 1,200 sick and asked for reinforcements.

It is clear from von Lettow's account that he had already decided upon the Mahenge country as the general direction of his retirement and that he had no intention of allowing himself to be separated from Kraut.

At this time too, the opinion had been formed that the German Commander-in-Chief's obvious and consistent guard of the Handeni road on his right flank at Kondoa Irangi—he had collected most of his strength there and left his other flank too weak to take offensive action—was due to a desire to prevent himself being forced away from his eastern detachment. With the advance of General Smuts developing at the rate at which it was materialising, every day made an attack upon van Deventer, which was never regarded as a serious probability after the failure of the first assault, less likely.

Ten days later, July 1, General von Lettow arrived at Kraut's headquarters at Turiani there to await the arrival of all the forces which had faced van Deventer except a detachment under Captain Klinghardt which he left " in front of the Kondoa force ". General Smuts seemed to be " the most dangerous and important " of his opponents.

The information which had reached van Deventer as to an attack upon him was once more suspect.

(v) THE ACTION AT KANGATA.

The Director of Medical Services was now told to consider the formation of forward hospitals. The loss of personnel—for a man once left behind was lost for an unconscionable time, irrespective entirely of the degree of his disability—was becoming very serious.

Though the enemy had escaped anything like envelopment he had been hustled for some days, and there seemed to be just a chance of bringing him to action before long. Every effort was made to bring as many troops as possible into the field by speeding up hospital arrangements and handing over places garrisoned by field troops to the I.G. of Communications.

Still anxious to maintain touch with the retiring enemy, General Smuts on June 20 moved to Pongwe and at 2 p.m. sent Byron with his battalion on to Kangata.

Shortly afterwards the balance of Beves' force marched into Pongwe.

At 5.20 p.m. heavy and sustained firing to the south-west was heard at G.H.Q., indicating that Byron had become engaged with an enemy force.

Some 40 minutes later a motor cyclist rode into G.H.Q. and handed over a message from Byron asking for reinforcements, and two companies of the 6th S.A. Infantry were at once sent out to him.

The· pursuit of an enemy who is at once unbroken and enterprising, and the German force was both, is an operation calling for the nicest combination of boldness and caution.

While no opportunity of scoring a success must be missed, no chance must be given to your opponent, who will no doubt choose his place and occasion for his effort to inflict a heavy blow on an over-venturesome pursuer. Such choice is possible with deliberation on previously reconnoitred ground.

Rear guards have given many lessons to their enemies, and Freiherr von Bodecker proceeded to add another to the list. The " demoralisation " had clearly evaporated.

Byron reported that he was in touch with, and held up by, apparently 2 companies (" a strong force ") of the enemy.

The firing died down about 7 p.m.

Two hours later the signalling officer who was laying a line to Byron, rang up G.H.Q. from a point some 2 miles from Byron's camp and the latter asked for doctors, blankets, water carts and other necessaries. He reported about 50 wounded and others being brought in and an unknown number of killed.

His needs were met and Lyall, now 14 miles from Handeni and 10 from Kangata, was instructed to push on and gain touch with him.

On arrival at Byron's camp early on June 21, everything was found quiet, but the impression was that the enemy was in strength ahead and holding his position of the previous evening with outposts. Investigation, however, proved that this position was vacant, and that the enemy had again retired. He could not allow Lyall to get in behind him.

Byron's camp was in the bush. Just in front of it was a considerable depression in the ground. The enemy position lay on a level with that of Byron with the shallow hollow dividing the two forces.

Preoccupied with their desire to try conclusions with the retiring German force—and it must be remembered that on each occasion of contact during the past four or five days Byron's men had scored against their retreating opponents—the leading portion of the 5th Infantry had descended into the depression and were moving up the opposite slope without apparently noticing, or in any case giving the fact its proper significance, that the bush on either slope had been recently cleared away. The freshness of the cutting was plain on careful observation.

This clearing was to afford a field of fire which was delivered as soon as a considerable part of Byron's force was in view on either side of the hollow.

The rifle fire of the Askaris was, as usual, of small account, but heavy loss was caused by the skilful and daring use of the German machine guns used here, as always in this campaign, with consummate ability.

One machine gun was posted in the left rear of the advancing troops and others on the flanks.

A subsequent examination of the enemy position disclosed 409 rifle pits, in each of which were found from 100 to 300 cartridge cases, a striking illustration of the rate of fire—clearly mostly unaimed—of the average Askari.

Byron had about 400 rifles engaged, and a loss of 25 per cent. in about an hour and a half must be regarded as heavy. Von Bodecker's loss was 1 killed and 8 wounded.

While the check had little or no effect upon the South Africans, their success must have given enormous encouragement to the retreating Askaris, and von Bodecker is to be credited with a daring and opportune exhibition of tactical skill.

The episode emphasises very clearly the inadvisability of pushing forward a single detached force in bush country without support from a flank on parallel or converging roads. Incidentally it also suggests the need for caution in assuming too readily that a retiring force is necessarily a beaten force. It would have been wiser to have arranged more effective combination in respect of time and movement between Lyall and Byron.

G.H.Q., Beves and Lyall all camped at Kangata on the evening of June 21. Hannyngton was ordered to stand fast at Handeni. Sheppard was instructed to reach Kangata at midday on June 23 being preceded by the 1st Divisional Reserve on the previous evening.

(vi) THE MOVEMENT TO, AND ACTION AT, THE LUKIGURA RIVER.

General Smuts had ordered van Deventer to stand fast and rest his horses, with a view to moving as rapidly as possible when the Eastern Force should have " cut the railway east of Kondoa ".

In order to carry out his own share of the combined operations he continued his advance, though the long line of communications—precarious and calling for unremitting attention and improvement—and the ever increasing difficulties of supply and endless wastage of personnel from disease were growing obstacles to continued movement.

The enemy was reported as in position at the Lukigura river, and General Smuts decided on yet another attempt to outflank and capture the force opposed to him.

Accordingly, some special redistribution of the forces was temporarily made to give effect to the following plan.

While the advance along the motor road to the south was to be continued, a special column under Major General Hoskins was to come in on the enemy left flank, the main body holding the German force in front.

Hoskin's force—four infantry battalions, some scouts, a mountain battery, less a section, and a machine gun company—included the two South African Infantry Battalions (5th and 6th) under Beves.

During the night of June 23-24 this column marched to a point north of the Lukigura river and a bridge held by the enemy, and, after a further exhausting march, got astride a road in rear of the German position.

Sheppard, with whom were General Smuts and G.H.Q., moved from Kangata just after midnight on the 23rd and at daybreak was marching in column of route along the motor road here fringed by bush and forest.

The formation and the hour were unpleasantly reminiscent of Gatacre's situation in the Anglo-Boer War when he was caught at Stormberg moving parallel to the enemy's front.

Here the movement was against the hostile front, but some present were probably relieved when firing broke out ahead and not on a flank.

Just before the river was reached the road took a right-angled turn to the left, and continued parallel to the course of the river, and as soon as the leading troops of Sheppard came to the turning a soldier of the 17th (Indian) Cavalry was shot dead.

The armoured cars moved forward and were met by pom-pom and machine gun, as well as by rapid rifle fire. One car was temporarily disabled by a direct hit but was run back safely by its crew.

The 29th Punjabis deployed and came into action to their front.

Information of Hoskins being delayed came to hand and Sheppard was instructed to confine himself to holding the enemy in front of him.

Prominent on the right front of the Punjabis was a high hill rising from the tropical growth, which not only was a key position in the action which now ensued but was approximately the probable point of junction between the advances of Sheppard and Hoskins whose line of march it commanded.

The officer in command of the attack was instructed to seize it and the detachments which he sent forward to occupy it just reached the hill in time to drive off the enemy who, recognizing the importance of the point, was found advancing up the slope on the further side on a similar mission.

The flank next Hoskins thus secured, the engagement, still directed to holding the enemy to his ground, continued until sounds of Hoskins' approach became audible.

Soon after noon the latter engaged the enemy opposite him and Sheppard attacked strongly.

The enemy caught on three sides put up a stout resistance, and the action came to an end at 3 o'clock in the afternoon. The German Commander once more effected his retreat, but only after having been severely handled. The hasty retirement of the enemy Askaris in disorder through the bush and eluding Hoskins' troops was plainly visible from Sheppard's side.

4 Europeans and 30 Askaris were found dead on the enemy position.

This operation was the nearest approach to success in enveloping tactics which was attained throughout the whole campaign.

The march of Hoskins' column was exhausting in the extreme and his own conduct of the flanking movement admirable.

The bearing of the rank and file throughout their trying march and in the actual attack delivered when the movement had nearly exhausted them was deserving of the highest praise and earned the admiration of their opponents.

In addition to the enemy dead found on the field 21 Germans and 32 Askaris were taken prisoners by the two columns which had a total casualty list of 10 killed (Hoskins 6, Sheppard 4) and 36 wounded (Hoskins 26 and Sheppard 10).

Towards the end of the action a naval gun (8.8 c.m.) shelled the ridge above the Lukigura which had been captured and continued firing until dark from the further bank of the Msiha river 12,000 yards distant.

146

The force, once more combined, remained in this position for the next two days, reconnoitring in the vicinity.

(vii) A HALT ENSUES.

Nature, flouted by this time to her limit, here took command, as had been the case at Kondoa Irangi, and the eastern force was now reduced, as the western force under van Deventer had been earlier, to immobility.

That it had been possible to keep on the move so long was due solely to the indomitable spirit and courage of the fighting soldiers of all units and to the splendid work of the personnel of the administrative units, transport, supply, and medical, with them and along the difficult and drawn out lines of communication.

General Smuts was well aware that an advance from Handeni to the Lukigura would call for a tremendous effort by his men and it may be considered that the strain which it put upon them was excessive. There is no doubt that many suffered severe hardship in consequence of the immediate movement forward.

Hardship is, however, inseparable from war, and it is only when the result is not commensurate with, or can be secured without, the sacrifice that a commander may be fairly criticised for demanding the utmost exertion of which his troops may be capable.

The Commander-in-Chief considered that no chance which might offer of bringing the enemy to bay should be missed, and the very close approach to an outstanding success at the Lukigura was justification for the extra demands made upon the fighting soldier to achieve it.

It was also necessary to push the enemy further south than Handeni where he would be well placed for far more dangerous and effective action against the communications than he was able to take from 10 miles south of Msiha.

But in any case, there was no real choice.

The neighbourhood of Handeni was without water in quantity enough for the subsistence of any considerable force, and much of what there was was bad.

The natives who gave information about the waters ahead stated clearly, and, as it proved, correctly, that the Lukigura and Msiha were the first waters which would be adequate for the strength of the advancing columns.

General Smuts therefore had two alternatives.

To return to the Pangani, a course which, after the fine work of the troops and the great measure of success that had attended it, was unthinkable, or to go on.

He went on.

(viii) LINES OF COMMUNICATION.

Map number ten shows the communications of the forces under the Commander-in-Chief and General van Deventer at this time.

They stretched back from Msiha on the east and Kondoa Irangi on the west to Mombasa by rail and road.

From Mombasa to Moschi the railway was complete and working. From Moschi to Kondoa Irangi and Msiha approximately, respectively, 150 and 80 miles of road—the " road " was at its best, fairly level, unmetalled soil, and at its worst a rough track—intervened between the nearest railway and the forward field force.

The motor transport of every conceivable date and model lacked spares, which were in any case quite unstandardized, the personnel of the administrative services were just as liable to disease as the fighting soldier forward and succumbed wholesale, and any man who became sick was lost for months in some unknown hospital to which he had eventually found his way.

The transport was quite inadequate to supply bare essentials to the troops who had never had a full ration for many weeks and were therefore easy prey to disease.

All the lines of communication were liable to sniping and mines were freely used on them, though the actual posts on them were secure.

(ix) SUPPLY.

The supply position at this time may perhaps be judged by the following quotation from Volume II of " The Royal Army Service Corps ", dealing with the East African campaign:—

" At Buiko the position had been serious. At Handeni it seemed desperate. Rations had been short for many days. No white flour had been issued for some time, hard biscuit eked out with mealie flour being provided in lieu. The only meat available was the fly-stricken trek ox which had to be eaten at once as it would not keep."

On June 24, when 250 miles had been covered "General Smuts who had started with 15,000 men had 20,000", and these numbers must be considered in the light of the fact that the forward movement of reinforcements and the backward movement of numerous casualties was continuous. "These accretions complicated the task of maintenance beyond that of the additional mouths to be fed, as all had to be fitted out with their first line transport while the proportionate increase required in the supply columns was a task to which the existing resources were unequal. There were, quite apart from the conditions of the country, too many troops for the transport at the disposal of the army; and all the time that the administrative services were grapling with the problem involved by the main force, it was compelled to deal with General van Deventer's division at Kondoa Irangi. That the army was enabled to keep moving testifies to the unsparing efforts of the Army Service Corps and the South and East Africans associated with it. As it was, it was only dire necessity that made General Smuts call a halt at Makindu (Msiha). The fighting strength had been reduced to one half of its establishments by sickness and the casualties among transport animals had been enormous. It was impossible further to extend the communications and numbers of sick required evacuation. Towards this last purpose and of the bringing up of supplies every vehicle was brought into action and employed without ceasing".

(x) THE MEDICAL SITUATION.

It was clear that the conditions to be met by the medical authorities were of a peculiar nature and called for arrangements departing very materially from those applicable in theatres where lines of communication were less drawn out, means of communication were more plentiful, and disease less of a factor. The influence of this last drawback may perhaps be realized when it is recalled that in this campaign non-battle casualties were to battle casualties as 31.40 to 1, by far the greatest proportion on any front, Mesopotamia coming next with 20.25 to 1.

The shrinkage of the forces—mainly due to sickness—had reached proportions which made it a grave danger and a serious obstacle to the successful prosecution of the campaign.

Men who went sick and were evacuated along the lines of communication remained away for inordinate periods. This was not necessarily due to tardy discharge from the hospitals which they eventually reached, but was largely due to the distance to which they went back, irrespective of their original degree of disability.

It was now suggested to the medical authorities that the position which had arisen was largely due to a lack of forward hospitals where slight cases could be treated adequately at once, thus obviating long periods of absence and the aggravation of small ailments caused by delay of suitable treatment.

It was recommended that forward hospitals should be established behind the fighting troops, situated as occasion might demand. The equipment of such hospitals could not of course be elaborate, nor did anything but medical personnel, drugs and medical comforts and a supply of blankets seem to be needed.

At such places would be treated, for example, the numerous cases of stomach trouble which only needed a few days' rest and diet under medical supervision for recovery. Such cases at this time were all sent back and lost for weeks on end to their units, though they need be only casualties for a few days during which, however, it was impossible for them to march or fight.

The native " bandas "—grass huts—put up in an hour or so would provide shelter and the native form of bed—made from wood and fibre to be had in abundance—would serve admirably for all minor cases of sickness.

The location of larger hospitals to be arranged so that cases should be sent back further in proportion to their gravity, in other words, all hospitals to be graded on the basis of probable duration of incapacity of the casualties and their distance from the front line.

The situation called for a considerable degree of improvisation to meet a very serious loss of man-power.

It was typical of the state of affairs that the first difficulty which presented itself in the adoption of some such system was want of transport.

(xi) GENERAL SMUTS LEAVES FOR THE LINES OF COMMUNICATION.

A great master of the art of war laid it down that " The secret of war lies in the communications ".

General von Lettow now proceeded to give some point to this dictum of Napoleon.

The lines of communication of the eastern force at this time have just been described. Though the posts were secure, the lines themselves were exceedingly vulnerable.

The portion between Handeni and Korogwe was especially liable to enemy interference as the area bounded by the coast, and lines joining Tanga, Korogwe, Handeni and Msiha was unoccupied by British forces.

In his despatch of the 27th October, 1916, General Smuts writes: " I had deliberately left the East Usambara area alone while pushing the enemy forces in front of me back as fast and as far as possible ". In consequence, however, of evidence of serious determination on the part of the enemy to give trouble there and, in doing so, to jeopardize the communications, the Commander-in-Chief decided that " the time had come to secure his rear and left from this guerilla warfare ".

Accordingly, having arranged that the eastern force should move to the Msiha river, some 8 miles on from the scene of the action at the Lukigura, and occupy a position at the first named place, General Smuts handed over local command to Major-General Hoskins and on June 26 left for an examination of the situation in the East Usambara area.

The first objective of the Commander-in-Chief was the camp of Major-General Brits who had reached Luchomo on his march down the Pangani. Here General Smuts succumbed temporarily to a severe attack of malaria which bestowed its attention indiscriminately on the Commander-in-Chief and private soldier, at the front and all along the communications.

Mombo and Wilhelmstal, at each of which places an examination of local conditions was of importance, had been included in General Smuts' itinerary, but the inspection had to be carried out by a deputy while the Commander-in-Chief received medical treatment in Brits' camp.

Excellent work had been done on the communications and all bridges along the route which was traversed had been made good.

Nothing seemed to call for any special attention at Mombo, but at Wilhelmstal the position was more complicated.

(xii) THE ENEMY CIVIL POPULATION AT WILHELMSTAL.

This town lies high—nearly 5,000 feet above sea level—in the Usambara range, in surroundings which bring to mind some parts of Switzerland. It is situate in a mountain basin, the climate is cool and good, but the pallor of the German children there was remarkable.

A good wood fire at night was much appreciated.

There were good farms surrounding the town where 500 white women and children were collected.

It seemed that the Usambara country was to be regarded as a kind of sanctuary, for at Lukigura a request had been received from the German women at Wilhelmstal for permission to send a letter to their Governor, Dr. Schnee, protesting against the presence of German patrols in these mountains which they believed to be contrary to the wishes of Dr. Schnee and General von Lettow alike.

The situation at Wilhelmstal was largely due to circumstances in which, in consequence of a long and rapid advance, co-ordination of the different services in the territory left behind was lacking because the control of a co-ordinating authority had lost touch.

The Political Officer and the Post Commandant were at cross purposes.

The former, under the Chief Political Officer, was concerned with the supervision and control of the enemy civil population and of all matters directly affecting them, apart from any military measures, responsibility for which rested with the Post Commandant who was responsible to the Inspector-General of Communications. The temperaments of the two men concerned were antagonistic, though each was competent enough, and their respective chiefs, at a distance from the scene, were naturally enough inclined to support each his own man.

Dual control inevitably connotes friction, and it was clear that either there should be a military commandant with a political officer—as his adviser—or a political officer with a small military force to act under, and maintain, his authority.

The second course seemed to be the more advisable and was adopted. Wilhelmstal lay actually off the lines of communication, it was clearly designed to remain outside the sphere of active military operations so far as the German authorities were concerned and the situation was eminently one for careful handling from a political point of view.

A carefully selected Political Officer was appointed, and, with a subaltern and 25 mounted men at his disposal, handled the position without further trouble.

(xiii) EVENTS ON OTHER FRONTS.

Information was now received of the withdrawal of several enemy detachments from Kondoa Irangi, via Kimbe (12 miles north-west of Msiha camp), where Pretorius had watched, and was still watching, all their movements. Turiani, south of Msiha, on the Morogoro road was mentioned as the point of their concentration, and the intelligence proved to be correct.

The Inspector-General of L. of C., Brig.-General Edwards, the D.A. and Q.M.G., Brig.-General Ewart, and other administrative staff officers were summoned to Luchomo to see General Smuts who took the opportunity of discussing important details of staff work.

The main trouble was shortage of men and inadequate medical arrangements.

It had now become necessary to take steps for the occupation of the coast ports with the ultimate object of securing Dar-es-Salaam, with a view to changing the main base to that place with a consequent shortening of the lines of communication.

As a preliminary step, the Commander-in-Chief acceded to a suggestion by General Edwards that the latter should arrange to land a force at Vanga slowly to work its way down to Tanga. By this action a more satisfactory method of occupying Tanga would be achieved than by a bombardment of the latter place followed by a landing to find the place in all probability unoccupied by any enemy force.

On June 29 van Deventer repeated the gist of various enemy messages—picked up or intercepted—he was at this time working with his patrols though still held to Kondoa Irangi, and among them was one which sent to the German Chief Command by the subordinate commander in the west, stated that some Belgian Askaris had been captured and were willing to serve

under their captors. The message continued " impossible serve
my units as my opponent will be Belgian ", thus clearly
indicating that the German *main* body would not retire upon
Tabora.

General Gil, the recently arrived Portuguese Commander-
in-Chief, advised General Smuts of the arrival of two transports
with Portuguese troops which he was sending to the frontier.

Bombs were now being placed from time to time on the
Usambara railway and the Director of Railways, by whose unremitting effort, backed by the unceasing hard work of his
subordinates the railway was rapidly being repaired, asked that
retaliatory measures should be taken against the civil population
in British hands. While the annoyance of the Director of
Railways was natural enough, and though General Smuts, who
had urged him, and not vainly, to stupendous exertions,
sympathised with him, the request was not met, as, in the
absence of clear proof that civilians or natives had done the
damage, " such measures would most likely only affect innocent
people ".

On June 29 British troops occupied Bukoba in the north-
west which the enemy had evacuated five days earlier.

Intelligence now pointed to the retirement of von Lettow
with his main force to Iringa and Mahenge. Governor Schnee
was reported to have gone to the former place, and the
increased importance of closer co-operation with Northey's force
and the Portuguese became apparent on the assumption that
the information was correct.

Steps accordingly were taken to arrange that Northey in the
south-west should be placed under General Smuts' general
direction to ensure a co-ordination of effort and movements.

The delimitation on general lines, of the Belgians and
Portuguese spheres of operation was also a matter for consideration.

Van Deventer reported at this date difficulties which were
more or less common to all the field forces.

He had over 700 men in hospital and more than 300 in
convalescent camps, but shortage of such strengthening foods
as oatmeal, bacon, cheese and milk made it " almost
hopeless to expect convalescents to become fit for active service ".
Most of his sick were lying on the ground, and there was a
dearth of clothing, boots and soap.

Lack of transport and the appalling condition of the roads had contributed to this state of affairs, and it cannot be too strongly emphasised that in a campaign in a country like tropical Africa, hospital accommodation on a graduated scale such as was described on page 150 and moving as rapidly and as close as possible behind the fighting troops is absolutely indispensable to the efficiency of the latter, and to the maintenance of an adequate force.

The nearest hospital at which a moderate degree of comfort could be assured to van Deventer's sick was back at Ufiome.

As a further instance of the wastage which was occurring, it may be mentioned that in the month after May 20, 1,500 of all ranks had disappeared from sickness among the 5,500 of the 1st Division (Hoskins).

Large movements of enemy companies along the railway eastwards towards Morogoro were now reported.

By July 3 General Smuts was recovered enough to admit of his return to Lukigura which he reached on the afternoon of that day.

Before leaving Luchomo the Commander-in-Chief ordered Brits to begin his movement—one regiment at a time—towards Lukigura on the evening of the following day and van Deventer was instructed to come to G.H.Q. and discuss future plans.

(xiv) ENEMY ACTIVITY ON THE LINES OF COMMUNICATION.

Since the beginning of July reports had been coming in of stock raiding and other activities of the enemy in the districts to the east of the line of advance from Korogwe. Snipers were active about Zindeni, between Korogwe and Handen, and on June 30 General Hoskins had been fired on in his car between Lukigura and Msiha, practically in his own lines, and his aide-de-camp, Captain Mullins, had been killed by his side.

These episodes marked the beginning of attempts "to interrupt the motor traffic between Korogwe and Handeni" ordered by von Lettow and they extended later south of the last-mentioned place. Sniping from the long grass and bush which bordered all the routes, land mines laid in the roads, attacks on porter convoys and constant cutting of telegraph and telephone lines were all features of this interference with the communications.

It was such an effective, and from the point of view of the enemy, who knew the whole country, simple way of adding to the difficulties which encumbered the advance that it is surprising that it was not far more freely resorted to.

In point of fact this was the sole persistent effort of the enemy in this direction, and it could not have come more conveniently, for the whole force was compulsorily at a standstill and the advance was not delayed further by these actions.

The position had become critical in consequence of wastage of personnel and breakage and loss of transport. There was thus no possibility of an advance until the situation should have improved.

Raids against the communications are enterprises which appeal to the imagination, but, unless they achieve a result commensurate with the risk they entail and the wear and tear they impose upon the troops which carry them out, are merely spectacular and do not attract the sound commander. The raids of " Jeb " Stuart in the American Civil War are famous and did as a rule serious, if temporary, damage to the Union lines of communication, but the damage which they inflicted on their enemies was infinitely less than, say, that which resulted to the confederate arms at Gettysburg, as a consequence of the absence of Stuart's cavalry on one of the enterprises of the kind mentioned.

It is probable that General von Lettow attached more importance to keeping his small army compact under his hand than to occasional successful ventures of quite temporary value.

In any case, there were no systematic efforts against the communications except upon this occasion.

(xv) GENERAL SMUTS REJOINS THE EASTERN FORCE.

On July 5 General Smuts moved to Sheppard's camp on the Msiha river.

On the same day General Gil, the recently arrived Portuguese Commander south of the Rovuma river, was told of the apparent intention of the enemy main body to retire to Mahenge and Iringa, and was asked to advance towards the former place. General Northey reported his strength as 700 whites, 1,000 natives and 24 machine guns, and added that he usually had 25 per cent. sick with little permanent wastage.

Daily reconnaissances and bombing operations were carried out by the Air Force during the halt at Msiha, with little, if any, material damage to the enemy, but they procured useful information as to the country ahead.

The difficulty of reconnaissance from the air in such country as East Africa may perhaps be judged from a normal report, which, describing a reconnaissance over Turiani where, as was well known, the main enemy concentration had taken place, stated: " one man seen crossing bridge, no other movement observed ".

All movements of enemy patrols in the Nguru mountains were reported by Pretorius, who with his natives, was occupying a vantage post of his own selection near Pembe in advance, and to the west, of the Msiha position.

It was now known that General von Lettow was back again in front of the eastern force.

An interesting communication from an enemy subject received at this time contained a request to be allowed to visit the German Governor with the object of " inducing the latter to end the war and preserve Kultur in the country ". It was explained to the self appointed missionary that any open letter would be sent through the lines to the enemy, and any answer forwarded by the same route, but the personal touch was evidently an indispensable feature of the proposed transaction which was not carried any further.

General van Deventer arrived at G.H.Q. on July 1 and after a full discussion, left for his command at Kondoa Irangi on the following day.

157

CHAPTER X

(i) FURTHER ENEMY ACTIVITY AGAINST THE LINES OF COMMUNICATION.

THE activities of enemy parties against the lines of communication of the eastern force, especially between, and to the east of, Korogwe and Handeni, were now becoming an increasing annoyance, and on July 10, Brig.-General Edwards, I.G. Lines of Communication, was ordered to take certain steps and himself to proceed to Korogwe and take charge of the local operations.

Brig.-General Hannyngton with his brigade was moved back from Lukigura to the area mentioned above.

Though these efforts of the enemy did not prevent any advance, for the simple reason that, as has been explained, to advance was out of the question, they were bad for *moral* and especially in the case of the porters, some of whom needed slight excuse for bolting in any emergency, and the situation had in any case to be cleared up before any further forward movement could be resumed.

General Smuts' instructions were broadly as follows:—

The enemy was to be cleared from the area north and east of the Pangani, all bridges were to be destroyed and native chiefs were to be held responsible that no fresh bridges were built and that the former ones were not repaired. Forces were to move against Hale and Kofi, and the enemy was to be driven south to Manga. Commanding Officers were advised that, in the opinion of G.H.Q., the enemy numbers were greatly exaggerated by informants, a view borne out by experience shortly afterwards. Reports of large enemy forces in the area under consideration were persistent and regular and were thought to be spread intentionally.

The Handeni-Korogwe road was not to be used until Kofi should have been cleared of the enemy.

An attack on Korogwe in the early morning of July 13 was beaten off without difficulty and information from a captured Askari justified the view of a great exaggeration of the German forces in this area.

Hannyngton was ordered to assume command of all troops at Handeni on his arrival there, and was to take his orders temporarily from advanced G.H.Q. at Msiha. His brigade was, of course, normally one of those of the 1st Division under General Hoskins. Hannyngton, who had previously served in East Africa, was an admirable commander of a detached force and invariably acquitted himself well when sent on an independent mission such as this. He never made difficulties, and joined to his experience of the country sound professional competence.

He was also instructed to take over command of the forces which Edwards was sending out from Korogwe when he should gain contact with them, thus allowing the I.G.C. to attend to his normal duties which were arduous enough.

A minor difficulty arose at this time in consequence of the attack on Korogwe, already mentioned, which to a small extent recompensed General von Lettow for the abortive attempt on the place. The attack caused the entire porter personnel of the I.G.C. to disappear with consequent delay to the operations which he had been instructed to set in train.

(ii) OPERATIONS ON THE LINES OF COMMUNICATION.

At this time the situation on the Lines of Communication was confusing. It may be mentioned that, in order to be in close touch with events, General Smuts had returned to Nderema, near Handeni, on July 18. General Botha, too, was expected to visit the scene of operations and Nderema was regarded as a more suitable centre at which to receive him than a place further forward.

Hannyngton and Wilkinson—the Commanding Officer of the Railway Companies of Sappers and Miners—whom the I.G.C. had made available with a force of some 500 rifles (including his own companies), were dealing with small bodies of the enemy who were moving about the area roughly bounded by the Pangani, the Indian Ocean, the road from Korogwe and Lukigura and a line from Lukigura through Manga to the coast. See map number eleven.

Wilkinson was working under General Edwards, and Hannyngton under General Smuts, an arrangement which, though unavoidable, made the co-ordination of operations in an area virtually without any communications unusually difficult.

By the end of July the area had been cleared as the result of some admirable work in difficult circumstances by Hannyngton and Wilkinson, later aided by the 57th Wilde's Rifles, an Indian battalion, recently arrived from the Western Front in Europe.

Hard marching, short commons—the normal lot of the fighting soldier in this campaign—and frequent actions in thick bush had been the features of this side undertaking to which all concerned had given their best endeavour. The operations were made more difficult by the absence of means of inter-communication which prevented co-operation by columns ignorant of each other's whereabouts. The staff work was much complicated by the fact that many places had several names which were used indifferently to denote the same spot.

Korogwe, Amani, Segera Hill, Zindeni, and Kwa Mugwe were all scenes of engagements.

At the end of the operations Hannyngton rejoined the main force at Msiha, and Wilkinson, with his Sappers and Miners, resumed his normal work on the railway which had been interrupted by his effective excursions into the field.

Meanwhile, with the co-operation of the Navy (Vengeance, Talbot, Severn and Mersey) the ports as far south as and including Sadani were occupied on the following dates:—Tanga, July 7; Pangani, July 23; Sadani, July 30.

While Hannyngton's brigade marched back to Lukigura, his 40th Pathans under Lieut.-Colonel Mitchell moved on Manga via Rugusi, reaching the former place on August 3 whence they patrolled the surrounding country.

The pause at Msiha was occupied generally in consolidating the lines of communication, bringing up reinforcements, building up advanced supply depots, and repairing damaged mechanical transport and increasing the animal transport.

(iii) GENERAL SMUTS AT NDEREMA ISSUES GENERAL INSTRUCTIONS.

Arrived at Nderema which he made his headquarters, General Smuts on the day following went to Korogwe where base G.H.Q. were now established. The visit was of much advantage as it enabled the two sections of G.H.Q.—it has already been explained that G.H.Q. were divided into advanced and base portions—to adjust many important matters under the direction of the Commander-in-Chief.

Northey, who had now come under General Smuts' general control for operations, was advised of the local situation and of that of van Deventer and informed that the enemy forces in the Lake area were retreating, apparently to Tabora, and that the Portuguese had been asked to move on Mahenge but had not replied to the suggestion.

It may here be observed that neither at this time nor at any other did the Portuguese find it possible apparently to effect any movement calculated to aid the general plan.

Northey was further told that no idea could then be given to him as to whether the general retirement of the enemy would be to the east or the south, that it was thought safe for him to move towards Iringa and that any warning which it might be possible to give him as to enemy movements in that direction would be conveyed to him.

General Crewe in the north-west was advised that the Commander-in-Chief hoped that he would be able to be the first allied commander to occupy Tabora, and, if possible, to arrange that General Tombeur's (Belgian) forces should move, parallel with his own, on Mariahilf.

In the event Crewe was forestalled at Tabora by the Belgians.

The situation in respect of the occupation of enemy territory was, as may be supposed, always delicate as regarded different allied interests and " persuasion " was indicated to General Crewe as his chief instrument in the achievement of what was required of him.

Crewe was at this time continuing a pursuit of the enemy force which he had ejected from Mwansa on July 14.

As an instance of the continuous heavy reduction which went on in the fighting strength the following is illuminating.

On July 20 the Commanding Officer of the 129th Baluchis reported his regiment as being " totally unfit to march " and his medical officer stated that two months' complete rest and feeding (the unit had been for some time on half rations) were absolutely necessary to make the regiment fit for any work in the field. 800 were in hospital and some 200 doing duty.

(iv) GENERAL BOTHA ARRIVES.

On July 21 General Botha arrived at Nderema with the small party which had accompanied him from the Union.

Exactly a year earlier he had returned to Cape Town at the conclusion of his successful campaign on the other side of the continent in German South-West Africa.

Nearly every South African who was at this time serving under General Smuts had taken part in the operations in German South-West Africa, and the sight of their former Commander-in-Chief produced the extraordinary effect of encouragement and confidence which his presence never failed to arouse.

He was at once keenly interested in the local situation and during his stay he and General Smuts spent all their time, when not moving about, in discussing the campaign and affairs in the Union in the manner to which they were accustomed and always found to be of such great mutual benefit.

On the 23rd the two Generals went to Lukigura and thence to Msiha where they inspected the forward positions.

General Botha left on the following day, and, after a visit to van Deventer at Kondoa Irangi, returned to South Africa.

(v) A REDISTRIBUTION OF FORCES.

The Commander-in-Chief remained another week at Nderema clearing up the situation to the east of the lines of communication and giving his personal attention to the work of reinforcing and refitting his force for its next advance.

He visited Wilhelmstal—his first projected visit had been prevented by his severe attack of malaria—and Korogwe and then returned to Lukigura to complete his plans and arrangements for his forward movement.

A redistribution of units in the 1st Division was now necessary. Detached duties and other factors had caused some confusion and the two Brigades were now reconstituted as follows:—

1st East African Brigade.
Sheppard.

Rhodesians.
29th Punjabis.
130th Baluchis.
2nd Kashmirs.
3rd Kashmirs.
40th Pathans.

2nd East African Brigade.
Hannyngton.
57th Rifles.
2nd K.A.R.
3rd K.A.R.
Gold Coast Regiment.

(The first and last of the above units in the 2nd Brigade were reinforcements from India and the West Coast of Africa, respectively.)

The Gold Coast Regiment, which had fought in the Cameroons, was about 1,000 strong with 12 machine guns and two 2.5 guns and was reported by the I.G.C. as in his opinion " a valuable asset ", an estimate which they justified to the full in the ensuing months.

The two brigades formed the 1st Division under Major-General Hoskins with the 25th Fusiliers and the Cape Corps (a coloured unit from the Cape Province under European Officers) as his divisional troops.

(vi) VAN DEVENTER MOVES AGAIN.

Meanwhile van Deventer had found himself able to move from Kondoa Irangi where he had been held up by lack of transport and rations and by heavy casualties from sickness among his troops for three months.

His force—the 2nd Division—was composed of the following uits:—

1st South African Mounted Brigade.
Nussey,
who had taken the place of Manie Botha who had returned to the Union on urgent private grounds.

The 1st, 2nd, 3rd, 4th and 9th S.A. Horse.
(The last a recent reinforcement.)
3rd South African Infantry Brigade.
Berrangé.
The 9th, 10th, 11th and 12th S.A. Infantry.
E.A. Volunteer Machine Gun Company.

Two of Beves' regiments from the 2nd S.A. Infantry Brigade, the 7th and 8th, were with van Deventer, having been detached, it will be remembered, when the situation at Kondoa Irangi had given ground for some anxiety.

They were to be returned to Brits to whose 3rd Division they belonged on reaching the Central Railway.

Van Deventer also had 4 batteries of artillery, the 1st, 2nd and 4th Permanent S.A. Field Batteries and the 28th Mountain (Indian) Battery.

His Divisional Troops were the S.A. Motor Cycle Corps and a light armoured car battery.

A detachment of the Royal Naval Air Service also accompanied him.

By the end of July, having started his main advance on the 19th, van Deventer had occupied with advanced troops, pushed forward for the purpose, Dodoma on the 29th, Kikombo on the 30th and Saranda and Kilimatinde on the same day.

The German forces opposed to him were under the command of Captain Klinghardt whom von Lettow had left to delay the advance when he himself " marched his main body back to Dodoma in support of Kraut opposite General Smuts ".

Von Lettow gives the strength of Klinghardt's detachment as 5 companies but later, and correct, information indicates that in all 8 companies and a small detachment at Singida faced van Deventer.

Hard marching, brisk fighting and sound tactics characterised these operations of van Deventer as they did all his work in the field.

Klinghardt after stout resistance wherever it was possible to offer it, in the words of von Lettow " slipped off to the east along the railway " but was almost at once laid low by enteric fever and handed over his command to Otto.

So that when General Smuts rejoined his eastern force in its forward positions at the end of July van Deventer was astride the Central Railway between Morogoro and Tabora with the bulk of his force under his own hand at Nyangalo.

In the north-west at the same time the Belgians, advancing from Ruanda, had occupied Kitega, the capital of Urundi, on June 17 and Biaramulo on June 24 while Bukoba had been occupied by a column under Lieut.-Colonel Burgess of Crewe's force on June 28.

As has been stated, Mwanza fell to Crewe on July 14 and on July 28 the Belgians reached Kigoma, the western terminus of the Central Railway on Lake Tanganyika.

To the south Northey had also been on the move and had reached Madibira and Beni by the end of July. He had received none of the promised help from the Portuguese who, as far as could be ascertained, were far from ready to take the field.

He was accordingly ordered not to advance further towards Iringa but to consolidate his positions and only deal with an enemy force, reported as at Lupembe, for the time being.

The situation at this date, the end of July, just before the resumption of the general advance, may be estimated from map number twelve.

(vii) AN APPRECIATION OF THE GENERAL SITUATION AT THE END OF JULY, 1916.

At this time there was correspondence with the War Office about the future conduct of the campaign on the assumption that further fighting would be necessary after the capture of the Central Railway.

Certain Indian regiments were needed for Egypt, and it is interesting to note that some Indian battalions were not suitable for service in Egypt on religious grounds. A sidelight on the many complications which attend the administration of the British Empire.

The advance, after pushing the enemy south from Handeni as far as Lukigura and occupying Msiha as the forward position in the east, was suspended on June 25.

This was unavoidable, as the force was in no shape to move any further without rest, reinforcement, and fresh supply and medical arrangements, and it was necessary to make plans for dealing with the coming work in the Nguru mountains, and for the employment of the freshly arrived mounted brigade as well as for properly timed co-operation with the troops of General van Deventer.

The following was the position at this time:—

On the east Lukigura and Msiha were the most advanced posts: Handeni, Korogwe and Tanga were occupied.

Substantial reinforcements were on the way.

The 57th Rifles (Indian), the 2nd West Indies Regiment (a war unit not to be confused with the regular West India Regiment) and a battalion of the Gold Coast Regiment were due at Tanga.

On the western line of advance the retirement of the enemy from before van Deventer had taken place.

The trouble on the lines of communication had been ended.

It had served as a warning not to omit to clear up the flanks in an advance, a precaution now specially necessary as in front of the eastern force was the strongest enemy concentration which the opposing commander was capable of effecting, with due regard to his several other responsibilities.

The actual direction of the enemy retirement from opposite van Deventer was unknown, but it was probable that some strength would go towards Iringa by way of Saranda and Dodoma, partly to occupy that suitable country, and partly to maintain touch throughout the enemy forces which would otherwise be impossible so far as the north-western command and the troops facing Northey were concerned.

It seemed probable that the main enemy strength would gravitate towards Morogoro, for in this direction was General von Lettow's chief opponent, and that Kilossa would prove to be the most westerly point of any real resistance.

Thus the German Commander would cover Dar-es-Salaam and the railway—the value of which to his adversary was obvious—as long as it was possible to do so and be able to go south towards Mahenge as easily as, and later than, in any other posture he might elect to assume.

It was accordingly necessary to refrain from an advance from the side of Msiha until (a) the forces there should be as strong as they could be made, and (b) the approach of van Deventer's main force (after detachments towards Dodoma and Saranda) should have arrived at a point where he would become a factor to be considered by the enemy commander in his resistance to the advance on the east. Mpapua seemed to be the point indicated, though the first point where such enemy resistance was to be looked for was largely a matter of speculation and could only be estimated on a view as to what was his soundest course.

Immediately before General Smuts the enemy—according to available information—was disposed as follows:—

He held strongly as the left of his line, the hills from Mahase-Kwa-Ngage about Wuworu, Feruka and Hesapo, the right of his position resting on Ruhungu. The ground between being held lightly by posts chiefly for purposes of communication. Patrols and posts extended north from Mahase to Kilindi.

These arrangements effectively guarded against surprise by a flanking movement, covered strongly a line of retreat through the mountains, and threatened General Smuts' flank should he elect to advance against the German right or left without effectively screening himself.

Information had been received from van Deventer who had procured it by means of his scouts, that all Europeans had gone to Gulwe from Saranda, that many troops had left Saranda for Uhehe, that no trains were running further eastward than to Kimamba (30-40 miles west of Morogoro) and that every native village had been taxed 3 cows in calf which had been driven to the south.

This intelligence, which was valuable, as it came from van Deventer's own sources of information by reconnaissance and from escaped or captured enemy natives, indicated a wholesale withdrawal to the south.

At this time opinion was still divided as to whether von Lettow would stand and fight in the vicinity of the Central Railway—his own view of such a proceeding has already been given on page 123—but there seemed to be no reason for such action on his part unless he attached such importance to the maintenance of his hold upon that part as to pivot himself upon it and take up a position astride the railway.

The information taken in all its bearings, however, seemed to indicate an intention to leave Dar-es-Salaam to a speedy and inevitable occupation and to withdraw his force intact south of the Central Railway towards Mahenge and Iringa.

This last course suggested itself as eminently sound on the part of a commander whose sole object was to prolong the campaign and keep a force in the field which would prevent the occupation of the territory until that force should have been captured or completely dispersed.

The retirement on the two places named was in the end carried out.

With the resumption of the general advance as an immediate prospect several considerations presented themselves.

It was already plain that upon General Smuts' arrival at the Central Railway his mounted troops would cease to be available.

Their mobility, though it is true that they were once more on the move, was not what it had been before the advance to Kondoa Irangi in the case of van Deventer's men, and those of Brits, at this time collected at Lukigura, would probably cease to be of any use for any hard work after the conclusion of the coming operations.

South of the railway tsetse would preclude their employment in the field, as their horses would die at a rate which would put replacement out of the question.

It was also becoming increasingly apparent that, if a decisive result could not be obtained as a consequence of the operations which were about to be undertaken, white troops, sooner or later, would have to be replaced by natives who, if not absolutely immune from deadly tropical disease, were far less affected by it than were Europeans who succumbed to it in alarming numbers.

(viii) GENERAL SMUTS SUGGESTS CONSIDERING TERMS.

With the considerations last mentioned in mind, General Smuts sought permission to treat with the enemy, and tentatively approached the British Government to ascertain if it would be prepared to consider some generous treatment to his opponents on the lines of the arrangements made by his own Government in German South-West Africa a year earlier.

After interchange of views—including a discussion by Major the Hon. F. Guest of the General Staff (representing General Smuts) with Sir Henry Belfield, the Governor of British East Africa—the proposal was dropped. The conditions on the east were admittedly different from those in German South-West Africa, where the whole of the German force was composed of Europeans, but General Smuts' suggestions were largely misunderstood by those to whom he addressed them.

General Smuts stated that he was " not at all hopeful that any overtures would be successful as all captured Germans said that von Lettow was determined to hold out to the end of the war and all supply arrangements were already made to that end in Mahenge area ". A correct appreciation.

General Smuts' object in suggesting the possibility of terms was in his own words " only to save millions on expenditure which would be involved in prolonging the campaign in the far south ".

Eventually, in September, 1916, two months later, General Smuts, on his own responsibility addressed a non-committal letter to Dr. Schnee, the Imperial Governor, suggesting that this " resistance might well now cease in a manner honourable to yourselves ", a suggestion which was courteously but firmly set aside.

General von Lettow's own view is contained in his book: " General Smuts realised that his blow had failed. He sent me a letter calling upon me to surrender, by which he showed that, as far as force was concerned, he had reached the end of his resources ".

This opinion was certainly optimistic from the enemy point of view.

General von Lettow's reply was what was to be expected from a soldier of his calibre.

General Smuts took the opportunity of offering his opponent his congratulations upon the award of the " Ordre pour le Mérite " bestowed upon the latter by the German Emperor.

This act of courtesy was referred to with appreciation by General von Lettow when, years later, he was the guest at the annual dinner of the East African Expeditionary Force in London, and the two Generals met in happier circumstances.

An interesting example of the difficulties of administration in a mixed army such as that commanded by General Smuts was afforded by a reference to the Commander-in-Chief from the Administrative Staff on the marked disparity between the sentences awarded to Imperial and Union soldiers by Courts Martial. The latter were composed of officers from each service for the trial of their own troops, and the reason for the difference in treatment was obvious.

On the one side were professional soldiers used to enforce and accustomed to obey the rules of military discipline.

On the other, for the professional soldiers were a very small part of the whole of the South African forces, " colonials ", presenting all their characteristic independence and impatience of what they regarded as red tape.

Such was one of the innumerable smaller difficulties which daily beset the commander of—to use his own words—" a most heterogeneous army, drawn from almost all continents, and speaking a babel of languages ".

CHAPTER XI

(i) THE SITUATION TO BE DEALT WITH BY THE EASTERN FORCE.

THE operations which were now to be taken in hand under the personal control and direction of General Smuts were designed—see General Smuts' despatch of October 27, 1916— "to corner the enemy in the Nguru mountains" and, if this purpose were not achieved, "to bring him to bay at Kilossa on the Central Railway".

The country ahead was at its best as difficult and trying as that which had been left behind; in the mountains is was even more formidable, and the chances of cornering the enemy were slight, unless he elected to stand deliberately. The unsoundness of such action on his part has already been discussed and made clear.

He would be retiring on a line or lines of his own choice and the composition of his forces which were highly mobile, well acquainted, as always hitherto, with the country, little troubled by sickness and not dependent upon large supply trains for their sustenance, was such that they could be moved in any direction and without dislocating or really affecting any general arrangements.

General Smuts possessed none of these great advantages.

He was tied to one line of supply, as was van Deventer, whose circumstances were the same as his own; for the service of this line large supply columns would be required; his fighting strength—indeed his whole strength—would again start to shrink with the first march of his forces; any alteration in a line of advance which had been decided upon and prepared for would inevitably entail delay and rearrangement. His troops would be groping in the dense bush while their adversaries watched them.

The German Commander would retire upon his supplies on a prearranged line or lines, while the British lines of communication which were to serve General Smuts and General van Deventer would steadily lengthen and would have to be organised as they developed. They would also become more vulnerable with every mile.

These last conditions would obtain until, with the Central Railway held between Morogoro or some other spot and Dar-es-Salaam, the latter port should become available as a base of supply.

When van Deventer's troops—still supplied from Moschi—reached Kilossa from Kondoa Irangi, they had marched 220 miles from the last-named place by the shortest route. They were then more than 400 miles from Moschi.

A far less able commander than General von Lettow would easily have avoided the capture of his forces or any damage to them in such circumstances as these.

Up to a point it had been done in German South-West Africa by the simple expedient of avoiding action, but this was not the method of General Smuts' skilful opponent.

The advancing columns were compelled to deploy and fight on every occasion which presented itself as suitable to their determined enemy who maintained contact until the last possible moment, always with counter-attack, which was often delivered with great effect, in mind.

It was in his handling of a force, numerically inferior, but from the nature of its personnel far more mobile, against one of which occasionally even the strength and always the comparative inflexibility were drawbacks to it, and in his employment of all the advantages that nature gave him in this tropical country that General von Lettow showed his special ability.

There have been other instances of such conditions in warfare in Africa, and the lessons which are to be derived from a study of these conditions remain to-day of high importance to the forces of the Union.

(ii) THE ADVANCE OF THE EASTERN FORCE RESUMED.

On August 3 General Smuts returned to Msiha to put his troops in motion for the advance which was to carry him to Morogoro, and result in the occupation of the Central Railway from Dodoma to Dar-es-Salaam, some 300 miles.

The country immediately facing the eastern force at the beginning of August is described in the despatch of October 27, 1916, already quoted.

(The general dispositions of the enemy were given on page 166.)

" For a distance of about forty-five miles the main road to the Central Railway passes close under the Nguru and Kanga mountains. The enemy had skilfully disposed about twenty companies or 3,000 rifles with much heavy and light artillery in the mountains and athwart the main road which had been entrenched along the numerous foothills which the road crosses. If we forced our way down the road against these formidable obstacles or moved by our left flank through the bush and tall elephant grass, part of the enemy force in the mountains on our right would get behind us and endanger our communications. It was therefore necessary to advance by way of the mountains themselves and to clear them as the advance proceeded southward. This could best be done by wide turning movements through the mountains which would have the effect of threatening or cutting off the enemy's retreat if he delayed his retirement unduly."

Scouts sent to reconnoitre the main mass of the Nguru mountains reported that the route by the Mdjonga valley was practicable, as were two lines of advance into the Mdjonga valley by way of the valleys of the Mgasi and Lwale.

The relative strengths of the contending forces were, stated in terms of rifles, 7,000 British to 3,000 German. The effect of artillery, once the advance started, was in such country negligible on either side.

In order to conceal the initial movements from the enemy, who had the camp at Msiha under constant observation and had taken advantage of this rare circumstance to shell it frequently and with considerable accuracy and effect, the westward movements were initiated from Kwa Ngero on the Lukigura.

The movements to that locality were taken by the Germans to be due to their long range artillery fire.

The forces taking part were as follows:—

1st Division.

Major-General Hoskins.

1st East African Brigade.

Brig.-General Sheppard.

29th Punjabis.
130th Baluchis.
2nd Kashmir Rifles.
M.G., 2nd Detachment.
27th Mountain Battery (less one Section).

172

No. 5 S.A. Field Battery.
No. 6 Field Battery.
One double company, 61st Pioneers.
One section, E.A. Pioneers and the following
  Army Troops attached:—
    134th How. Battery.
    No. 1 L.A.M. Battery.
    Squadron, 17th (Indian) Cavalry.
        2nd East African Brigade.
        Brig.-General Hannyngton.
57th (Wildes) Rifles.
3rd Kashmir Rifles.
3rd K.A. Rifles.
M.G. Detachment, 129th Baluchis.
One section, 27th Mountain Battery.
Mounted Infantry, K.A.R.
        Divisional Troops.
25th Royal Fusiliers.
2nd Rhodesian Regiment.
Cape Corps Battalion.
Loyal North Lancs.
M.G. Company.
No. 7 Field Battery.
East African Mounted Rifles.
One section, E.A. Pioneers.
        3rd Division.
        Major-General Brits.

    2nd South African Mounted Brigade.
        Brig.-General Enslin.
5th South African Horse.
6th South African Horse.
7th South African Horse.
8th South African Horse.
(No. 3 S.A. Field Battery was attached to this mounted
brigade, but was compelled to turn back at Pembe.)
    2nd South African Infantry Brigade.
        Brig.-General Beves.
5th South African Infantry.
6th South African Infantry.
        Divisional Troops.
Volunteer Machine Gun Company.

173

No. 1 S.A. Field Battery.
No. 3 S.A. Field Battery.
No. 8 Field Battery.

And the following from Army Troops:—

No. 13 How. Battery.
No. 5 L.A.M. Battery.

The average strength of the eleven infantry battalions was below 500 rifles.

(iii) GENERAL PLAN OF THE NGURU OPERATIONS.

The general plan of the advance was as follows:—

The 2nd S.A. Mounted Brigade (Enslin) was to move westward from the Lukigura against the German detachments at Kimbe and Msunga (see map number thirteen) and thence, by the valley of the Lwale, on Turiani. Brits with the balance of his division would follow Enslin and at Turiani co-operate in an attempt to cut the retreat of the enemy main body in position at Ruhungu.

Hannyngton was to move down the Mdjonga valley against the enemy detachment at Kwa Tschengo, while to Sheppard was assigned the task of demonstrating before Ruhungu and holding the enemy main body to its positions there.

General van Deventer was advised of the coming advance, and was told that, if the enemy should stand, Brits would try to come down the mountains behind them at Mhonda and Turiani. If the enemy were to retreat past Turiani, Brits would proceed round the west of the Nguru to Mkundi (some 10 miles to the west, and a little south, of Kwedihombo). General Smuts added that if the enemy were not cornered by these movements his encirclement must be effected on the Central Railway and that, to this end, the 2nd Mounted Brigade would be sent towards Kimamba and Kilossa to co-operate with the 2nd Division. Van Deventer himself was ordered to move early towards Mpapua and on to Kilossa. The Commander-in-Chief expressed the view that, if van Deventer could by a sudden move south capture these places, the enemy might not be mobile enough to retreat.

In the event, these plans were altered under the pressure of circumstances and in consequence of the line of retirement adopted by the enemy.

(iv) THE MOVEMENTS START.

Brits with his mounted and infantry brigades moved westward from the Lukigura on the morning of August 5.

Enslin with his mounted men, less the 7th S.A. Horse which he sent to attend to Msunga, captured the German post at Kimbe and pressed on to Pembe, and, crossing the Mdjonga there on the 6th, continued his way along the Mdjonga valley. The enemy detachment at Msunga eluded the 7th S.A. Horse which lost touch with Enslin and strayed into the mountains.

On the 5th G.H.Q. and the 2nd E.A. Brigade (Hannyngton) remained on the Lukigura and the 1st E.A. Brigade (Sheppard) at Msiha. Brits with his infantry and transport was laboriously and with difficulty making his way through long grass, thick bush, tree stumps and rough ground behind Enslin.

The intelligence scouts had, in the light of events, evidently not taken transport into consideration when they reported the several lines of advance through the mountains as " practicable." It became clear that considerable time and damage might have been saved if the scouts had been accompanied by competent administrative staff officers.

On August 6 General Smuts decided to follow Brits and left Lukigura at 9 a.m., reaching Kimbe in the afternoon, an hour and a half ahead of the infantry of Brits' division. On his way he had passed the transport which had sustained much damage in consequence of the roughness of the route.

By the evening, G.H.Q., 1st Divisional H.Q. and 3rd Divisional H.Q. were at Kimbe, the 2nd S.A. Infantry Brigade had one regiment, the 6th, with Beves at Kimbe, and the 5th S.A. Infantry some miles short of that place. Rather further back was the 1st Divisional Reserve. The 1st E.A. Brigade (Sheppard) was still at Msiha.

On August 7 the Commander-in-Chief with G.H.Q., Brits and his infantry, moved to Pembe, 1st Divisional H.Q. returning to Lukigura with its Divisional Reserve.

An entry in the War Diary on this date gives an idea of the transport problem.

" The roads traversed so far did not exist two days ago and have had to be cut as the columns moved. They are very bad with extremely steep inclines which results in the transport continually breaking down and coming up long after the columns."

Sheppard who had moved from Msiha now reported (August 8) that he was east of Ruhungu, which was held by the enemy, and without water and that he proposed to retire and move again down the motor road. He was ordered not to retire but to push forward and engage the enemy. He then reported that attack from where he was was not feasible and that he was compelled to retire. This message was soon followed by another reporting the resumption of his advance by the right bank of the Lukigura.

Despite every possible effort it was now found that to send any heavy transport further on through the mountains was out of the question, and General Smuts ordered it all back to Lukigura and the columns to proceed with two wheeled transport only.

By night Hannyngton had reached Kwatschengo after a patrol action and some half dozen casualties.

G.H.Q. remained at Pembe on the Mdjonga river, as did Brits with Beves' infantry. Strenuous efforts were made to improve the crossing over the river. Enslin, who had reached Mhonda, was experiencing resistance there. He had two regiments with him and his two others were on their way behind him. The 7th S.A. Horse were still unaccounted for.

At 10 p.m. heavy firing was heard at Pembe from Hannyngton's direction and continued until the early morning.

On August 9 Hannyngton resumed his advance and at 7 a.m. came into touch with mounted troops which turned out to be the missing 7th S.A. Horse which had lost touch with Enslin and had been the cause of the firing of the previous night. Endeavouring to reach Enslin through the mountains by a night march they had come in contact with a strong enemy force and became seriously engaged with it. The action ended in the withdrawal of the German force, and the 7th S.A. Horse now joined Hannyngton, who by evening had occupied a hill 2 miles north of Matamondo after some resistance on the way.

Meanwhile General Smuts had ordered Brits with Beves' infantry forward in support of Hannyngton and the former moved on Kongo from Pembe, and reached the former place in the evening of the 9th. On joining Hannyngton, Brits was to assume local command of the combined force.

Hannyngton was advised of this arrangement by telephone from Pembe in the evening.

Sheppard was now reinforced by the Gold Coast Battalion and ordered to move round the east side of Ruhungu and force the enemy to fight or retire.

On August 10 Hannyngton advanced against the enemy in front of him at Matamondo and became engaged early in the morning. A patrol of the 57th Rifles captured a machine gun by action which is described by von Lettow as " very skilful ". The engagement continued until 11 a.m. when Brits arrived, and Beves' two infantry regiments were put into the fight and drove back the German right.

Darkness supervened without a decision having been reached. On the following morning, however (the 11th), it was found that the enemy had retired.

Enslin was at this time still holding his position at Mhonda against a reinforced body of the enemy, but was held up and unable to advance in any direction.

On August 11, however, touch was established by helio with Brits who, on the next day, joined hands with Enslin at Mhonda.

For the last four or five days Sheppard had been moving below the mountains to the east against Ruhungu. On August 9 he had started his second venture against this position down the right bank of the Lukigura.

Two days later the Ruhungu position was found by scouts to have been deserted and it was occupied by a detached column, and Sheppard pushed on to Kipera where he secured a crossing over the Wami river.

On the evening of the 12th General Smuts' forces were disposed as follows:—

G.H.Q., Russongo*; 1st Division, H.Q. and Reserve, Russongo; Sheppard, Mafleta, to move on Kipera; Brits (with Beves, Hannyngton and Enslin), Mhonda; Van Deventer was at this time at and about Mpapua.

It was now clear that the withdrawal of the enemy was complete, but the direction of his retirement was not known. It might have been to Morogoro or to Kilossa, for at Kwedi Hombo the road forked in either direction.

Brits had sent in a message from Mhonda that until the evening of the 11th Turiani had been strongly held, but that

---

* Russongo, a river crossing the motor road roughly midway between Msiha and Turiani.

many guns had passed through that place, and he was of opinion that the enemy had gone south, a view which proved to be correct.

The 12th had been spent largely in clearing obstructions from the motor road and in bridging the Russongo.

On August 13 G.H.Q., Brits' Division and Hannyngton reached Turiani where the bridge had been completely destroyed. It was some 40 feet high and steps were taken to cut a drift and build a low bridge.

Sheppard was now feeling his way in the vicinity of the Wami river.

The advance had been opposed by the following enemy forces:—

At Ruhungu under Kraut: 7 companies;

at Massimbani under Stemmermann: 3 companies (Massimbani lay some 5 miles south of Ruhungu and rather less to the east of the motor road and covered Kraut's right rear);

at Kongo (and then Kwatschengo and Matamondo): 2 companies under Poppe;

at Turiani: 1 company under Schelke;

while at Dakawa (12 miles due south of Kwedihombo) where the road to Morogoro crossed the Wami was posted Schulz with 4 companies. Here he secured the line of retirement to the south.

(v) COMMENTS ON THE NGURU OPERATIONS.

Though General Smuts did not stay his hand and the movement southward continued without a check, the operations between Msiha and Morogoro fall into two clearly defined parts.

From Msiha to Turiani the effort to head off the main body of the enemy under General von Lettow was undertaken solely by the forces under the immediate control of General Smuts. Van Deventer was still too far off to demand more than a close watch from the German chief command, and this could be well effected by a small detachment well led. This duty was efficiently carried out by Otto. As will be seen, after the retirement from Turiani, General von Lettow sent Kraut over to face van Deventer, no doubt in view of the greater importance of the latter's movements.

The effort to capture the enemy force having failed in the Nguru mountains, it at once became obvious that, without close strategic, and, before very long, tactical co-operation with van Deventer, there was no hope whatever of bringing the enemy to bay.

Before proceeding to the operations between the south of the Nguru mountains and Morogoro, therefore, it will be well to consider those which have just been described and which present several important features.

They demonstrate afresh two factors of the utmost importance in considering the strategy and tactics of warfare in tropical bush country.

The immense difficulty of strategic surprise and the remarkable strength of tactical defence.

General Smuts' general plan was to pin the main body of the enemy to his Ruhungu position, while, moving through the mountains by his own right he should get in behind the German force at Turiani on its line of retreat.

A holding attack is a most difficult tactical undertaking. Once the enemy grasps its nature he ceases to regard it seriously and looks for the real motive which it covers, in this case the movement to the west round his left flank.

The attack therefore has to be pressed with all vigour and apparent determination to push it home, but without so committing the attacking force that its withdrawal *at any time* is compromised.

In country such as that round Ruhungu to *hold* an enemy force meant virtually to surround it for, otherwise, it could withdraw, bearing in mind its extremely mobile character and its thorough acquaintance with the terrain, in any one of several directions at its commander's will.

Sheppard would therefore have to be far stronger than the force against which he moved at Ruhungu.

The total number of rifles in General Smuts' whole force was only 7,000 as against the enemy strength of 3,500, and a proportion of 2 to 1 as against a defending force in such a terrain was a very slight advantage, if indeed the advantage did not actually lie with the defence against an enemy on interior lines as was General von Lettow.

Sheppard's approximate strength was 1,500 rifles, while at Ruhungu in position were 7 companies, with 3 more close at hand at Massimbani, representing a total strength of 10 enemy companies or *at least* as many as were at the disposal of Sheppard.

An effective holding attack in such circumstances was impossible, but the strength of Sheppard's brigade was all that could be made available for the purpose.

Even had a holding attack at Ruhungu been feasible, the enemy could not be cornered unless the strategic movements into the Nguru could be concealed long enough to guarantee his surprise.

This again was, unfortunately, impossible.

As has been stated, even the initial movement back to the Lukigura of the forces designed for the advance through the mountains was observed by the enemy, though he at first assigned a mistaken reason—his own long range gun fire—for it.

As soon as Enslin started, the German observation posts at Kimbe and Msunga became aware of his movement and his *sole* chance of surprising the enemy was a rapid movement, unchecked, to Turiani.

At Mhonda he was held up for 5 days by a German detachment which was strongly reinforced by Kraut as soon as the arrival of the South African mounted troops was notified. Kraut also reinforced Poppe at Matamondo, and any slight chance of his eventual retirement being interfered with, if it ever existed, disappeared.

The British, South African and Indian troops displayed their customary dogged courage and patience to give effect to their commander's plans which were the best possible for snatching a success in circumstances little calculated to make it likely.

The great strength of the defence coupled with the mobility of the German forces and the impossibility of surprising them strategically in close proximity to them in bush and mountainous country were as powerful auxiliaries to General von Lettow as they were almost insuperable hindrances to General Smuts.

Assuming strategic surprise in such a theatre to be practicable, the movements which are to effect it, *which must proceed unchecked*, must be carried out at a far greater distance than was possible in the Nguru operations. The question will be discussed generally in the final chapter.

(vi) THE ADVANCE CONTINUED.

(Map number fourteen should be referred to.)

On August 12 General Smuts ordered the following movements:—

The 3rd K.A.R. to relieve units of the 2nd S.A. Mounted Brigade on the motor road south of Turiani. The latter had been held up by enemy rearguards and the mountain torrents emptying themselves into the Wami. All the bridges had been destroyed, and it seemed probable that a strong enemy force was holding the point of junction of the two roads at Kwedihombo.

The mounted troops were then to move by the left bank of the Lwale-Liwale river from the east towards Ngulu-Kwa-Bogwa endeavouring to intercept the retreat of the enemy if found in position.

Beves with his two infantry regiments was instructed to continue a movement which he had put into execution towards Pangala, and, keeping well up on the Nguru foothills, to try to intercept the enemy retreat from the west.

Hannyngton, reinforcing his K.A.R. unit, would move with his brigade south along the motor road.

Sheppard was to remain at Komssonga, which he had reached, to clear up the left flank, throwing out a battalion to Ngulu-Kwa-Bogwa to gain contact with the left of Hannyngton's Brigade.

Contact with the enemy was not regained as a consequence of these movements until Hannyngton reached the Mkindu late on the afternoon of the 14th when his troops came upon a party engaged on destroying a bridge. Four companies were now reported to be in a position near Kwedi Hombo which Hannyngton was ordered to attack on the following morning (15th) under arrangements to be settled with Beves. The latter would co-operate on his right flank leaving 50 rifles on Pangana Hill. Enslin, with 130th Baluchis (Dyke) from Sheppard, was instructed to move early on the morning of the 15th and join in the attack from south of Kwedi Hombo trying to get astride the Morogoro and Kilossa roads. He was also warned to be able to deal with any reinforcements from Mwomero should they appear.

Hannyngton camped on the Mkindu river for the night of August 14-15 with Beves behind him on the motor road.

Enslin was advised of the importance of information as to the direction of the enemy retirement and to endeavour to secure this intelligence by means of patrols along the Mkindu river to the motor road, towards Kwedi Hombo, and in a southerly direction towards Mwomero.

On the morning of the 15th Kwedi Hombo was occupied, three enemy companies there retiring in some haste and confusion in consequence of the apparently unlooked for approach of Enslin's mounted men.

Some prisoners were taken and information, though still inconclusive, again pointed to a main retirement to Morogoro.

In these circumstances General Smuts decided, while watching the Kilossa road, to make his main advance along that to Morogoro. Even if the principal enemy retirement should prove to be on Kilossa, he himself, with the bulk of his forces on the Morogoro road, would be on the enemy outer flank in relation to van Deventer.

(vii) THE ACTION ON THE WAMI RIVER.

Having decided on his advance to Morogoro, General Smuts made his dispositions for crossing the Wami, a river reported by Sheppard as " similar to the Pangani at Buiko but broader ". This indicated a strong defensive feature of which the enemy might be expected to take full advantage. Sheppard's cavalry patrols along the east bank of the river 3 miles from his camp had been forced to retire, and to deal with the situation the following arrangements were made.

Brits, retaining for the purpose of the immediate operations the 130th Baluchis from Sheppard lent to Enslin, to move with his 3rd Division by the Morogoro road so as to be at the Dakawa crossing on the afternoon of the 16th.

If the enemy were holding the crossing, he was to reconnoitre the position so as to be able to attack on the morning of the 17th. Brits was advised that Sheppard was to co-operate with him in the attack and was moving down the right bank of the Wami for the purpose.

After securing the crossing he would rest his troops on the river, sending mounted patrols along the Morogoro road and the right bank of the river.

Sheppard received instructions in agreement with the above plan and was told to be near Dakawa by the night of August 16-17. Advancing through thick bush his brigade bivouacked about 5 miles from Dakawa on the evening of the 16th, by which time Brits had arrived at Dakawa to find the crossing strongly held, and the latter accordingly arranged that the 130th Baluchis should move against the enemy front while his mounted troops looked for a crossing to the south-west pending the development of Sheppard's movement.

At dawn on the 17th, after patrols had been fired upon, the action at the Dakawa crossing became general.

The mountain guns (section 27th Battery) came into action, silencing three enemy machine guns, while the Baluchis, aided by the two South African battalions, endeavoured to overcome the strong resistance of the enemy.

Meanwhile, Sheppard, reduced as a consequence of several detachments to about 500 rifles, was advancing south-west through difficult country, and Enslin crossed the river but immediately turned sharply to his left and became engaged with the enemy left. Here he was stopped and could not get behind the German force nor was he able to gain contact with Sheppard.

At nightfall the enemy still held his positions with his line of retreat open, Sheppard having been held since 2 p.m. at Sokoto after a casualty list of 70. He was afterwards twice attacked and remained at Sokoto for the night.

Orders were given for a resumption of movement on the same plan on the following day in the unlikely event of the enemy electing to remain in his positions.

On the following morning, however, the German commander had retired, and the retirement in the direction of Morogoro was finally established by reconnaissance from the air which the comparatively open country and the return of fine weather made possible. The establishment of an aerodrome at Dakawa, too, brought the air force once more within easy distance of the enemy lines and advantage was taken of this to bomb Morogoro.

General Smuts' supplies had now failed again and the advance on the east was once more arrested.

His forces had been opposed by Schulz and Stemmermann with 4 and 3 companies, respectively, together with 2 companies under Heyden-Linden, 9 companies in all. They were distributed in a dug-in position on the right bank with their right flank well thrown back and entrenched in dense bush.

The right flank was held by Stemmermann with 4 companies while Schulz faced Brits across the Wami. The remaining companies were in reserve and the total German force amounted to 1,200 rifles.

The British casualties were 120, of which 75 were in Sheppard's brigade, the 29th Punjabis sustaining the heaviest losses, 54 with 10 per cent. killed. The losses of the enemy were probably considerably less.

(viii) THE COMBINED ADVANCE TO THE CENTRAL RAILWAY.

The close co-operation of van Deventer now became of extreme importance, a fact of which General von Lettow showed appreciation by sending Kraut with 2 companies and one 4.1" gun together with other lighter guns, to Kilossa where, joining Lincke with 3 companies and some mounted troops, he took up Otto's task of resistance to van Deventer.

Otto was withdrawn to Morogoro with 5 companies to carry out the evacuation of stores required for the southward retirement, while Schulz, with whom was Stemmermann, remained at Dakawa and fought the delaying action which has just been described.

After the engagement at Nyangalo on July 27, van Deventer's Division had been held up at that place in consequence of his transport having been run once more to a standstill in the strenuous work which it had performed since leaving Kondoa Irangi.

On August 10, in response to an order from General Smuts to co-operate with him with the least possible delay, van Deventer again moved forward though supplies had only just reached him as the last he had gave out and there was no time to issue them in full quantity before the advance began.

Van Deventer directed the 9th S.A. Horse on Chunya, with detachments of the regiment thrown out, one moving on Kongwa and Chelwe, the other well out on the left flank to reconnoitre the country about Chelwe and Tubugwe.

On his right flank the 3rd S.A. Horse and 11th S.A. Infantry moved from Kikombo on Msagali clearing up the country south of the central railway in the direction of Gulwe.

The remainder of the Division marched behind the 9th S.A. Horse in the centre, and late in the afternoon contact was regained with the enemy at Chunya. Van Deventer's infantry charging up the slope—a fine performance after a particularly trying march all day—scattered the enemy who occupied a second position ahead.

On August 11 the German forces had retreated and were not picked up again until van Deventer's advanced mounted patrols came into touch with them round Mpapua. The enemy was attacked by Nussey with his mounted brigade in the afternoon. Leaving the 2nd S.A. Horse to attack the front of the enemy position, Nussey took the 1st Regiment to seize a position in rear of the enemy, sending the 9th Regiment to cut off the German retreat south of the town.

Late in the afternoon the 12th S.A. Infantry came up and at once joined in the frontal attack, the 10th Infantry at the same time moving round the enemy right flank.

The enemy, driven from their position and through the town, by a resolute counter-attack made good their escape to the south-east in the direction of Gode-Gode.

30 Hours of hard marching and manoeuvring, without water and without food, for the supply wagons were far behind, over 32 miles of appalling roads had once more reduced the South Africans to exhaustion and temporary immobility, and they occupied Mpapua whence they scoured the country for food of any kind which would keep them till supplies should come up, and van Deventer pushed his mounted patrols to Gulwe and Kimagai establishing the retirement of the enemy to Kidete.

At Mpapua the 11th S.A. Infantry rejoined the Division on the 14th, followed on the 16th by the 9th Infantry, both suffering from the effects of their hard marching and trying work.

Moving on again after supplies had reached him, but without the two battalions last mentioned, van Deventer advanced against the enemy found on August 16 holding a position at Kidete. After an attack, in which the 10th S.A. Infantry sustained 30 out of a total list of 45 casualties, and, after a trying march in great heat, delivered a spirited assault, the enemy retained his positions at nightfall.

At daybreak, Otto, who had retired at 2 a.m., was out of touch and van Deventer bivouacked on the Kidete river.

On this date, August 17, General Smuts' troops had fought the action at the Wami, and the positions of the eastern force and the 2nd Division are shown in map number fifteen.

At this juncture Major Kraut and his detachment arrived at Kilossa from Kwedi Hombo and Otto moved back to Morogoro.

The retirement of the enemy had been rapid, for, although bridges, points and tanks on the railway were mined, there had evidently not been time for their destruction. A train had been derailed with considerable casualties to the Askaris who were being conveyed by it.

The country now immediately ahead of the 2nd Division was formidable indeed, and van Deventer's own account gives a good idea of the situation which faced him between Kidete and Kilossa as also of the nature of the fighting undertaken by his South Africans, which was a daily occurrence from the 15th to the 22nd of August.

Van Deventer writes: " The railway from Kidete to Kilossa for a distance of 25 miles follows a narrow defile cut through the Osagara mountains by the Mkondokwa river; *every yard of advance was contested by the enemy* . . , The fighting consisted of the enemy receiving our advance guard with one or several ambushes, then falling back on a well prepared position and retiring from that on to further well-selected ambush places and positions ". An ideal system of defence in such country which, be it once more observed, *depended for its full effect upon previous exhaustive reconnaissance* which is of course always possible over ground which is held and is to be the scene of a deliberate retirement.

Von Lettow's own account of these operations is of interest and value. He writes: " Otto's Detachment frequently found itself exposed to an attack on its front while being enveloped on both flanks. The enemy did not always succeed in timing these movements correctly.*

He goes on to say: " the short range of visibility always enabled us either to avoid the danger, or, if the opportunity was favourable, to *attack the troops outflanking us in detail.*† In any event, these outflanking tactics of the enemy when followed, as in this case, in extraordinarily thick bush, and

---

* Perhaps in the circumstances hardly to be wondered at.

† Another valuable comment on " Bush Fighting " by a master of the art.

among numerous rocks, demanded great exertions and used up his strength ".

To quote van Deventer again: " The operations called for an extraordinary amount of mountain climbing and constant fighting. The slight casualties sustained over an enormous track of country, bristling with dongas and difficulties at every point, were mainly due to the advance being carried out by avoiding as far as possible frontal attacks ".

Van Deventer's employment of his mounted troops in forward reconnaissance and tactical envelopment in country reported as " impossible even for *dismounted troops*" was in the best tradition of the mounted riflemen of South Africa.

His richly deserved tribute to his men might have been written by any commander of fighting troops, wherever they may have come from, in this country of East Africa calculated to impose strict caution on the boldest leader.

" Their endurance and hardships through dry and waterless stretches on scanty rations form an achievement worthy of South African troops."

These experiences were the daily lot of all the soldiers, who fought on every front in this campaign.

Van Deventer received supplies on August 18, and in the afternoon moved on Msagara with his infantry brigade which, early on the following morning—19th—climbed the heights of the enemy position. The German forces, however, vacated the latter without offering resistance and made a rapid retreat in the direction of Kilossa.

Van Deventer's mounted men followed in pursuit and early in the afternoon were checked by the fire of a Königsberg gun before a high position in very difficult country. Here they were opposed by Kraut, while Otto passed on to Morogoro. On August 21, when van Deventer had got some of his artillery forward—most of his heavy guns were held up for want of petrol—the 3rd Infantry Brigade—once more collected—moved up the heights before the enemy position until fire from it checked their further advance.

Van Deventer had sent two mounted forces out on his flanks, the one north of the railway to Mundo and the other south via Kwasalimo directed to reach the railway east of Kilossa. The latter was to establish contact with the Cape Corps which General Smuts had detached from his own force and which was moving down the Kwedi Hombo-Kilossa road.

This unit had been detached on the 18th with a view to helping van Deventer in road and bridge making from Kilossa onward.

This threat to his flanks induced Kraut to vacate his strong positions before Kilossa. His decision was no doubt expedited by the arrival of one of van Deventer's mounted patrols to the south of the railway opposite a company of the enemy placed to protect a route from Kilossa to the south.

Van Deventer was now through the rugged country which had held him up and aided the enemy since he had moved from Nyangalo, and his worn out infantry, incapable of further marching, halted at Kilossa.

Mounted patrols verified Kraut's retirement in the direction of Myombo to the south.

(ix) THE MOVEMENT ON MOROGORO.

General Smuts with the bulk of his forces had meanwhile been held up at Dakawa, partly by the need for bridging the Wami before an onward movement could be undertaken but largely because of the lack of supplies. All reinforcements had been stopped on their way to enable supplies to reach the forward troops.

General von Lettow some time earlier had reconnoitred " the passes leading from Morogoro up the northern slopes of the gigantic Uluguru group and down again on the south side towards Kissaki " which " had to be examined on foot ".

General Smuts—see his despatch already quoted—says: " I was not then aware that a track went due south from Morogoro through the mountains to Kissaki and that the capture of the mountains would not achieve the end in view ", i.e. " to bottle the enemy up in Morogoro " by seizing Mlali on the road to the south by the west of the Uluguru range and blocking the road round these mountains to the east.

This last action was the object of the movements which General Smuts now set in train.

Advising van Deventer that two routes were open to the enemy, one round the west of the Uluguru by Mlali or Simbas and the other east and branching from the main road at Kwama-hedi, General Smuts added that the best plan to cut the enemy off would be to close both roads and pin him in Morogoro.

Considering that infantry would not be able to move fast enough to carry out this plan, General Smuts proposed to use his 2nd Mounted Brigade (Enslin) to deal with the eastern road while van Deventer's 1st Mounted Brigade (Nussey) was to reach Mlali at the same time as Enslin should reach the vicinity of Kwamahedi. The 1st and 3rd Divisions would move from Dakawa to Ngerengere and thence to the railway. Owing to the absence of water, van Deventer's mounted troops would have to go from Mkata to Mlali without a halt.

Van Deventer, at this time, August 21, being still held up before Kilossa, stated his inability to move to Mlali until he should have cleared up the situation in front of him, and General Smuts then ordered his own Mounted Brigade (Enslin) with a field battery to Mkata which place Enslin was ordered to reach on the morning of the 22nd and attack. Pursuant to this order the 2nd Mounted Brigade left Dakawa in the afternoon of August 21.

Van Deventer was ordered to send his mounted troops to meet Enslin at Mkata where Nussey would take the place of Enslin and the latter would return to move against Kwamahedi as at first planned.

As a consequence of van Deventer's occupation of Kilossa and Kraut's retirement to the south, Enslin was ordered on August 22 to march from Mkata so as to be at Mlali on the morning of the 24th and then to move towards Morogoro dealing with any enemy forces which might be retiring along his road. Van Deventer was ordered to pursue Kraut as far south as possible and to move his mounted troops so as to protect Enslin from any interference by the enemy retiring from Kilossa to Kissaki.

General Smuts, with the rest of his force, moved on the morning of August 23 from Dakawa, the 1st Division an hour and a half ahead of the 3rd, on Kimamba, camping for the night of the 23rd-24th six miles beyond that place, without fires or lights.

The advance was resumed and continued throughout the 24th without incident until the force reached the Ngerengere river at dark and camped there in considerable confusion which was attributable in no small measure to the fact that the two Divisional Generals with their staffs had remained with the Commander-in-Chief all day and not close to their commands. The 2nd E.A. Brigade (Hannyngton), as a consequence possibly of its Brigadier's knowledge of local conditions, formed an exception in the general confusion. 30 miles had been covered over rough waterless country in the same number of hours.

Colonel Brink, Chief Staff Officer to General Brits, was sent ahead with 200 mounted men to seize the high hill Mkogwa which he did, German patrols on Fulwe and Mkonge retiring on the following day.

Information came to hand that the enemy were evacuating Morogoro and on August 26 this place was occupied by the 2nd Rhodesian Regiment and a detachment of the 130th Baluchis.

While there was no cessation in the operations, the occupation of Morogoro and, with it, a large portion of the Central Railway marked the conclusion of a clearly defined phase of them and it may be well here to review the situation and what the strategy of General Smuts had achieved.

(x) THE RESULT OF GENERAL SMUTS' MOVEMENTS FROM MAY TO AUGUST, 1916.

There can be no doubt as to the general soundness of this strategy or its striking results. The latter are shown graphically on plans numbered sixteen and were remarkable.

On May 22, 1916, when the main advance from the Ruwu river line, south of Moschi began, van Deventer had seized Kondoa Irangi; the Kilimanjaro area had been occupied by General Smuts; Northey in the south had organised his forces since his arrival in the early part of the year and held them assembled on the frontiers of Nyasaland and Rhodesia ready to co-operate; while in the north-west the line of the Kagera river was held with the enemy opposite in occupation of a strong defensive line along the mountains of the Kigezi district, Lake Kivu and the Russisi river.

German territory was practically inviolate, the German Commander held all his towns, ports and railways except a very small portion of the Tanga line between Kahe and Moschi.

In the space of three months General von Lettow had been deprived of all his railways, his capital town and main port (Dar-es-Salaam)*, with all the sea ports to the north of that place, and to quote General Smuts: " every healthy or valuable part of the colony with the exception of the Mahenge plateau ".

* This place actually fell to General Smuts' forces on September 3 but its fate was sealed when he reached the Central Railway.

And this result was permanent, for, with the exception of a raid by Naumann at the end of 1917 which produced no result —he finally surrendered near Kilimanjaro—the territory gained remained intact and securely held till the end of the war.

Incidentally, as showing the uselessness of raids—spectacular as they may be—unless they achieve a definite purpose in a general scheme, the comment of von Lettow is of interest. He writes: "It is to be regretted that this operation (Naumann's), carried out with so much initiative and determination, became *separated so far from the main theatre of war as to be of little use* ".

When General Smuts' force reached Morogoro van Deventer had secured Dodoma and held all the railway between that place and Morogoro and was in tactical co-operation with the Commander-in-Chief. Northey in the south, on learning of the German retirement on the Central Railway, had pushed forward to, and held, Wuasa on the way to Iringa, which latter place he occupied on August 28 and a detachment was moving towards Mahenge; in the north-west the last German vessel had disappeared from Lake Tanganyika when the Graf von Götzen was scuttled off Kigoma, the Belgians held Ujiji and Kigoma, and Crewe was about to move south from Malero, 60 miles south of Mwanza.

These great results had been achieved only as a consequence of extraordinary efforts and endurance on the part of the troops in circumstances of extreme hardship which persisted throughout the operations.

The force which moved under General Smuts' own direction from Moschi marched a distance of 300 miles reckoned as the crow flies. It was actually considerably further. Add to this bare statement of distance the tropical heat, the constant, serious and enervating lack of food, the steady forward movement, checked only when a total absence of any means of sustenance compelled a halt, the daily experience of fighting and marching in dense bush where the nerves were constantly taut, with no prospect of respite till a wound or tropical disease should lay him low, then to be transported under trying and exhausting conditions in rough transport back to a distant base where some degree of comfort might at last be obtained, and an idea may be formed of the lot of the soldier in the ranks in this extraordinary campaign.

General Smuts' strategy was in accordance with sound principles.

With the capture of the Central Railway as his strategic and the main enemy concentration as his tactical objective, the move on Morogoro was the most dangerous which the enemy could look for, in view of the value of the stores of all kinds which were there. It was a point which it was essential that he should hold as long as he thought necessary for the execution of his plan of a retirement to south of the railway and its capture would entail, as it did, the retirement of the enemy on all fronts.

In other words it was strategically the decisive point.

As General von Lettow writes when he decided to leave the force before van Deventer at Kondoa Irangi: " I decided to march my main body back . . . and move up in support of Major Kraut " as " General Smuts seemed to be the most dangerous and important of our opponents ".

The loss of Morogoro entailed the hurried retirement of all the enemy forces before van Deventer as he started to move eastward from Nyangalo. In such country as he passed through the seasoned troops under Otto and Kraut would never have allowed him to advance so quickly and with such small casualties as he did unless their retirement was regulated by conditions elsewhere.

CHAPTER XII

(i) THE LINES OF COMMUNICATION ON
REACHING MOROGORO.

IN HIS despatch of the 27th October, 1916, General Smuts writes: " At Morogoro I found many proofs of the precipitate flight of the enemy forces, and I decided to continue the pursuit in spite of the fact that my forces and animals were worn out with the exertions of the last three weeks and that my transport had reached its extreme radius of action ".

The existence of a track through the heart of the Uluguru mountains made it once more impossible to head off the enemy, but this was not known at the time when the Commander-in-Chief decided to press on.

The advance therefore suffered no immediate check, but at this point it is necessary to interrupt the narrative of its progress and consider the state of the lines of communication and the effect of the occupation of the Central Railway and Dar-es-Salaam. The latter port was occupied on September 4, having surrendered without opposition on the day before.

The lines of communication now reached back 450 miles to Moschi and, as stated in the official record of the Royal Army Service Corps, " the supply situation still gave cause for anxiety. Everything had to come from the Handeni depot from whence the route was wholly dependent on the weather. The casualties in animals* had caused such a shortage that the transport in possession of the artillery had still to be retained for the carriage of supplies. It was a matter of getting everything possible forward before the rain came ".

Tsetse fly and an almost entire absence of grain feed had caused enormous wastage.

The actual lines of the communications of General Smuts and General van Deventer may be seen from map number seventeen.

On September 7 the 1st, 2nd and 3rd Division had reached 15 miles south of Matombo, Kidodi and Kissaki, respectively.

---

* 28,000 oxen died during the advance from Kahe to the Central Railway in 3 months. Later on in two months (September 15 to November 15) 10,000 horses, 10,000 mules, a further 11,000 oxen and 2,500 donkeys died.

Van Deventer had depended largely on mule transport.

Railhead at Korogwe was 225 miles from the 1st Division and 245 miles from the 3rd. Railhead, which in the case of the 2nd Division was at Sanja, was 362 miles away from it.

The intervening lines of communication were by road, and in the case of the 1st and 3rd Divisions ran through Handeni, Msiha, Turiani, Dakawa to Morogoro, while the 362 miles of road necessary to reach van Deventer's force (2nd Division) passed by Lolkissale, Ufiome, Kondoa Irangi, Nyangalo, Mpapua, Kilossa and Uleia.

On the arrival of the " small rains " the tracks along which supplies were forwarded became a mass of mud, bridges once more were swept away, all along the lines delay, congestion, and damage to vehicles, added to fresh attacks of disease, crippled the whole service of supply and medical work alike. Any chance of getting an adequate ration to the troops if they moved much further would disappear, and, though a short effort might be made, the advance was bound to be held up entirely before very long.

To shorten the lines of communication by a very substantial distance was thus imperative.

(ii) MEDICAL ARRANGEMENTS.

During the whole advance along the Pangani to Morogoro the main problems which faced the medical authorities were the evacuation of hundreds of sick, the wounded cases were *comparatively* few in number, and the forwarding of medical comforts and other essential supplies.

To evacuate the sick it was necessary to get them back to Moschi and Taveta for transport by rail to Voi.

The sick admitted to field medical units were left at various points and sent back by motor ambulances and empty returning supply lorries. Medical officers with some personnel and comforts were detached from the field units for this purpose.

The routes by which the sick were sent back were of course the same as supplied the forces, and are shown in map number seventeen.

On these routes were stationary hospitals at Mbuyuni and in a German hospital on the lower slopes of the Usambara range. Clearing hospitals were established at Handeni where also a convalescent depot was established, and, to meet the views of the General Staff (see page 150), it was arranged that only those patients whose recovery was improbable, were to be sent back to Korogwe for ultimate evacuation.

During van Deventer's forward movement from Kondoa Irangi various field ambulances were opened as the advance went on and were compelled to remain behind until cleared by motor vehicles or a temporarily stationary hospital was formed. In the official history of the medical services it is stated that " transport for the evacuation of cases was always inadequate, and this was frequently represented to G.H.Q. ".

At G.H.Q. at this time, as always throughout the campaign, every responsible officer was at his wits' end to keep the forces moving, and the shortage of transport was common to every separate unit and service of the field army, and remained so until some time later.

A serious shortage of medical comforts here as elsewhere added to the wretchedness of the hundreds of sick who were dropped along the track of the advance.

The sanitary equipment too, it is recorded in the history, was so deficient that the 2nd Division was without any water testing cabinet.

A casualty clearing station was opened at Dodoma which was a healthy spot. This became practically a standing hospital, and was an instance of initiative and capacity for making the best of things on the part of the officer who was charged with its supervision and who received a well merited reward when the hospital was seen later by the Commander-in-Chief.

When van Deventer had reached Kidodi his chief medical officer reported that the troops of his Division were " in need of rest and change to a more salubrious climate being debilitated by continuous marching, road-making, drift-making, fighting and lack of food, and by malaria and dysentery ". Such a report might well serve to describe the condition of every component part of the British Expeditionary Force in German East Africa on all fronts more often than not.

The experiences with General Smuts' force differed in no substantial degree from those which have been described.

With regard to the medical work in the Nguru operations the Medical History states: " There is no evidence that any well-considered scheme (of evacuation) was evolved or that medical units were instructed regarding the part they would play during the operations. The medical arrangements appear to have been hap-hazard and sections of field ambulances were apparently attached to any formation that happened to be at hand ".

There is justice in this criticism, and it may be well to record two of the causes which contributed to confusion and lack of order.

Though these last conditions were not confined to the South African formations they were more prevalent there than in the 1st Division which had the advantage of the presence of many subordinate commanders and staff officers who were professional soldiers.

Such experienced officers were by no means plentiful in the units from South Africa, and the lack of trained staff officers and the inexperience of most of the commanders in handling comparatively large formations had already caused similar confusion in administrative staff arrangements in the campaign in German South-West Africa, though the results, in view of the healthy climate there, were perhaps less generally noticed. They were certainly far less serious to the sick who emerged from their experiences in East Africa all considerably affected—many for the rest of their lives—in health.

Another cause of want of system was that no senior medical officer, representing the D.M.S., was ever attached to advanced G.H.Q., nor did the D.M.S. himself come up there, at all events during 1916. To expect a junior officer to co-ordinate medical duties in a force of two divisions was unreasonable.

After Hannyngton's action at Matamondo his casualties had to be evacuated through rugged mountainous country by stretcher bearers, eight to a stretcher.

A hospital was established at Mhonda mission and Turiani was the chief evacuating centre. Here again delay was caused by the absence of preparations for removing the sick from the lorries. As all lorries were urgently needed for the conveyance of supplies, they could not be delayed for the evacuation of the sick, and this added to the medical difficulties.

In a steady increase of sickness, smallpox and other infectious diseases and black water, the consequence of repeated attacks of malaria, appeared soon after the occupation of Morogoro.

(iii) THE OCCUPATION OF DAR-ES-SALAAM.

The effect of the occupation of Dar-es-Salaam will be apparent from the map.

The substitution of a railway line running parallel to the deployment of the advancing forces for long and difficult roads, subject to frequent interruption from the various causes which have been made clear in the foregoing pages, and at right angles to the general line of advance was an enormous advantage.

As General Smuts wrote in his despatch of the 27th October, 1916: " Much was to be said for an advance inland from Dar-es-Salaam, which would much facilitate the transport and supply arrangements for the campaign into the interior ". After very careful consideration, however, the Commander-in-Chief had ruled out the project as at the time when such an enterprise against the capital would have to be undertaken the S.E. monsoon would make a landing very difficult and even dangerous, and a prolonged campaign on the coast would mean the disappearance of a very large percentage of his troops from tropical disease.

It is interesting to speculate whether the percentage of loss would have been as large as that which attended the advances from the north in view of the far shorter distance which it would have been necessary to traverse to reach the same objective. However, an advance from Dar-es-Salaam in the first instance would have called for very considerable increase in British strength, as the decisive point of the Uganda railway would otherwise have been jeopardised to some extent, a risk which could not have been taken with impunity.

Dar-es-Salaam was occupied on September 4, and the Inspector-General of Communications moved his headquarters there on September 12, and, reaching out by means of patrols, very soon established contact with the force of the Commander-in-Chief.

The Central Railway from Dar-es-Salaam to Dodoma was now in the hands of General Smuts.

The destruction to the railway had been extensive so far as the bridges were concerned—some 60 having been demolished between Kilossa and Dar-es-Salaam—but the permanent way had been little damaged though prepared for destruction, and the rapidity of the final advance to the railway had most probably prevented enemy action. The enemy had no doubt decided that the disappearance of the bridges would make it impossible to pass locomotives over the line for some time, and with reason, for it was not until January, 1917, that locomotives could be put into use.

An ingenious alternative had, however, been devised by Lieut.-Colonel Dobson and the South African Pioneers with van Deventer. The bridges were temporarily repaired with such material as was at hand—wood in any quantity was always available for bridge work in this country—so as to carry a weight of 6 tons, and narrowing the gauge of the heavy motor lorries, and placing them on railway trolley wheels, the Pioneers conveyed by rail all van Deventer's supplies during his advance from Dodoma to Kilossa. A converted lorry carried 5 tons while its trailer conveyed another 10.

This was a highly creditable and valuable piece of extemporisation by the South Africans which eased the supply position very greatly. Immediately General Smuts became aware of the plan it was extended generally, with the result that, by October 6, it was in operation from Dar-es-Salaam to Dodoma, and stores were conveyed from the sea-base at the former place.

(iv) THE ADVANCE FROM MOROGORO.

As has been stated, there was no cessation of movement after Morogoro had been reached on August 27.

General von Lettow, according to his practice, had carefully reconnoitered in person " by cycle " and in the case of the passes through the heart of the Uluguru mountains, " on foot " all his lines of retreat.

While holding on as long as possible " to retain the power of delivering counter-strokes " he called back Otto and Schulz to Morogoro, and Kraut took up a position " immediately south of Kilossa on the road to Mahenge ".

In the light of information *now* available the following were his dispositions just before the occupation of Morogoro.

Just north of the town were Schulz and Stemmermann who had retired before the advance from Dakawa; Otto was in, and round, the town itself.

At the Catholic mission on the lower foothills of the Uluguru, but well above the town, were two mountain guns, while a little to the south-west, guarding the left rear of the German force, was a field company.

These forces comprised 14 companies, with a small mounted detachment, of between 2,000 and 2,500 seasoned Askaris, a formidable force, once more on the defence in extraordinarily difficult country which they had well reconnoitred.

It will be remembered that on August 21 Enslin, with his (2nd) mounted brigade, had been directed from the Wami on Mkata on the railway line with orders to move from that place against the rear of Kraut engaged with van Deventer at Kilossa.

When, on the following day, it was learned at G.H.Q. that Kraut had moved south towards Uleia, it was the Commander-in-Chief's first intention that van Deventer should move on and block the enemy line of retreat to the west of the Uluguru. This further effort, however, was quite impossible of execution by van Deventer's infantry at a pace which would make it of any use, and, accordingly, the task was assigned to Enslin and van Deventer was ordered to send his mounted brigade (the 1st) under Nussey to reinforce the 2nd, Enslin being instructed to move on Mlali.

The ensuing operations may be followed· on map number eighteen.

Enslin reached Mlali on the 23rd. His force was approximately 1,000 strong and he had with him the 4 guns of the 3rd S.A. Field Battery.

Nussey, on leaving Kilossa on the 24th, had 1,117 mounted and 236 dismounted men together with the 4th S.A. Field Battery, also 4 guns. It is eloquent of the wastage which always occurred as a movement against the enemy was made that two days later when he joined Enslin his strength had shrunk to 850 rifles. He was compelled to leave all his dismounted men and 249 of his horses at Mkata en route.

(v) THE ACTION AT MLALI.

Enlin's scouts on reaching Mlali seized a prominent feature, Kisagale Hill, which commanded the road and the Mlali river, and Enslin sent a portion of his force across the river to surround and capture an enemy detachment entrenched in a house. The effort was supported by the artillery but repulsed, and, on the arrival of enemy reinforcements, Enslin withdrew his detachment across the river. He then contented himself with holding on to what he had gained, viz.: Kisagale Hill, being soon inferior in numbers to the enemy who were strongly reinforced.

Von Lettow had observed Enslin's movement and intended to let the latter become committed and then to counter-attack him with the whole strength at his disposal and Otto was despatched to hold the 2nd Brigade with 3 companies. Stemmermann was ordered to " fall back along the eastern slopes of the Uluguru mountains and delay the enemy there ".

The rest of his forces the German Commander-in-Chief ordered to reinforce Otto.

The passes actually over the mountains he closed by " weak patrols ".

It being of the utmost importance that the 600 tons of supplies removed from Morogoro to Kissaki should not be lost, as a consequence of his being forestalled at the latter place, General von Lettow withdrew his forces and broke off the fight, retiring southwards through the mountains. Nussey reaching Mlali on the 26th co-operated with Enslin in pursuing the enemy as far as Mgeta Mission.

The casualties of the South Africans were 1 killed and 7 wounded.

The seizure of Kisagale by the scouts was, incidentally, an instance of the tactical instinct of the soldier in the ranks of the commando, and, in view of Enslin's inferiority in strength and distance from support, a probably fortunate exhibition of initiative.

(vi) THE ADVANCE CONTINUED.

On reaching Morogoro, just as these operations concluded, General Smuts gave his orders for the continuance of the forward movement by the rest of his forces.

The latter were now regrouped to some extent after a certain dislocation during the operations in the Nguru and on the Wami, and organised as follows:—

1st Division.

Major-General Hoskins.

1st East Africa Brigade.

Brigadier-General Sheppard.

2nd Rhodesia Regiment.
29th Punjabis.
130th Baluchis.
2nd Kashmir Rifles.
5th Battery, S.A. Field Artillery.

One section, 27th Mountain Battery.
Squadron 17th (Indian) Cavalry.
2nd East Africa Brigade.
Brigadier-General Hannyngton.
57th Rifles.
3rd Kashmir Rifles ($\frac{1}{2}$ battalion).
3rd K.A.R.
7th Field Battery.
27th Mountain Battery (less a section).
E.A. Mounted Rifles.
K.A. Rifles M.I.
Divisional Troops.
25th Royal Fusiliers.
Gold Coast Regiment.
Cape Corps Battalion.
3rd Division.
Major-General Brits.
2nd S.A. Mounted Brigade.
Brigadier-General Enslin.
5th, 6th, 7th and 8th S.A. Horse.
2nd S.A. Infantry Brigade.
Brigadier-General Beves.
5th and 6th S.A. Infantry.
3rd and 8th Batteries S.A. Field Artillery.
Divisional Troops.
13th Howitzer Battery.
Army Troops.
9th Field Battery.
14th and 134th Howitzer Batteries.

On August 26 General Smuts ordered an advance by the 1st Division to the east of the Uluguru mountains.

Retaining under his hand at Morogoro Beves (2nd S.A. Infantry) Brigade and the Gold Coast Regiment, he directed Sheppard (1st E.A. Brigade) on Kiroka Pass and Hannyngton (2nd E.A. Brigade) on Mikesse for Kikundu.

Sheppard, after a check in consequence of the destruction of a bridge, negotiated the Kiroka Pass on the 27th, while on the same day Hannyngton reached Mikesse, and on August 28 the two brigades, Hannyngton leading, arrived at Pugu on the Msambisi river.

Advancing on the following morning they encountered stiff resistance, sustaining the loss of 5 killed and 19 wounded, in wet weather which had begun on the preceding evening.

Here, in consequence of the heavy rain, General Hoskins was compelled to order a halt, and his Division remained by the river until the afternoon of August 31, inactive except for patrol work.

At once the inevitable consequence ensued.

Rations were delayed, malaria and dysentery again broke out following exposure and lack of food, and nature once more resumed her active aid to General von Lettow by creating havoc in the ranks of his enemy.

(vii) GENERAL BRITS' MOVEMENT ON KISSAKI.

Meanwhile, the Commander-in-Chief had instituted other movements to the west of the mountains.

On August 28 General van Deventer had reached G.H.Q., and on the following day accompanied General Smuts, with whom was also General Brits, to Mlali, where it was ascertained that the enemy had retired through the mountains southward to Kissaki.

At this time Nussey's troops held the Mgeta Mission and those of Enslin had occupied Hombossa, a little to the south-west of Mlali.

The following moves were now verbally ordered by General Smuts.

Nussey with his brigade to move on Kissaki through the mountains along the Mgeta river track. Enslin at the same time to move on the same objective by way of the Mahalaka road.

The whole movement was placed under the command of General Brits who remained at Mlali to await the arrival of his infantry—Beves with his two battalions, 5th and 6th S.A. Infantry. Beves was ordered to march from Morogoro, taking the 3rd Divisional Artillery, so as to reach Mlali on the evening of the 31st.

The country through which these troops and the 1st Division on the east were to operate was entirely unknown to them, very difficult and mountainous, with deep rivers, dense bush and tropical primeval forest, and all movements called for the exercise of great caution.

202

Awaiting the advance was General von Lettow, once more on interior lines, once more with a knowledge of the terrain and once more with his force concentrated and under his own command.

While the 1st Division was concentrated, with its two brigades in close touch, Brits' infantry and his two mounted brigades, much reduced in numbers, would, in country such as that which has just been described, find themselves completely out of communication with each other, even if only a few miles apart, unless the command common to the three detachments could achieve the effective combination and accurate timing of all their movements, always matters of extreme difficulty in bush and mountain country such as the Uluguru mountains.

Any shortcomings in the respects mentioned would afford their opponent an opportunity of dealing with each detachment in detail and with superior numbers.

Brits' task was therefore likely to be very difficult.

It would appear that, before the movements ordered by General Smuts were put into execution, Generals Brits, Enslin and Nussey discussed together the situation and its possibilities. It was agreed, as a result of this consultation, that the 3rd Division (Brits' force) would in all probability meet with slight opposition on its march to the west of the mountains and would therefore reach the neighbourhood of Kissaki some days before Nussey's brigade and that the enemy, in view of the nature of the country to be negotiated, would " make matters uncomfortable for the latter ".

Nussey, too, " thoroughly understood " that immediately the 3rd Division should reach the vicinity of Little Whigu and Big Whigu Hills these vantage points would be held and every possible effort made (by means of visual signalling and patrols, failing wireless communication) to get into touch with him.

It was by this time accepted that any such operations as those now planned inevitably entailed severe hardships upon the troops engaged, and Nussey's own account of the condition of his brigade before moving south through the Uluguru gives a striking description of the straits to which troops campaigning in country like the Uluguru range may be reduced and of the difficulties which may confront their commander.

He says: " My Brigade was in a pitiable state, over 60 per cent. of my strength were dismounted and their boots and clothing were in an awful state. I had no pack mules or porters. My Battery became hopelessly immobile at this stage. The only roads through the Uluguru mountains were native tracks which led from one native town to another. They were all situated on the heights. My greatest embarrassment, however, was ' ammunition ' so I sent out and commandeered 200 porters. The second night after I set out a large number of these impressed men escaped during a thunderstorm and I had to bury 80 cases of ammunition on the top of a mountain. The balance was issued to the men. The mule carrying my wireless set fell over a precipice the second day after I left Mlali ".

(viii) GENERAL NUSSEY ADVANCES FROM MLALI.

Moving through the heart of the mountains, having left all his dismounted men at Mlali, Nussey, on September 1, marched down the Mgeta to find that the track marked on the map which had been selected as his route did not exist. Another constant difficulty which was met with, as, with the many changes of habitation by the natives, tracks disappeared in a few weeks. On September 2 the 1st Mounted Brigade had turned enemy outposts out of Kibuhu and ascertained that their main body was at Kikeo.

It may be mentioned that efforts by Nussey to communicate with General Brits by runner, after learning that the route assigned to him was non-existent, failed of course, as the latter had left Mlali.

On the advance of the South Africans the enemy vacated Kikeo, blowing up large dumps of ammunition and supplies.

By this time, however, Nussey's men who had started with only one day's rations were exhausted from want of food and their rate of progress became very slow, and it was not until 5 p.m. on September 7 that the enemy was again encountered at Sungamero and withdrew rapidly towards Kissaki after setting fire to several large bandas containing small arm ammunition, gun ammunition, soap, grain, meal and other valuable stores.

(ix) GENERAL BRITS ADVANCES.

It is now necessary to follow Brits' advance with the 2nd Mounted Brigade (Enslin) and the 2nd Infantry Brigade (Beves) along the Mahalaka track.

On August 31, Enslin, now reduced to 150 rifles per regiment or 600 rifles in all, moved to the south-west of Mlali on Msongosi and the 2nd Infantry Brigade marched from Morogoro on the same day behind the mounted men. It was found impossible for the Field Batteries to accompany the infantry, so the guns were turned back. Later all wheeled transport had to be returned and for the next three weeks the infantry were without greatcoats or blankets, and, after the second, were reduced to half rations, and even this reduced allowance would often have been welcome in the next week or so.

The mounted men reached the vicinity of Tyaduma and on September 5 were overtaken by the infantry, a very fine performance in their circumstances. In all probability many of Beves' men had taken part in his outstanding march of 200 miles a year earlier in German South-West Africa.

At Mahalaka all wheeled transport was turned back and the supply situation, always precarious, again became acute.

Brits' two brigades could now only muster 1,200 rifles between them, a small strength with which to move against the enemy in such country.

Nothing had been heard of Nussey's Brigade and—as far as can be ascertained—with the disappearance of the wireless sets nothing was done to supplement the deficiency by the means agreed upon by the three commanders in conference before the start.

General Brits, however, left to his own devices, and with no means of rapidly communicating with the Commander-in-Chief, decided that an immediate effort must be made to capture Kissaki, though he was without information as to the enemy strength at that place. The interception of the enemy was of course the main object of the operations.

Accordingly, he directed the two battalions of the Infantry —some 600 rifles—to move on Kissaki by way of the Mgeta river while Enslin with the mounted troops—about the same strength—was to reach the Iringa-Kissaki road and thence move on the same objective.

Two comparatively small forces would thus be moving in country which would very probably preclude the exchange of information between them, against the concentrated enemy who was on interior lines.

Though Brits was ignorant of the strength opposed to him, it might be assumed at least to be as much as his own with the usual added advantage of complete knowledge of the ground.

The enemy was in point of fact stronger than Brits and Nussey together, for von Lettow at Kissaki had at his disposal the detachments of Otto, Schulz, von Liebermann and Tafel, in all probably not less than 2,500 rifles with some 30 machine guns.

Stemmermann was opposing the advance of Hoskins. The German defences had been prepared at some distance from Kissaki, "covered from the view of aircraft and so arranged that they could be occupied and evacuated unobserved".

Early on the morning of September 7, Enslin and Beves moved in agreement with the plan already mentioned.

(x) BEVES' ENGAGEMENT NEAR KISSAKI.

Beves' infantry, preceded by a screen of native scouts and one company with two machine guns as its advanced guard, and warned to move slowly in view of expected opposition, moved on as broad a front as possible through dense elephant grass and bush, and after six hours marching had covered only five miles! At this point, at 1.15 p.m., Beves reported by mounted orderly to 3rd Divisional Headquarters near Tyaduma that his advanced guard was "being fired upon but that it was nothing serious". He added that his progress was being badly interrupted by swarms of bees interfering with the animals. It will be remembered that at Tanga these insects had taken the side of the enemy. As indicating the severity of this obstacle to the advance, it may be mentioned that bees killed the horse of the Brigade Major that he was riding as well as his spare mount.

By 4.30 p.m. the two regiments had crossed the Mgeta and located the enemy position across, and barring, the road to Kissaki.

Receiving information from his scouts that two enemy companies with machine guns were entrenched near the town and in view of the lateness of the hour, Beves very properly decided to dig in for the night on the left bank of the Mgeta and to resume his advance in the morning, and informed his Divisional Headquarters of his intention.

Immediately after the information to the above effect had been despatched, an orderly reached Beves' camp from Enslin who asked whether the former were not firing on his men. Beves answered in the negative and at the same time advised Enslin of his whereabouts and intentions as described above.

As an example of the invariable difficulty of estimating correctly any tactical situation in the bush, even close at hand, it may be mentioned that heavy maxim and rifle fire was heard by those at Beves' camp at the time, apparently about two miles away, but that it was " extremely difficult to locate its exact direction and impossible to distinguish whether our fire or the enemy's ".

At 10 p.m. the enemy delivered an attack upon the western portion of Beves' perimeter, but was beaten off without difficulty at 10.40 p.m.

At 11.30 p.m. orders reached Beves from General Brits to retire to Whigu Hill, where Divisional H.Q. was posted, and reach that point before daybreak.

Posting a strong rear guard to cover his movement, Beves effected a skilful withdrawal in darkness—having waited for the disappearance of the moon—and reached Whigu at 4.30 a.m. on September 8.

On receipt of the order to withdraw both the regimental commanders (of the 5th and 6th S.A. Infantry) urged Beves to request the Divisional Commander to reconsider the order, but their Brigadier took the view that the written order left him no discretion, and that Divisional Headquarters were best able to judge of what was necessary in view of what might have happened to Enslin and his mounted men.

The narrative of this campaign has already shown the delicate nature of any tactical withdrawal in bush country, and the successful performance *in darkness* of this manoeuvre by Beves and his infantry reflects the highest credit upon all ranks from the Brigadier downwards. The South African infantry-man had learned much since Salaita only six months earlier.

The two companies reported by Beves' scouts were, in point of fact, four under the command of Otto. A heavy attack was delivered by this force on Beves' empty trenches at 2.30 a.m. and again at 4 a.m. on the 8th.

(xi) ENSLIN'S ENGAGEMENT NEAR KISSAKI.

While the infantry had been toiling through the bush and elephant grass, Brits' (2nd) Mounted Brigade had proceeded under Enslin in the direction of the Iringa-Kissaki road, and at noon came up against a strong enemy force—Schulz, 4 companies and von Liebermann, 3 companies, some 1,200 rifles with 14 machine guns. Enslin had barely half the number of rifles that were opposed to him.

Moving to the attack the South Africans were speedily out-flanked in the thick bush where their mobility ceased to be effective, and they were compelled to fight at close quarters against greatly superior numbers. A decisive counter-attack, delivered at the point of withdrawal by Enslin of one of his regiments, by the 11th Field Company under Lieutenant von Volkwein compelled the hurried and confused retirement of Enslin's men with a loss of 16 killed and 24 wounded as well as some missing. Aided by the thick bush, the 2nd Mounted Brigade made its way back to Tyaduma.

On September 8 Brits' Mounted Brigade and Infantry were once more together with their commander at Whigu.

(xii) NUSSEY'S ENGAGEMENT NEAR KISSAKI.

It will be remembered that upon the evening of the previous day, the 7th, the 1st Mounted Brigade under Nussey had reached Sungomero.

At 6 a.m. on September 8 Nussey, in complete ignorance of what had happened during the previous twenty-four hours and of the whereabouts of General Brits or any of the latter's troops, moved forward on Kissaki. No sound of the engagements which had taken place the day before had reached the 1st Mounted Brigade.

The latter moved in the following order: 3rd S.A. Horse, 4th S.A. Horse, 9th S.A. Horse, and the 2nd S.A. Horse (in reserve). The last regiment was followed by all dismounted men and men with weak horses as an additional reserve.

The Brigade was ordered, if the enemy were encountered, to deploy, the 3rd S.A. Horse in the centre and the 4th and 9th S.A. Horse to the left and right, respectively. All horses were to be sent immediately to the rear.

At 8 a.m., from Little Whigu, Kissaki was sighted and half an hour later Nussey's advanced guard was fired on and drove back the enemy outposts.

The Brigade deployed in agreement with the orders it had received, and at once became engaged. Its strength by this time was rather less than 500 rifles with 4 machine guns. The enemy opposed to them was Tafel's detachment of 4 companies, 700 rifles and 8 machine guns.

The Brigade now, 9 a.m., was ordered to dig in and hold on at all costs, and Nussey reinforced his right with van Deventer's Scouts, at the same time ordering an attack on the enemy's left. Three attempts were made against this objective but all failed with the loss of several killed and wounded.

All the line was now heavily engaged and at 9.30 a.m. the enemy rushed the South African centre, but after 15 minutes' fighting, practically hand to hand, was repulsed.

By 10 o'clock the severity of the fighting had diminished to some extent, and it was ascertained that the German force was in an entrenched position some 100 yards ahead.

Nussey now withdrew his Scouts (" van Deventer's ") and sent them in a westerly direction " to endeavour to take the Mgeta river and obtain information of the 3rd Division ".

At 11 o'clock heavy and sustained rifle and machine gun fire broke out from the enemy lines and lasted for 40 minutes, being only answered when a target presented itself. This was followed by another determined attack on the South Africans' left which was beaten off.

Nussey reinforced his left by 40 men under Lieutenant Anderson at 2 o'clock, and half an hour later, feinting at the centre, the enemy again charged the left flank, and was again beaten off after 15 minutes' hand to hand fighting. Lieutenant Anderson was killed here gallantly leading his men.

Von Lettow had by this time reinforced his original strength by the detachment of von Liebermann called up from Kissaki, an additional 400 rifles, and the 1st Mounted Brigade was heavily outnumbered.

Another attack was delivered on the left at 3 o'clock and repulsed.

At 3.30 p.m. Nussey sent Captain Heavingham with 60 men of the 2nd S.A. Horse to act as a reserve " in front of and to the left of the (South African) left flank " and to counter-attack the enemy, should the latter attempt to come round again.

Heavingham had only just reached a suitable point from which to carry out his mission when the enemy " with bugles sounding and Askaris yelling " once more determinedly assailed Nussey's centre and left.

Heavingham now delivered his counter-stroke from behind the enemy, dispersing the attack and capturing a German officer and several Askaris. This fine enterprise which had most valuable result, was, however, carried out at the cost of its leader's life, for Captain Heavingham was shot at close quarters in the fight.

Fighting continued until shortly after 5 p.m. when the enemy retired and Nussey remained on the scene of action. His men, however, had been without food or water for 48 hours and he withdrew his force after dark to Sungomero, the nearest place at which water was available.

The action had cost the Brigade 44 casualties of which 23 were killed. The latter included 4 officers, Major Cowie and Lieutenants Flynn and Anderson in addition to the gallant Heavingham. All these officers were shot at close quarters leading their men who responded nobly to their example.

Heavily outnumbered, the South Africans had fought a fine fight. Brigadier-General Nussey, who had already done good work in command of van Deventer's mounted troops, conducted the action with skill and determination, his handling of his reserves and their employment in counter-attack being especially creditable.

One is compelled to speculate as to why—having disposed of Brits so conclusively the day before—General von Lettow, with such advantages as he possessed in respect of numbers and knowledge of the terrain, did not attempt the destruction of Nussey's force by more extended action against its rear, for he must have been well aware that he could concentrate the whole of his force (except a very small detachment to watch Brits) on Nussey who could look for no assistance.

The explanation may perhaps lie in fear for his own communications—his escape from Kissaki was of course *vital* to him—from the movements of Hoskins on the east and van Deventer on the west which were designed to forestall him at Kissaki, if possible.

(xiii) COMMENTS ON THE KISSAKI ENGAGEMENTS.

The operations which have just been described emphasise, perhaps more clearly than ever, what has been referred to constantly in this narrative. The great importance and extraordinary difficulty of maintaining communication in bush country between forces for the effective action of which their close co-operation is indispensable.

As far back as the action at Tanga in 1914 the difficulty of lateral communication had been noticed.

It was hoped that communication might be maintained by means of the wireless apparatus with which the forces of Brits and Nussey were furnished. The reason why this arrangement for inter-communication failed has been made clear. As to whether it would have functioned adequately if no mishap had occurred to Nussey's equipment, and Brits had retained his, instead of leaving it behind, is at least open to question.

Any interchange of information between the two forces, in order to be of use, would have to be prompt and free from interruption, and experience in East Africa showed that the pack wireless sets of the " spark " type were quite unreliable in bush country, and these were the only type with the forces.

The loss of the wireless sets then was possibly of small consequence in the circumstances and, in the absence of this method of communication, it would seem that, in view of the understanding arrived at between Generals Brits, Enslin and Nussey before separating, the other means agreed upon, viz.: visual signalling, patrols and runners should have been tried continuously from the time that reliance upon wireless became obviously useless.

It does not seem that any effort in the above direction was made, except by Nussey after the loss of his wireless and again on the morning of the 8th.

General Brits, presumably considering that his instructions from the Commander-in-Chief implied pressing on to Kissaki in any circumstances, clearly undertook the advance from Tyaduma without taking Nussey's force into consideration as a factor in his own arrangements.

This may be assumed from Beves' Operation Order of September 6, issued for his own advance on Kissaki, in which he gives as the information available that " General Nussey is still opposed by the enemy on the upper reaches of the Mgeta river ". The order was of course based on information received from Brits' Divisional Headquarters where, obviously, possible action by Nussey was not taken into definite calculation.

On September 7 Beves issued an addendum to the order mentioned, to the effect that Nussey had occupied Kikeo on the afternoon of the 5th. This intelligence, however, came from G.H.Q. and not as a consequence of communication between Brits and Nussey.

The latter on the 7th was, in point of fact, not more than 10 miles away from Beves. At this distance a serious effort to get across from one force to the other by patrols or runners would have been well worth while and might have succeeded with good result.

There was also a very distinct danger that the respective lines of advance of Beves and Nussey might cross, and serious consequences ensue before either force could establish the identity of the other. Point is lent to this comment by the difficulty (see page 207) experienced in deciding whether firing two miles away was that of Enslin or the enemy.

The lack of co-ordination of the movements of Enslin and Beves on September 7 may be accounted for to some extent by the abnormally slow advance of the latter because of the nature of the ground (see page 206).

Co-operation between the two forces, however, would seem to have been left largely to chance. Even with the greatest care it would have been difficult, but, again to quote the operation order mentioned above, the only information given as to Enslin is that " General Enslin's Mounted Brigade moves to-morrow morning at 7 a.m. from here (1 mile west of Tyaduma) in a S.E. direction to strike road leading into Kissaki from a S.W. direction and then to press on into that town ".

This again is based on what must have been communicated from Divisional H.Q., and there is nothing to suggest any pre-arranged co-operation. Possibly a quicker rate of advance by Beves (it was of course unusually slow for unavoidable reasons) may have been relied upon, but in this country to depend upon a definite rate of progress was at all events risky.

The wisdom of withdrawing Beves from the position which he had reached on the evening of September 7 seems doubtful.

Beves had two seasoned infantry battalions with machine guns in a position of his own selection, which he had entrenched,

212

on the north bank of the Mgeta river, and he had two days'
supplies on the hoof with him and an abundance of water, for
the flanks of his perimeter rested on the river. The only attack
which had been made upon him he had beaten off without
using his machine guns. His communications with his
Divisional Commander, at Whigu Hill, were open. He was in
fact, as comfortably and safely situated as he well could be.

In this posture he might well have·inflicted severe casualties
on the attacks which were made upon his empty trenches in
the early morning of the 8th, for 600 South Africans entrenched
and ready for an attack—as they of course would have been—
represented, at this stage of the campaign, an exceedingly hard
nut to crack.

The result of such an encounter would have gone very far
to adjust the balance of *moral,* and Beves, entrenched, would
have been an invaluable pivot and very strong support for
Nussey on the following morning. With Beves stationary, the
chances of any serious misunderstanding or clash between the
two forces would have been very slight.

The representations of the two battalion commanders—both
competent and experienced—seem to have been sound,
and, though General Beves considered he had no discretion,
he did, presumably, have time to refer to General Brits in the
light of his own knowledge of the local position which the
Divisional Commander was without.

In all the circumstances it seems fair to conclude that to
commit Beves and Enslin to an attack in such country without
the most careful efforts to ensure their co-operation and
especially *without knowing the whereabouts of Nussey* was an
error of judgment.

General Brits was out of *quick* communication with G.H.Q.
—whence to obtain the Commander-in-Chief's orders in view
of any unforeseen developments—but his own position as a
detachment commander and his prestige were adequate to
support him if he should elect to deal with the situation as it
appeared to him on the spot, even if it involved a departure
from the orders of his chief. He seems to have judged the
situation wrongly.

There is no doubt that General von Lettow failed to take
full advantage of the opportunities which the same situation
offered him.

The detachments of Beves, Enslin and Nussey each in turn, furnished an objective for a heavy attack in superior numbers, and this in circumstances which precluded any aid for its quarry.

The ground had been well reconnoitred and the necessarily slow advance of the South Africans had been watched.

Under such conditions a total casualty list between the three forces of 40 killed and 50 wounded must be regarded as fortunately light, especially if it be considered in the experience of more or less similar experiences earlier in the campaign.

While the terrain was difficult, even with the advantage of prior reconnaissance, General von Lettow's troops were extraordinarily mobile and should have been able to achieve a far greater tactical success than they did.

A master of the art of war has laid it down that "Moral force is to the physical as three to one".

It seems clear that moral factors were at work here.

Von Lettow himself writes: "It was my opinion that these satisfactory successes at Kissaki had not brought us a final decision against the troops of General Brits, and I still believe that in the dense bush and the rugged country an energetic pursuit, which alone would have secured the desired result, was impossible of execution. My attention was all the more drawn towards the force (Hoskins on the east) pursuing Stemmermann's Detachment, as it had already come within two days' march north-east of Kissaki. During the last few days the situation there had not been favourable; the broken ground had in several instances caused our already weak forces to be disseminated. Some portions had been ambushed, *the troops were very fatigued, and several people were suffering badly from nerves*".

Add to this that over one thousand Askaris had deserted and been rounded up in Morogoro, and it becomes clear that for the time being the *moral* of the German troops was lower than it had been since General Smuts had taken command.

Even the restrained admissions of General von Lettow indicate a state of affairs which did not lend itself to vigorous action on his part.

It was all the more to be regretted that the engagements, to use General Smuts' own words in his despatch, should lead "to a double retirement and a regrettable recovery of enemy morale".

But the physical obstacle of the huge Uluguru range, prepared—as might be inferred from the large dumps of stores placed at intervals—for an obstinate defence, had been surmounted in a week, and this great strategic result outweighed any tactical rebuffs which might have been sustained in the course of the operations.

Nevertheless the actions round Kissaki *were* tactical reverses to the South African troops, and they have been described at length, as they teach many of the most important lessons that are to be learned in bush warfare.

General von Lettow had by this time become aware that sheer exhaustion alone would hold up the unceasing, if occasionally slow, advance against him, and with van Deventer to the south-west at Kidodi, and Hoskins a cause of anxiety to him two days march from Kissaki, he could not take any risk in remaining at the latter place, even if he had been more successful than he actually was against Brits. The preservation of his force and its spirit, always a governing factor in his strategy, was at the moment more important than ever.

(xiv) HOSKINS' MOVEMENTS ON THE EAST.

General Smuts, sensible of the difficulties which might, and did, arise in connection with Brits' movements, left Morogoro on September 3 with the object of overtaking the latter. Faced with the same obstacles that had caused the whole of Brits' wheeled transport to be turned back, he found the venture impossible and returned to Morogoro.

On September 8 the Commander-in-Chief was apprised of Brits' repulse, and at once instructed the latter to refrain from further attack until the advance of Hoskins on the east should make co-operation between them both possible.

At the same time he ordered the latter to move south in order to take off enemy attention from Brits and ease the pressure upon him.

We left General Hoskins held up by weather on August 28 at Pugu on the Msambisi river.

On the afternoon of August 31 the 1st Division resumed its advance and on September 1 Hoskins sent forward a battalion with a section of mountain guns to seize the Ruwu river crossing. This river runs deep in a valley closed in by steep heights rising to 1,500 feet, and the approach from the north is through luxuriant primeval forest and thick bush.

The detachment found a rope stretched across the river which was running rapidly and breast high.

A company crossed the river and the remainder of the force bivouacked for the night on the northern bank. Here they were fired upon by some machine guns and sustained a few casualties, but at daybreak an attack by the whole force compelled the retirement of the enemy and the ground was held until support made it secure.

On September 3 the 2nd E.A. Brigade (Hannyngton) reached Matombo Mission to find that the enemy had retired and were holding the mountain of Kingarunga (3,000 feet).

Here Hannyngton gained a notable accession of strength by the arrival of the Gold Coast Regiment (1,428 strong with 12 machine guns and two 2.95″ mountain guns) which was a veteran unit which had done hard service in the Cameroons.

On September 4 it advanced on the enemy position at Kikarunga and after some considerable loss occupied some of the lower slopes of the mountain by dark.

By the 6th Kikarunga had been occupied after three days fighting and exhausting climbing, and the enemy fell back out of touch.

While Hannyngton was engaged on these operations, the 1st E.A. Brigade (Sheppard) was co-operating on a parallel road to the east moving by way of Tunungo on Tulo in the direction of which a column of about the same strength as that of Hannyngton was pushed ahead.

On September 9 Hoskins was in occupation of Tulo.

All the troops which he could spare were put to improving and making the road from the north. The Commanding Officer of the 1st E.A. Brigade, who was from the Royal Engineers, used his technical skill to great advantage.

At Tulo it was ascertained that the enemy had retired on Kissaki and the task assigned to Hoskins—to push the enemy back towards the South African columns on the west—had been carried out.

General Smuts' order to press on in view of Brits' position now reached Hoskins who accordingly moved at once on Dutumi on September 10.

General von Lettow, on interior lines and secure from any immediate interference by Brits, was now able to concentrate his full available strength to oppose Hoskins.

The latter therefore found the enemy strongly entrenched on the eastern (nearer) bank of the Dutumi river, while beyond the further bank strong German forces were reported as at Nkessa.

By noon the 57th Rifles had seized Kitoho Hill on the right of the advance and pushed back some enemy detachments. The 57th Rifles were reinforced by the 3rd K.A.R. which unit was instructed to pass the former and turn the enemy left flank.

Along the main road the 3rd Kashmir Rifles aided by mountain guns, endeavoured to push forward, but were being held when darkness fell.

On the following day the 3rd K.A.R. advanced down both banks of the Dutumi until checked by heavy fire at noon and forced back at 5 p.m. by a German counter-attack to higher ground.

Despite reinforcement by the Gold Coast Regiment and a battery of South African Field Artillery (5th) the attack was held all day.

On September 12 the enemy had withdrawn from Kitoho Hill and the attacking line was extended to the right.

On the left, where the enemy still held his original positions, the Schulz Detachment attempted a counter-attack in dense bush and failed, and each side remained stationary, pending developments on the British right.

Late in the afternoon on this flank headway had been made to a point which commanded the German left flank and line of retreat. After a heavy burst of firing all along the line every-thing became quiet and in the morning, September 13, the enemy was away and out of touch. The operations had resulted in casualties to the number of nearly 100.

Meanwhile General Smuts had ordered Brits on the 11th to move against Kissaki once more from the north and west.

Brits was again without supplies and Nussey's Brigade had been without rations for two days, but on September 12 the Commander of the 3rd Division sent his two mounted brigades (1,200 strong in all) to the east to Mgasi, whence on September 14 they moved to the south. They now learned that the enemy had evacuated Kissaki and crossed the Mgeta river, and on September 15 Beves with his infantry marched into the boma where they found many German sick and wounded.

At Dakawa Brits and Hoskins joined hands by means of their patrols.

(xv) VON LETTOW'S MOVEMENTS ON INTERIOR LINES.

General von Lettow took full advantage here of his position on interior lines.

On September 7 Otto (4 companies) was opposite Brits, and Tafel (4 companies) on the road before Nussey. Stemmermann (6 companies) was retiring before Hoskins. Schulz and von Liebermann (4 and 3 companies, respectively) were in reserve at Kissaki.

In the engagement with Enslin Schulz and von Liebermann reinforced Otto on the 7th and on the following day (8th) went north to help Tafel against Nussey.

On September 10 von Lettow took Schulz, von Liebermann and Tafel to oppose the advance of Hoskins' brigades and left Otto alone opposite Brits to protect Kissaki.

CHAPTER XIII

(i) THE ADVANCE TO THE RUFIJI TEMPORARILY SUSPENDED.

GENERAL von Lettow had succeeded, by using the carriers belonging to his troops and all the people he could raise in the district, and by employing the waggons at his disposal, in evacuating all his stores to Behobeho en route for Kungulio on the Rufiji.

This was the object for the fulfilment of which he had been compelled to remain as long as possible at Kissaki, and his fortunate repulse of Brits and the extra week which he gained by it must have been of the utmost value to him.

Brits, on reaching Kissaki, found it empty of stores, but in its boma were many casualties left behind by the enemy.

The eliminating test of the Uluguru campaign and the preceding advance from the Wami had found out the weaklings —if soldiers who had already been campaigning hard for two years may be fairly so described—of the German troops, and their Commander now took with him across the Mgeta a concentrated force of some 3,500 first class fighting men who rapidly recovered their *moral* and spirits, temporarily lowered by their gruelling experience in the course of their opponent's recent relentless forward movement.

" Demoralisation " was from time to time reported as affecting the German forces, but the only instance of it in the case of those before General Smuts that was clearly apparent was here in the Uluguru and, just before the movement through the mountains, at Morogoro.

With the disappearance of over 1,000 Askaris round Morogoro, General von Lettow's force was purged of all except very determined fighters.

He now took up a position on the far (south) bank of the Mgeta with his right at Msogera and his left just opposite Dakawa.

On September 15 Brits' mounted troops passed over the Mgeta to the left of the enemy position and established themselves there, and the 2nd S.A. Infantry Brigade joined them.

The South Africans, however, were in no condition to attempt anything further and remained in their positions, beating off a counter-attack on September 20.

It was now clear that the enemy was determined to hang on unless compelled once more to retire, and on the night of the 18th-19th a column (3rd K.A.R.) crossed the Mgeta and advanced towards Msogera coming up against a strongly held and concealed position from which enemy fire effectually checked their further advance. Reinforcements failed to alter the position, and the K.A.R. established a bridge head on the right bank of the river.

The Commander-in-Chief decided to abandon further direct action against the strong enemy position in difficult country on September 20, contemplating an enterprise against the German left from Tulo by Brits.

Supply and transport difficulties were, however, acute, and all troops were ordered to abstain from any attack and to stand on the defensive.

It was now clear that any further forward movement from the south of the Uluguru was out of the question for the time. The South African forces were incapable of any further effort, medical, supply and transport services were all most severely overtaxed and had done their work under conditions which made it at times well-nigh impossible.

Apart from these considerations, from a purely military point of view it was necessary to consider the general strategic situation anew.

By the end of September General Smuts had given up any idea of a further advance towards the Rufiji until he should have reviewed the situation with a view to fresh plans.

(ii) THE ULUGURU OPERATIONS CONSIDERED.

There can be no doubt that almost superhuman exertions had been demanded by their Commander-in-Chief from the troops in this conquest of the huge Uluguru block. Their response, from every unit and service, had been beyond all praise, and this fact is in itself a justification of the call made upon them.

Soldiers such as those who served General Smuts from all parts of the Empire do not complain of hardship, provided the result justifies it. Resentment against undue severity is easily sensed in a body of men who feel it, and on no occasion could it be detected in this campaign, even when discomfort and privation were at their height.

The fact is that upon every occasion those who made the sacrifices and survived them saw some striking and tangible reward for their efforts.

Looking up at the northern end of the Uluguru mountains above Morogoro—a very limited view of a small part of a tremendous physical obstacle—the thought came that, if any defence were attempted, to surmount the difficulties attending heavy fighting in such country would entail enormous effort. As has been stated, all preparations for such a defence had been made, but were rendered practically nugatory by the sustained advance. It is clear *now* that the temporary discouragement of General von Lettow's troops was more far-reaching than was suspected by his opponent at the time, though evidence of it was not wanting, and that, as has been indicated already, the moral influences at work among the German forces at this time gained strength from the persistence of their opponents.

As a military achievement alone the conquest of the Uluguru mountains in a fortnight was a remarkable achievement by the troops who effected it, the safety of the Central Railway—with all that that condition implied—was a most substantial strategic advantage which well repaid their efforts.

The territory gained remained permanently in possession of the victors for the rest of the campaign, and General Smuts had found it possible to suggest the institution of civil control over the part of the country which he had now occupied.

Mr. (later Sir Horace) Byatt was selected by the Imperial Government as Administrator.

(iii) ADMINISTRATIVE SERVICES IN THE OPERATIONS.

The transport and supply position at this time is well summarised in the R.A.S.C. History by Colonel Beadon who, on page 314 of Volume II, writes:—

" All supplies and stores (at Kissaki) had been carried off or destroyed by the enemy and the troops were completely exhausted by these operations carried out on half rations (it will be remembered that on two occasions Nussey's men were without any rations at all for 48 hours); the force about Kissaki, cut off by a downpour of rain, itself actually lived for a fortnight on hippopotamus meat shot in the Mgeta river and on millet. It was not for some weeks after the occupation that it was found possible to run ambulances and other transport through the mountains, and, consequently, it was not possible to get food or medical comforts forward or evacuate the sick. The improvised hospitals were crowded with numbers down with malaria. The columns had pushed nearly a hundred miles beyond their original destination on the Central Railway, and there had been no real pause or opportunity for accumulating stores for the advance. The fighting front was then fed from a railhead at Korogwe on the Tanga-Moschi line, this step being one of the first fruits of the occupation of the port, but even then everything had to be brought up three hundred miles over winding tracks through bush and swamp. . . . . Although the rains were not due for some time there had been several spells of wet weather which involved holding up all traffic for several days at a time. On these occasions not only were roads impassable, but bridges were washed away and had to be rebuilt, and the embankments along the hillside sank and required bolstering up. Again for the transport and supply matters had reached a crisis. It was impossible to push the advance further."

This description serves as well for the lines of communication and medical services whose work was complicated by the same difficulties that affected that of transport and supply.

The official medical history once more deplores the want of a prepared scheme of medical arrangements for the advance from Morogoro to Kissaki and records that the lack of combination between the medical and combatant staffs was again responsible for increasing the difficulties associated with the evacuation of casualties in East Africa.

There is no record, as far as can be ascertained, that this lack of combination was ever brought to the notice of the Commander-in-Chief which was unfortunate, for no doubt some efforts might have been made to improve matters in this respect.

The lack of preparation generally—*and it affected every single service without exception*—was, as will be mentioned later, a most severe handicap on all concerned throughout the whole Expeditionary Force and it existed from the inception of hostilities.

A sudden decision, in view of the needs of the situation, to push without delay an advance beyond the point for which such arrangements as may have been possible have been made, means, in country like East Africa, extemporisation under extreme difficulty and a " prepared scheme " in such conditions is impossible. That all the services—of which the personnel was as liable to the ravages of disease as were the fighting troops—did what they did under the occasionally well-nigh insuperable difficulties which faced them is to their lasting credit.

(iv) THE OCCUPATION OF THE COAST PORTS.

Any detailed description of the admirable arrangements made by the Royal Navy and their military associates under the I.G.C. for the occupation of the coast ports is beyond the scope of this volume, but an outline of events in this connection is necessary to enable a reader to follow General Smuts' general strategy.

On August 15 Bagamoyo had been occupied and the capture of Dar-es-Salaam became the next venture to be undertaken.

Brigadier-General Edwards, the I.G.C., concentrated a force of 1,900 rifles and 20 machine guns at Bagamoyo. Included in this force were 300 South African Infantry (details for the units in the field) and the 2nd Loyal North Lancashire Regiment, recently returned from a five months' recuperative sojourn in the Union.

This force moved in four columns on a wide front, the two smallest directed, the one on Ruvu station to endeavour to seize the railway bridge over the river at that spot, the other to occupy Ngerengere railway station. " Mersey ", " Severn " and " Thistle " and the armed tug " Helmuth " were the ships associated with the undertaking.

On nearing Dar-es-Salaam, information was received that in all probability the town would not be defended, as it contained a large number of women and children and all troops had vacated it.

At 8 a.m. on September 4 the Deputy-Burgomaster accepted the terms which had been conveyed to him and the town and port were occupied.

The jetties were intact and landing facilities were easy of replacement.

223

The town had been emptied of war material.

The column directed on Ngerengere station found it empty, but a large viaduct had been blown up, and into the breach several trains had been run and smashed up. This obstacle was eventually circumvented by a deviation.

The 40th Pathans moved on Ruvu station and on September 1 surprised a small enemy detachment, the rear guard of a force which had moved southwards the day before after destroying the railway bridge. In an advance to Pugu the column came into contact with several retiring enemy parties, and, having captured 25 Germans, 20 Askaris and a considerable quantity of baggage and cattle, reached Dar-es-Salaam on September 6.

This marked the first step towards the sorely needed switch of communications to the Central Railway.

The new plan of the Commander-in-Chief made it necessary that bases should be secured on the coast to the south of Dar-es-Salaam and orders were given for the occupation of all sea ports to the Rovuma.

Kilwa Kivinje, an open roadstead, and Kilwa Kiswani— a magnificent land-locked deep water natural harbour—were secured, and occupied on September 7. Mikindani was occupied on the 13th without incident, Ssudi followed, and on the 17th Lindi was taken, and, with the occupation of Kiswere on the following day, the entire enemy seaboard, except for the Rufiji Delta, was held.

For some time the various garrisons left in the ports were not interfered with.

(v) EVENTS IN THE NORTH-WEST.

It will be remembered that Brigadier-General Sir Charles Crewe, who had originally been sent on a mission to General Tombeur to arrange the details of Belgian co-operation, had been given the command of the forces in the Lake (N.W.) area.

Though reference has been made to his activities, it has been slight, and it may be well at this point to give a resumé in outline of the operations which he conducted.

Without an idea of the general situation, the movements which took place under General Smuts' direction in the ensuing three months before he relinquished his command will be difficult to follow.

Without a knowledge of all the enemy movements, too, the steps taken to deal with them cannot be appreciated.

Sir Charles Crewe assumed command of the Lake area on June 17, 1916.

Co-operation with the Belgian Forces was an essential condition of his own operations.

The Belgian troops were also mainly Askaris—and they were Askaris of a fine type—led of course by European officers, and were some 10,000 strong. The German forces opposed to them were about 3,000.

The difficulties attending any forward movement by the Belgians were the same (transport and supply and the hindrances incidental to weakness in these services) as confronted every advancing force in this country and with these the reader will now be familiar.

Subject to the conditions that British troops should take over a certain portion of their outpost line and that transport of which they were deficient should be furnished to them, the Belgian authorities undertook to assume the offensive.

Considerations of space forbid even the scantiest description of the difficulties which attended the various arrangements for co-operation and it can only be recorded that they were often serious and always present.

Nor can the details of the movements be given.

Before the assumption of command by General Crewe the patrol actions and occasional more ambitious enterprises which had been a feature on every front occurred here.

The Belgian forces were organised in three detachments: Molitor, Rouling and Olsen.

On May 6 Molitor had occupied Kigali, some 50 miles south of the German border, Rouling, five days later, had reached a German position on the Sebea river, about 50 miles to the north-west of Kigali, and on the same date a portion of Olsen's force under Major Muller had halted at Mutabili, on the way to Nyanza, 30 miles in a direct line south-west of Kigali. Pushing on, Muller occupied Nyanza on the 19th. Two days later Rouling's troops joined hands with Olsen's at Nyanza, and contact was established with Molitor at Kigali, and the Belgians now occupied the province of Ruanda.

On June 9 a small expedition was sent by Crewe to capture Ukerewe island, and, landing, effected the occupation, and by June 15 had captured all the small enemy detachments on the island.

Ukerewe, noted for its rice supply, became a useful base.

The next Belgian move was against the German forces which had retired to the south-east towards Kitega and Biaramulo and was undertaken by the two forces of Molitor and Olsen.—Kitega lies some 50 miles due east from the head of Lake Tanganyika and Biaramulo about half that distance due west from the southern end of Lake Victoria.

Starting on June 1, Olsen, after some engagements of a minor character, occupied Kitega, the capital of the Urundi district, on the 17th.

Molitor, moving also on the 1st, after some opposition, occupied Biaramulo on June 24. Here he was across the line of retreat of the German force at Bukoba (approximately in the centre of the western shore of Lake Victoria).

Extending his forces in positions in mountainous country, Molitor endeavoured to intercept the retreating German forces under Captain Godovius. An intercepted message, of which the purport had been conveyed to their Belgian allies by the British authorities, ordered Godovius to attack Biaramulo with a view to its recapture and notified him of the march of Wintgens from the west to his assistance.

On July 3 the German forces—as usual well posted as to the terrain—in an attempt to pass unobserved, came up against Rouling and a severe engagement ensued. The Belgians, heavily outnumbered, maintained their position until reinforcements arrived and the enemy retired. The action had cost the Belgians 68 casualties of which 33 were dead. Captain Godovius was wounded.

After further engagements the Belgian forces maintained their positions and the enemy retired to the south.

Meanwhile a column under Lieut.-Col. Burgess of Crewe's force had occupied Bukoba on June 28, and other small columns advancing south from the Kagera river had established touch with Molitor's forces to the north of Biaramulo.

Crewe, after endeavouring to secure the co-operation of his Belgian allies, which their recent efforts had made it impossible for them to extend, and regarding the early seizure of Mwansa on the southern shore of Lake Victoria as important, established his base for the operation on Ukerewe island.

Landing his force (about 1,900 rifles) on a promontory to the east of Mwansa during the night of June 11-12 he advanced on Mwansa. Early in the afternoon of the 14th it was discovered that the enemy was retiring and the town was occupied.

An effort at pursuit could not be sustained owing to want of supplies.

Moving again on July 5, Olsen—his forces in two columns —moved on Kigoma (the terminus of the German Central Railway) on Lake Tanganyika and Ujiji, a little to the south of Kigoma. After slight resistance the German forces retired and Olsen occupied both his objectives on July 28.

These operations freed the Belgians from the necessity for immobilising further any troops for the protection of the shores of Lake Tanganyika.

Crewe, on July 17, with pursuit of the enemy in mind, formed a base at Nyatembe on the Mwansa Gulf, which was the furthest point which his steamers could reach, covering the base next day by a force, landed and entrenched to the south.

After a conference with General Tombeur and the (British) Governor of Uganda it was decided that, using Mwansa as a common base, Crewe and Molitor should advance to Iwingo and St. Michael, respectively. Arrived at their destinations the two Commanders would make arrangements for a joint advance on Tabora.

Early in August, Molitor, with 2,500 rifles and 8 guns, and Crewe, with 1,500 rifles and 5 guns, stood ready for the forward movement agreed upon. Olsen, with 3,000 rifles, was at Kigoma and Ujiji and Belgian detachments, in all some 1,000 rifles, were to the south on the shores of Tanganyika. 1,500 German troops faced Crewe and Molitor, while 650 offered a front to Olsen at the broken bridge over the Malarasi river on the Central Railway.

Space forbids any account of the operations which followed, and it must suffice to say that on September 7 (the date of

Brits' action at Kissaki) Olsen had reached Usoke station, 40 miles west of Tabora on the Central Railway.

The day before Crewe, apparently only advised on September 3 that Olsen was on his way to Tabora, had ordered an advance from Shinyanga, 50 miles south of his base on Lake Victoria, and just over twice as far from Tabora.

On September 25 he occupied Ndala, 40 miles north-east of Tabora, where he became aware that the Belgians had taken Tabora five days earlier.

Olsen, who had advanced from Usoke on September 16, had occupied the heights—after some stiff fighting on the way— to the west of Tabora, and awaited news of the force of Molitor with which touch had been established 2 days earlier.

On the night of September 18-19 the German forces evacuated Tabora and retired in the direction of Iringa (i.e. towards Kraut). On the following day the Belgians occupied the town.

At this time General Smuts was halted at Kissaki and van Deventer at Kidodi, but, except for a few small brushes along the Central Railway, where on October 6 a K.A.R. detachment from Crewe met a mounted patrol from van Deventer's force in the direction of Kilimatinde, the occupation of Tabora marked the end of Sir Charles Crewe's operations.

The Lake Force ceased to exist as a detachment and Sir Charles Crewe returned to the Union.

(vi) BRIGADIER-GENERAL NORTHEY'S OPERATIONS.

A record of Brigadier-General Northey's operations would also seem to be opportune here.

Until the end of 1915 events in the south pursued a course in no essential particular different from that of those elsewhere in East Africa.

Minor encounters and enterprises took place with varying fortune, and it was until the advent of Brigadier-General Northey, early in 1916, that any considerable movement was undertaken.

General Northey arrived in his sphere of operations in February, 1916, as did General Smuts at Mombasa.

He found his command, a force of 2,500 rifles, strung out over 250 miles from Karonga on Nyasa to Abercorn near Tanganyika.

The troops at his disposal included 6 companies of the 1st K.A.R., the South African Rifles (a contingent from the Union), white volunteers from Rhodesia (North and South) and the Northern Rhodesia Police, a native unit officered by white officers.

1,500 German troops were opposite him, similarly spread out in small posts.

Northey arrived during the rainy season and occupied himself during an enforced period of abstention from move-ment in organising his forces.

His orders were first to secure British territory and then, to the best of his power, to aid generally the operations of General Smuts and the Belgians.

In consequence of a rumour that some ship building was in progress at Sphinxhaven, a small expedition was directed on that place, and on April 28 searched it and found the report to have been unfounded.

The enemy was reported to be holding Ipiana, near the extreme northern shore of Lake Nyasa, Igamba, 30 miles to the west, Luwiwa, opposite Fife, still further to the west, and Namema, on the river Saisi, nearly opposite Abercorn, and 200 miles west of Karonga.

Northey moved against these posts in 4 columns.

From Karonga: Lieut.-Col. Hawthorn, 800 rifles with 3 guns and 8 machine guns.

From Fort Hill, midway between Karonga and Fife: Major Flindt, 400 rifles, 4 guns, 2 machine guns.

From Fife: Lieut.-Col. Rodger, 600 rifles, 4 guns, 6 machine guns.

From Abercorn: Lieut.-Col. Murray, 800 rifles, 3 guns, 10 machine guns.

Rodger and Flindt were South African officers. Each of the three first-named columns contained portions of the South African Rifles and Rodger, Flindt and Murray each had two 12 pdr. Q.F. mountain guns manned by personnel from the South African Mounted Riflemen.

Hawthorn occupied Ipiana, evacuated by the enemy, on May 23 and thence moved in the direction of Neu Langenburg.

Flindt had a similar experience at Igamba on May 25 and advanced in the same direction as Hawthorn and on May 29 occupied Neu Langenburg. The enemy had retired along the road to Iringa and Hawthorn was charged by Northey with their pursuit towards Neu Utengule.

On the night of May 24-25 Rodger moved on Luwiwa and Murray on Namema. At each of these places resistance was encountered.

Rodger, after three days, found Luwiwa evacuated and followed the enemy towards Neu Langenburg.

Murray was engaged longer at Namema and it was not until June 3 that he found that the enemy had vacated their positions during the night and he in turn followed the retiring German forces and occupied Bismarckburg on June 8.

Northey now concentrated Murray, Hawthorn and Flindt at Neu Langenburg. By the middle of June Neu Langenburg, Bismarckburg and Neu Utengule were held, and the enemy retired out of touch.

Without going into great detail, which is here impossible, the course of the operations which ensued and which were directed and carried out efficiently under the difficult conditions which were experienced on all fronts cannot be presented without a danger of confusing a reader. It must therefore suffice to state the result of them.

They were attended by the invariable difficulties of supply, as a consequence of the rainfall which is in these southern districts heavier than in any other areas of East Africa.

General Smuts decided that the most useful assistance that General Northey could render him was by advancing north-eastwards on Iringa. The Commander-in-Chief therefore asked Northey to co-operate in the above sense, but, already aware of possible developments, suggested caution in the latter's movements.

On July 1 (General Smuts' main force was at this time on the Msiha river and van Deventer was at Kondoa Irangi) Hawthorn moved against an enemy detachment at Soliwaya covering a stronger concentration at Malangali which blocked the road to Iringa.

Northey now concentrated the columns of Hawthorn and Rodger for the capture of Malangali from which the enemy was ejected on July 24 after some heavy fighting, and retired to Wuasa, some 35 miles south-west of Iringa.

On August 7 Hawthorn was ordered to move south towards Lupembe, leaving Rodger and Murray opposite the enemy force at Wuasa, and on the 18th occupied Lupembe and thence undertook an arduous advance through most difficult country to Mahenge.

On August 22, Northey, having been made aware of van Deventer's occupation of Kilossa and General Smuts' successful negotiation of the Nguru mountains, ordered Murray and Rodger to seize Iringa which they did on August 28.

On September 9 (the date of Nussey's engagement at Kissaki) and 10, Murray and Rodger were engaged with the enemy from Iringa and drove them from Muhanga mission in the direction of Mahenge. Here the two columns halted to allow Hawthorn's advance, much impeded by dense bush and forest, along the Mnjera river to make headway.

General Smuts had conveyed to General Northey his sense of the importance of an early occupation of Mahenge with a view to forcing any enemy body retiring before van Deventer eastward.

Northey accordingly sent Murray to the south to co-operate with Hawthorn.

The latter, coping with severe difficulties, was now, September 27, facing an enemy force, strengthened by the arrival of Kraut.

The main advance had now come to a halt south of the Uluguru mountains and on the night of September 29-30, Hawthorn, who had established touch with Murray, withdrew over the Ruhudje river and, with Murray, took up a defensive position overlooking the river. For the next few weeks, until the end of October, the two forces remained opposite each othe without any important incident.

Northey meanwhile had occupied Songea and Wiedhaven

(vii) GENERAL WAHLE'S MOVEMENT SOUTHWARD FROM TABORA.

When General Smuts was compelled to call a halt at the end of September, the position, see map number nineteen, was as follows:—

The Main Force under the Commander-in-Chief was opposite von Lettow south of the Uluguru.

Van Deventer's advanced troops were at Kidodi.

Crewe and the Belgians at Tabora.

Northey held Iringa, Hawthorn's position, south, on the Ruhudje towards Mahenge, and Songea.

The concentric advance had brought all the forces under the command of General Smuts much closer to each other.

On September 20 the Belgian forces had occupied Tabora, and the German detachment in the north-west under General Wahle had retired in a south-easterly direction. It was not pursued; the Belgians, having attained the object of their military efforts—the occupation of Ruanda and Urundi and the capture of Tabora—declined to make any further movement without instructions from their Government, and Crewe's force was unequal to any such task as a pursuit.

Wahle therefore moved off unmolested at his leisure.

There was at this time doubt as to his intention.

Wahle's force was estimated at 1,500 rifles, but was in point of fact much stronger.

On September 21, Northey telegraphed, in explanation of a request that van Deventer should relieve him at Iringa: " Have been anxious for some time as to danger of enemy forces from Tabora district coming S.E.".

Northey had handled his small forces with much boldness and occupied a considerable portion of enemy country with detachments of comparatively weak strength.

Kraut's withdrawal from before van Deventer had brought an accession of strength to the enemy opposite Northey which placed the two opposing sides on equal terms in respect of numbers. The arrival of even 1,500—they proved to be not less than 2,300 rifles—seasoned troops, who, though they had retired, were full of fight, would make Northey's position precarious.

General Smuts was well aware of this, and, in a communication to the War Office on September 21, stated that in view of the possibility of a junction between Wahle and Kraut and the resultant danger from such an association to Northey's communications he was compelled to keep the greater part of van Deventer's force (in any case none too large by this time) between Kilimatinde and the Ruaha.

The position was all the more serious as the forces at the Commander-in-Chief's disposal were seriously diminished and, in the case of the Europeans (i.e. the South Africans) worn out by disease and overwork and incapable of any sustained movement.

The great difficulties of supply further aggravated the situation which gave ground for considerable anxiety.

General Smuts, however, ordered van Deventer to occupy Nyukwas, a crossing on the Ruaha river on the Kilossa-Iringa road. This was done and by October 3 a detachment of the 1st S.A. Horse held the post.

In these circumstances General Wahle, whose intentions could at the time only be guessed at, moved to the south-east in three columns; Wintgens, 1,000 rifles, 5 guns and 16 machine guns; Zingel, with whom was General Wahle, 600 rifles, 6 machine guns; von Langenn, 900 rifles, 2 guns and 8 machine guns. Carriers of a strength equal to that of the Askaris accompanied the detachments and carriers were always potential Askaris to some extent.

The force therefore was formidable.

On October 1 General Smuts expressed his approval of a withdrawal by Northey, in view of his inability to reinforce the latter, if the commander of the forces in the south-west should decide to retire, but Northey, naturally reluctant to abandon what the great exertions of his troops had secured, decided to hang on.

On September 19 one of van Deventer's patrols gained touch with Northey's forces near Iringa by heliograph, and as the ensuing operations brought van Deventer's and other South African units into their orbit some detail in connection with the different movements is perhaps desirable.

With a view to assisting Northey, the 8th S.A. Infantry under Lieut.-Col. Taylor, which had been retained by van Deventer at Kilimatinde on the railway line since early August, was designated as one of the units of a column which was to be collected at Kilimatinde and placed under its regimental commander. Among the units to be so assembled was the S.A. Motor Cyclist Corps.

The main difficulty in sending reinforcements to Northey (i.e. to the extent that comparatively fit personnel was available) was the ever present one of supply.

Relying, however, on the reported fertility of the Iringa district, General Smuts sent the 7th S.A. Infantry (Freeth) from Kilossa on October 12 to make its way to Iringa.

He also decided to send another of his infantry battalions—the 5th S.A.I. (Byron) round to Nyasaland. Leaving Morogoro on October 15, Byron sailed with 150 fit men, the remnant of his command, to Durban, embarked 600 recruits and reached Songea by way of Beira on November 20.

Wahle directed his columns, Wintgens on Madibira and von Langenn and Zingel on Iringa. It would seem that Wintgens dropped Lieutenant Hübner as a rear guard with 300 rifles. The exact role of this detachment is not clear, but it is possible that the escort of a 4.1″ howitzer, drawn by a large span of oxen, as were its three limbers, was its principal function. It was also its undoing for, far behind the rest of the German columns, the detachment was attacked at Ilembule by Murray of Northey's force and captured on November 26. Its wanderings exercised no more influence on the operations than the concentration of Murray's force for its capture.

Northey, to meet the threat from the north-west, ordered Rodger to concentrate round Iringa reinforcing him at the same time with a detachment under Major Baxendale. Rodgers' guns were sent to Ngominyi, an important supply depot on the communications some 50 miles south-west of Iringa, and held as a defended post. Rodgers' mobility was thus enhanced.

On October 11 word came of Wahle's approach and Northey despatched his only reserve, 250 rifles, to Neu Utengule on his lines of communication.

On October 12 enemy advanced troops engaged a patrol of the S.A. Rifles on the Ruaha river to the west of Iringa. Repulsing these forces, the South Africans learned that the main force from which their prisoners came was near and intended to attack Iringa. Though Freeth and his infantry had passed Nyukwa's he was not close enough to be of immediate help and the garrison of Iringa was left to its own resources.

Intelligence of the arrival of a strong enemy detachment near Madibira on October 20 indicated serious danger to Ngominyi and two days later Baxendale left Iringa with 50 rifles to reinforce Ngominyi.

On the same day, October 22, the enemy occupied a commanding position north of Ngominyi and isolated the post. The latter was occupied by some 50 rifles with Rodgers' returned guns and commanded by Captain Clark of the S.A. Permanent Force.

On October 23 the enemy ambushed Baxendale on his way to strengthen Clark, killed the former and annihilated his detachment. A wounded member of it made his way to Ngominyi and warned Clark of the incident.

Meanwhile Rodger with 100 rifles had moved from Alt Iringa on October 24 to Clark's support. He became engaged near the scene of the ambush of the day before and was unable to proceed.

The day before Freeth had reached Iringa and two days later Colonel Fairweather with some of his motor cyclists arrived at the same place.

The latter assumed command and ordered Freeth to Rodgers' assistance.

Zingel who had appeared at Ngominyi was now joined by Wintgens.

Clark was now cut off and surrounded by a very greatly superior force. Making the best of a very bad situation and having repulsed an attempt by the enemy to capture the post about dusk on October 28, he gave his detachment permission to escape, if possible, during the night. 30 of the detachment took advantage of this in the hopeless position in which they found themselves.

At dawn on October 29 a bayonet charge covered by machine gun fire resulted in the death or capture of those who had remained, the gallant Clark being mortally wounded and his second-in-command, Lieutenant Bones, killed.

Freeth and Rodger, apprised of the fall of the post in the evening, were attacked on the following morning by superior forces, but maintained their position and on November 1 found the enemy had withdrawn.

Freeth himself then withdrew under cover of darkness and reached Alt Iringa on November 4.

Northey's situation was grave, but elsewhere his troops had scored a victory.

Hawthorn had, it will be remembered, occupied a defensive position on the Ruhudje river towards Mahenge in the direction of which his advance had been stopped. Murray had joined him.

Against this position the enemy, under Kraut, advanced on October 22.

Colonel Hawthorn had foreseen the possibility of attack and arranged for it by storing supplies and securing communication with General Northey, and on the night of October 29-30, by a carefully devised counter-attack, inflicted a heavy defeat on Kraut's force which he dispersed with serious loss and slight casualties on his own side on the morning of October 31.

Kraut was temporarily put out of action at the critical moment at which his co-operation with the advancing forces of Wahle might have seriously aggravated a difficult situation.

General Wahle had contemplated an attack in force by his converging columns on Iringa. Difficulties of communication, however, brought this plan to nought.

Malangali, another supply depot on the lines of communication, 40 miles south-west of Ngominyi, was the next objective of the enemy.

Here were 100 native Rhodesian recruits under Captain Marriott of the S.A. Rifles. The position was now strengthened and Murray, who was with Hawthorn and had just shared in his success, was ordered to move immediately to the succour of the post and reached Lupembe, 50 miles south and slightly east of Malangali on November 4. Sending on a company to Malangali, Murray halted at Lupembe.

On November 8 the enemy surrounded the post and on the following day, additional German troops having arrived, three heavy attacks at close quarters were repulsed.

The roads on the lines of communication had received careful attention and had been much improved and 50 light cars were now sent to Lupembe where they arrived on November 8.

Murray sent 125 rifles to strengthen the garrison of Njombe, a post 40 miles west of Lupembe on Hawthorn's communications, and, with 130 rifles in the light cars, himself proceeded towards Malangali, reaching the close vicinity of the post on the evening of the 9th, having covered 120 miles of rough roads.

Here he took a hand in the operations by engaging the enemy to such extent as was possible.

On the night of November 11-12 Murray was joined by a detachment which he had despatched from Lupembe on the 6th.

On November 11 the enemy withdrew, leaving a weakened detachment to deal with the Malangali post, which Murray promptly attacked and dispersed, capturing cattle and carriers and inflicting heavy loss.

The enemy next attacked Lupembe.

This important post on Hawthorn's communications was held by 250 rifles of which 200 were native K.A.R. recruits.

Attacked with determination by bayonet charges on November 13 and 14 the garrison held the enemy at bay and inflicted heavy damage on their opponents, who, on the 15th made off to the north-east, and in the evening the leading troops of Hawthorn, who had been recalled from Mkapira, 40 miles to the westward, reached Lupembe.

Four days later Murray joined Hawthorn at Lupembe and the enemy, evidently aware of this strong concentration, passed on eastward.

On November 22 Wahle and Kraut appear to have joined forces in the valley of the Mnyera.

At the end of the month, after the capture of Hübner's force, the enemy was all to the east of Northey's front and his position was far less dangerous.

On October 30 General Smuts, from Dar-es-Salaam, on his way to Kilwa, placed van Deventer in command of all operations round Iringa as " Northey is cut off from there and can give no orders ". Van Deventer was also instructed to keep Northey well posted as to the situation.

The 2nd Division at this time was in a parlous state, the infantry were far below establishment, and disease, short commons and unceasing hard work had reduced the whole force to a remnant, and a weak and worn out remnant at that.

However, in order to send much needed help towards Iringa, what was left of the mounted troops was formed into a mounted force.

On October 31 just over 330 mounted men left Morogoro* for Iringa and on November 4, Nussey, with 120 more, left for the same destination.

The following figures are of interest as showing the effect of tsetse fly.

300 horses were abandoned between Morogoro and Kilossa and on November 23 (in some three weeks) only the balance were with the force at Iringa, and these were rapidly disappearing. Nearly 100 men had also fallen out along the route, but those who reached Iringa were hardened troops whose presence there was of the utmost value.

Kidodi which was extremely unhealthy and had been under long range gun fire since the end of September, was evacuated and its diminished garrison moved back 10 miles to Kikumi.

Close on the heels of the mounted troops came the 17th (Indian Infantry) on November 25, van Deventer himself having arrived there three days earlier.

He took up positions round Iringa and released Rodger's force which rejoined Northey.

A German advance and attack on Songea failed and the position there was made secure by the arrival of Byron with his 5th S.A. Infantry on November 20.

At the end of November General von Lettow had all the forces at his disposal together in the south-eastern portion of the Protectorate, a result which had been attained by a fine march of 300 miles by the forces under Wahle who brought with him 1,600 excellent troops.

General Smuts now had all the forces opposing him opposite his different fronts.

A feature of the British operations had been the employment of light motor transport for the conveyance of Murray's troops from point to point, and this will be referred to again.

---

* 900 men of the two South African Mounted Brigades had been collected at Morogoro 3 weeks earlier for reorganisation and re-equipment.

CHAPTER XIV

(i) GENERAL SMUTS' FRESH PLANS.

BY THE end of September, General Smuts, for reasons which have already been explained, found himself compelled to halt and consider the situation which had arisen from the retreat of the enemy actually before him from Morogoro and the Central Railway to positions just south of the Uluguru mountains covering the Rufiji river.

The circumstances which had combined to make any further forward movement impossible and in consequence of which any general advance proved to be out of the question before the end of the year, are perhaps best described by reference to General Smuts' despatch of 28th February, 1917.

" Disease had played havoc amongst the troops of whom large numbers were totally unfit without medical attention, prolonged rest, change of climate and nourishment to make any sustained effort.

The wastage . . . . was enormous.

The Mechanical Transport was in a seriously damaged condition in consequence of the strain of continuous work over appalling roads or trackless country and extensive repairs for which there had been no time were essential.

. . . .

Animal disease had wiped out horses, mules and oxen by thousands and it was necessary to replace this transport in some way or other before movement was possible.

The strain upon all ranks of all units and services due to the steadily increasing effect of disease had reached the limit endurable ".

12,000 South Africans were sent back to the Union after the Uluguru operations.

This reduced the South African formations, as they stood, to skeleton units, and reorganisation became necessary.

(ii) REORGANISATION OF THE SOUTH AFRICAN FORMATIONS.

As has already been stated, the personnel which was available from the two mounted brigades, and fit for duty, 900 in all, was mergen in the 1st Mounted Brigade of which a diminished strength proceeded to Iringa where it almost immediately became dismounted from the loss of all its horses.

The 3rd Division and the 2nd Mounted Brigade were abolished, and Generals Brits and Enslin, their respective Commanders, returned to the Union.

Beves' (2nd) Infantry Brigade was, as a result of this step, reduced to the 6th S.A. Infantry and the Cape Corps, and reverted to its old rôle of Force Reserve at the disposal of the Commander-in-Chief.

The experience of a draft of South African infantry reinforcements gives a good example of the wastage which went on endlessly in this campaign.

A draft of 1,000 recruits which reached Korogwe, on leaving Handeni on their march south to the front numbered 330! By the time the survivors reached the units they were to reinforce the additional strength was negligible.

At the beginning of November the fighting strength of Berrangé's 3rd S.A. Infantry Brigade was 460 rifles.

It had become clear that, in view of the extent of their wastage and the rapidity with which it occurred, European troops were unsuitable in such country as was to be encountered. The difficulty of supply would soon again arise, and there was no chance that the conditions which they would have to face would make it possible to keep them fit for their task.

The 3rd Infantry Brigade (Berrangé) with van Deventer now became one composite regiment, the 10th S.A. Infantry.

Many of the Indian regiments were reduced to sore straits as well by exposure, hardship and disease.

Generally the loss of strength was made up by reinforcements consisting of a Nigerian Brigade* under Brigadier-General Cunliffe, 2,600 rifles and 4 guns, the 30th Punjabis, and an increase in the King's African Rifles.

The East African Mounted Rifles, to which reference has been made earlier and which had done admirable service, was disbanded, and its personnel distributed to the best advantage in the forces generally.

---

* This unit, mostly of trained men who had served in the Cameroons, was a valuable accession.

(iii) FIELD FORCE LANDED ON THE COAST.

On September 7 General Smuts cabled to the War Office indicating the probability, which afterwards became a fact, that the main enemy force would retire to the lower Rufiji instead of to Mahenge, and conveyed his intention, should the event bear out the information at his disposal, of landing a strong force at Kilwa to operate from the coast and attempt to confine the enemy in an area north of the Matandu river.

This area is roughly that included between the Rufiji and Ruaha rivers to the north, the coast from the Rufiji Delta to Kilwa on the east, a line bending southward between Kilwa and Mahenge on the south and a line from Mahenge to Iringa on the west. In other words, the area in which the entire enemy forces concentrated after the arrival of General Wahle's force and his junction towards the end of November with Kraut which was recorded in the last chapter.

The occupation of Songea which, it will be remembered, was effected by a force of Northey's on September 20, was ordered by the Commander-in-Chief to prevent an attempt by the enemy to break south-west.

General Smuts also ordered that Kilwa Kiwindje to which he attached the greatest importance, was to be held strongly by a garrison which should be able to repel any attack which the enemy might attempt. Kilwa Kiswani was to be held as well.

On October 1 the garrison at Kilwa was warned of the approach of an enemy force, and on the following day the defence was tested by two attacks by a German detachment under von Boehmken. The latter found the defence too strong and retired to Kimbarambara, 15 miles inland.

Brigadier-General Hannyngton was selected for the command of the Field Force to operate from Kilwa.

Rain had fallen in considerable quantities on the Mgeta front, and it is eloquent of the difficulties of transport to record that when General Hannyngton left his brigade to go to Kilwa on September 23 he did so on foot.

On October 8 he telegraphed from Kilwa, at which place he had arrived two days earlier, that his concentration was incomplete, but on October 10 he was able to institute a forward movement to meet General Smuts' injunction to gain ground as rapidly as possible to the north with a view to co-operation with the main field force on the Mgeta in due course.

(iv) OPERATIONS SOUTH OF DAR-ES-SALAAM.

The passage of some of the reinforcements for Kilwa had been interfered with by a situation which had arisen south of the Central Railway to the south-west of Dar-es-Salaam.

After leaving that place and withdrawing to south of the Central Railway, the enemy had left a detachment at Kissangire, 40 miles due south of Ruwu railway station.

From this spot could be launched enterprises against the railway communications over which were now working the converted petrol-driven lorries and cars already mentioned.

Accordingly General Smuts ordered the capture of the post.

On October 4 a half-battalion (Jhind Infantry), 250 rifles with 2 machine guns under Major-General Katha Singh, left Dar-es-Salaam, and on the 7th arrived at Manero Mango, 25 miles north of Kissangire on the Dar-es-Salaam road and was reinforced by 40 Intelligence Scouts.

On the morning of October 9 the detachment attacked the German post at Kissangire but was repulsed with a loss of 50 and retired to Manero Mango.

300 South African infantry reinforcements at Dar-es-Salaam were sent to Manero Mango, and orders were given that a battalion and two mountain guns should proceed to the same spot from the 1st Division on the Mgeta front.

The 57th Rifles under Lieut.-Colonel Willans, on receipt of this order, marched across country from the 1st Division on October 14, and a week later joined the Manero Mango detachment which had moved forward some 15 miles to Mssanga.

Willans now expressed the opinion that he was too weak to deal with the enemy at Kissangire, and, ordered to make a feint to the south-west of the latter place, detached 300 rifles to Kongo, 10 miles west of his own position.

Von Lettow at this time was concerned with the covering of an extensive collection of supplies which was taking place in the fertile area south of the Rufiji, and to protect his activities moved up reinforcements to Makima south of Kissangire.

Nothing of importance, however, took place, activity being confined to the usual patrol encounters.

By mid-December the enemy forces in the area had been reduced to dimensions which made them negligible as a menace and no further detachments than those which have been mentioned proved to be needed.

(v) OPERATIONS FROM KILWA.

Early in October the new motor system, which has been described, was working from Dar-es-Salaam to Dodoma, and Colonel Dobson and his S.A. Pioneers were moved on to complete the work to Tabora.

General Smuts took early advantage of the facility thus afforded him, and on October 5 left by rail car for Kilossa to visit van Deventer.

Here he took the opportunity of reconnoitring the road to south of Uleia and the railway to Kidete. He also inspected van Deventer's infantrymen who bore in their appearance striking evidence of the physical condition to which their continued hardships had reduced them.

The Commander-in-Chief returned to Morogoro on October 7 to find that Hannyngton had just reported his arrival at Kilwa.

The country through which Hannyngton's troops were now to operate was difficult, as usual, and was the more awkward to negotiate as it had not been surveyed, and maps were few and very inaccurate.

The best route inland from Kilwa was along the Matandu river which, it will be remembered, was the feature to the north of which General Smuts desired that the enemy should be kept.

The route in this direction (towards Liwale and eventually Songea) ran to Njinjo, 50 miles inland, and from that place tracks to Utete (north) Nambanye (west) and Liwale (south-west) branched.

The Kilwe-Utete road, running north-west from the former place, reached a large mountain block, the Mtumbei, where in the high country there was an enemy post, Kibata. The vicinity was reported as comparatively healthy, the coast country round Kilwa being notoriously the reverse.

Immediately after the occupation of Kilwa Kivindje the fine harbour of Kilwa Kiswani was developed as a landing base.

As has been recorded, an attack on Kilwa on October 2 had been repulsed.

On October 7 Njinjo was occupied by a column from Kilwa which ambushed a German detachment.

General Hannyngton on his arrival took in hand the occupation of Kibata, and to achieve this end despatched a force of 900 rifles from Kilwa on October 10.

After two skirmishes en route, this force, under Lieut.-Colonel Hulseberg, found Kibata abandoned and occupied the place on October 14.

A battalion of K.A. Rifles was left to hold the position.

By the end of October posts had been established at Kitambi and Mtumbei, distant some 10 miles from Kibata and Njinjo, respectively, and at a similar distance from each other.

There were thus four posts west of Kilwa at 10 miles interval on a 30 mile arc of 40 to 50 miles radius from the coast.

Kibata was a place of importance as a centre from which roads radiated in all directions.

General Smuts on October 28, left Morogoro and arrived at Dar-es-Salaam on the following morning. Thence he embarked on H.M.S. Talbot and reached Kilwa Kivindje early on October 31. Spending the day at Kilwa Kivindje arranging various matters with Hannyngton he returned to " Talbot " via Kilwa Kiswani and reached Dar-es-Salaam on November 1. On the following day he returned to Morogoro.

An important consequence of the visit of the Commander-in-Chief to the coast was his decision to put into effect certain arrangements proposed some time earlier but postponed in consequence of the position on the Mgeta front.

(vi) FURTHER RE-ARRANGEMENTS.

Major-General Hoskins (with one of his Brigades of the 1st Division) was transferred to Kilwa to take charge of the arrangements for an eventual execution of the advance inland from the coast.

These alterations resulted in the formation of a fresh 1st Division at Kilwa composed of the 2nd E.A. Brigade (formerly Hannyngton's and now to be commanded by Colonel O'Grady), transferred from the Mgeta front, and a new 3rd E.A. Brigade under Hannyngton made up of units which had been sent to Kilwa.

On the departure of General Hoskins for the coast, the 1st E.A. Brigade (Sheppard), holding the Mgeta line, came under G.H.Q., i.e. the Commander-in-Chief, who also held the Force Reserve (Beves) with him at Morogoro.

Sheppard took over the Mgeta line on November 7.

On this date General Smuts, in view of the need for close co-operation in the next operations asked that General Northey might be placed under his command for movements and operations. While the joint efforts at a distance had been arranged and carried out with the best results, it was felt that with closer touch established one command should be exercised over all operations.

This arrangement came into force on November 12.

General Smuts also indicated his intention, if the enemy stood on the Rufiji long enough, to try to envelop him there when the Nigerian Brigade should have arrived.

(vii) FURTHER OPERATIONS IN KILWA AREA.

Hoskins, on arrival at Kilwa, apportioned his front between the brigades of Hannyngton and O'Grady. The former to the north, the latter to the south.

On December 8 Hoskins held a chain of posts from Kibata, to the north, to Mchemera on the Matandu river as his southernmost position. In front of this line Ngarambi Chini, 25 miles due west of Kibata and Nambanye at a rather less distance to the west of Mchemera were also occupied, the former by the 40th Pathans, the latter by a company of the Gold Coast regiment.

The garrison of Kibata, 800 rifles under Lieut.-Colonel Hulseberg, had entrenched their position and prepared it for defence.

On December 5 the enemy attacked this post aided by a 4.1" Königsberg gun, a 4.1" Howitzer and a field gun and until the 7th fighting was continued in heavy rain.

On the night of December 8-9 the 2nd K.A.R. reached Kibata sent up to the help of the garrison.

The regiment at Ngarambi was also withdrawn and directed on Kibata.

A counter-attack by the garrison on the evening of the 9th was repulsed and the siege continued.

Hannyngton then directed that the Gold Coast Regiment and 40th Pathans should on December 14 attack the enemy right flank to the north of Kibata, and, in the engagement which ensued on the 15th, the Gold Coast Regiment, after a loss of a third of its strength, succeeded in holding on to a feature which it had gained and from which it was possible to enfilade the enemy position.

On the same day an offensive movement was undertaken with success by the garrison of Kibata, and resulted in the capture of the portion of the enemy position against which it was directed.

Each side now remained in position until the end of December by which time General Smuts had begun the final operations which he was to direct in East Africa.

(viii) A PORTUGUESE ADVANCE.

An offensive by the Portuguese, in response to a request by General Smuts to their Commander, General Gil, had started from the Rovuma, and on October 4 a reconnaissance party of two companies was ambushed, heavily defeated and driven back. The detachment was joined by two others sent out to reinforce it.

On October 26 a field force of six companies with some machine guns and a mounted detachment reached the vicinity of Newala which it found unoccupied and took possession of.

After several minor episodes General von Lettow sent a force under Captain Looff (Commander of the Königsberg) which ejected the Portuguese force from Newala and the latter retired across the Rovuma. Its activities had slight influence on the course of events.

(ix) THE ADMINISTRATIVE STAFF POSITION.

Before giving an account of General Smuts' final operations, it will be well to refer to the position of the Administrative Staff and Services whose work in the endeavour to improve matters and prepare for a fresh advance had gone on unceasingly during the enforced halt on the Mgeta river.

The situation which they had to face and remedy has been described.

The period of the halt south of the Uluguru, with the exception of the pause on the Msiha, was the only check in the forward movements of which the Administrative Staff was able to avail itself.

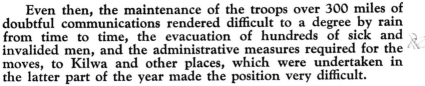

Even then, the maintenance of the troops over 300 miles of doubtful communications rendered difficult to a degree by rain from time to time, the evacuation of hundreds of sick and invalided men, and the administrative measures required for the moves, to Kilwa and other places, which were undertaken in the latter part of the year made the position very difficult.

The first great advantage was that in early October it was possible to use Dar-es-Salaam on the coast as a base. The accumulation of supplies at that place was comparatively simple.

Then, the capture of the Central Railway and employment of motor transport along it made it possible to cut out the precarious road communications north to Handeni and Korogwe, and the railway running behind the advance took their place.

From the railway south, of course, roads and tracks, liable to the same interruptions and obstacles as were those to the north, ran to the advancing columns, but the lines of communication were far less insecure than they had been before.

During August additional mechanical transport arrived, including a number of light Ford vans. Some 90 of these, dubbed by a wag the " Jigger Fleet ", were of enormous help along the Morogoro-Mgeta line. Here, however, too, was the usual snag, for the smaller carrying capacity of the light transport involved the provision of more personnel to drive them in numbers which would make up for the considerably greater lift of the heavier vehicles which they largely replaced.

(x) THE SITUATION TO BE DEALT WITH AT THE END OF DECEMBER.

The position of the different forces when General Smuts undertook his final advance was as follows. See map number twenty.

Those of the enemy were divided broadly into the troops under command of General von Lettow on the Lower Rufiji and those under Wahle and Kraut in the Mahenge Iringa area.

General Smuts' forces stood in the following positions.

The main force (its composition will be given later when its operations are described) under his own command on the Mgeta line.

Opposite him were Otto and 8 companies. Of these, 5 under his own command were based on Kiderengwa (see map number twenty) while he placed von Chappuis with the three remaining companies on his left to the west, covering the Beho-Beho Kissaki road. Between them they mustered some 1,000 rifles, 14 machine guns and a howitzer.

Van Deventer*, his force organised in three columns,
  Nussey, 1,450 rifles, 8 machine guns;
  Berrangé, 1,150 rifles, 8 machine guns;
  Taylor, 790 rifles, 8 machine guns;
was concentrated at Iringa and faced by Lincke, 500 rifles and 6 machine guns on the road to Muhanga.

Northey, his field force in two columns under Hawthorn and Murray, held Lupembe with the former and Njombe with the latter, while to the south Byron occupied Songea.

  Hawthorn: 1,000 rifles, 18 machine guns, 2 guns.
  Murray: 900 rifles, 14 machine guns.

In Northey's front lay Wahle's detachments; Kraut, Wintgens and Langenn, and Grawert before Byron at Songea.

Hoskins on the coast at Kilwa held the chain of posts inland already described, and in this quarter was Schulz' detachment with some minor additions—nine companies in all.

The German Commander-in-Chief was also in this district concerned to safeguard the Utete-Mohoro district which he describes as of " simply fabulous fertility ".

Here, as a consequence of the advance from the coast, he had found himself " obliged to proceed to a prolonged operation in the mountains of Kibata which offered but little prospect of leading to a decision ".

(xi) THE ADVANCE BEGINS.

The enemy, divided into two portions, was to be dealt with in such a manner as to keep them apart with a view to closing in on the main enemy forces on the Rufiji. After crossing the river it was the intention of General Smuts to swing eastwards towards Utete and with the co-operation of Hoskins from the south to confine the enemy force between them within a small

---

* His force was now as follows:—
  1st S.A. Mounted Brigade—now completely dismounted except for one troop—1,500 rifles.
  3rd S.A. Infantry Brigade, comprising 3 shrunken S.A. Infantry Battalions, 17th Infantry (Indian), and the 1/4th K.A.R.—2,000 rifles, approximately 3,500 rifles in all. 24 machine guns and 2 field guns.

area and then deal with it together. The main force would join hands with the detachment at Mssanga south of Maneromango which was to clear the country north of the Rufiji on its way south.

The general plan contemplated an advance by Northey and van Deventer at the same time as that of the main force and they were instructed to communicate direct with each other, repeating information to G.H.Q.

Their instructions were to press the enemy everywhere over the Ulanga and Ruhudje rivers.

The advance was planned to begin on December 24, but towards the end of the month heavy rain on all fronts made it doubtful whether any move would be possible so early.

On December 22 General Smuts left Morogoro for Dutumi where he established his headquarters.

Reports came in from all fronts of heavy rain, transport and supply difficulties and, their inevitable sequel, casualties from disease.

On December 23 General Northey reported his own arrival at Lupembe as his advanced G.H.Q., and van Deventer on the following day advanced to attack the enemy before him.

On the same day to the south Hawthorn and Murray moved on Mfrika, the enemy position opposite Lupembe.

Meanwhile, General Smuts' own advance was held up by rain until December 31, when his first movements began.

The forces on the Mgeta, reorganised as under, were now under the direct orders of the Commander-in-Chief:—

1st E.A. Brigade.
(Sheppard.)

25th Royal Fusiliers.
30th Punjabis.
130th Baluchis.
3rd Kashmir Rifles.
No. 3 Field Battery (4 guns).
No. 6 Field Battery (2 guns).
No. 7 Field Battery (less one section) (2 guns).
No. 13 Howitzer Battery (1 gun).
½ Double company, 61st Pioneers.
One section, E.A. Pioneers.
One section, Faridkot Sappers and Miners.

No. 1 Armoured Motor Battery.
One section, No. 5 Armoured Car Battery.
1,300 rifles, 9 guns, 14 machine guns.

Force Reserve.
(Beves.)

6th S.A. Infantry.
Cape Corps (less 350 rifles).
Kashmir Mountain Battery (4 guns).
½ Double Company, 61st Pioneers.
Faridkot Sappers and Miners.
1,400 rifles, 4 guns, 10 machine guns.

Duthumi Column.
(Cunliffe.)*

1st Nigerian Regiment.
4th Nigerian Regiment.
Cape Corps (350 rifles).
One section, Nigerian Battery.
1,250 rifles, 2 guns, 12 machine guns.

Kiburu Column.
(Lyall.)

2nd Kashmir Rifles.
2nd Nigerian Regiment.
One section, Nigerian Battery.
800 rifles, 2 guns, 7 machine guns.

G.H.Q. Reserve.

2nd Rhodesian Regiment.
African Scouts (local natives under Major
    Pretorius).
3rd Nigerian Regiment.
Detachment Cape Corps.
One section, No. 7 Field Battery (2 guns).
15th Heavy Battery (2 guns).
134th Howitzer Battery (4 guns).
One section, No. 5 Armoured Car Battery.
1,450 rifles, 8 guns, 8 machine guns.

The ensuing operations may be followed from map number twenty-one.

---

* The Nigerian Brigade, 4 battalions, 2,400 rifles, 16 machine guns under Brigadier-General Cunliffe and four 2.95" howitzers had arrived in time for the operations.

The various units were placed under their Column Commanders as from midnight on December 24-25 and then stood to await the cessation of the rain.

The lines of communication of General Smuts' force ran back along the east of the Uluguru mountains to Tulo, thence to the crossing at the Ruwu river and via Pugu to Morogoro and Mkesse station railhead.

By this time the Central Railway was in a condition to allow of the use of locomotives and ordinary rolling stock.

(xii) THE PLAN.

The plan for the local operations was as follows:—

The objective of the forces was the Kibambawe crossing over the Rufiji.

The first object of the movements was to endeavour to surround the enemy forces which had faced Sheppard on the Mgeta line, and to this end the following orders were given:—

Sheppard was instructed to concentrate at a bridge over the Mgeta, marked X on the map, and to detail a strong battalion— he selected the 130th Baluchis under Lieut.-Colonel Dyke—to march to the Wiransi road, on the afternoon of December 31, moving well behind the Dakawa position. Having reached the road, Dyke would leave a small post on it and move eastward on Kidergede and Kiderengwa on January 1, sending forward parties to obtain contact with Lyall.

The latter was ordered to march to Kiruru early on December 31 and halt there for the night of December 31-January 1. From Kiruru he was to move early on January 1 to a point on the Kiderengwa-Beho-Beho road in the vicinity of Chimbe which was indicated in his orders. Dropping suitable posts on the day he would, on arrival at the destination indicated, entrench and send forward parties to establish contact with Dyke.

He was to do his best to intercept the enemy and, if the latter were " enclosed ", would come under Sheppard's orders for operations towards Kiderengwa.

Sheppard, with his brigade, less the 130th Baluchis, was ordered to move against the Dakawa position at daybreak, 5.30 a.m., on January 1, with a view to the envelopment of the enemy force in the position. Generally, the enemy was to be forced to the east. A company was to be sent to Wiransi to mask or occupy it on January 1 and, if the occupation were effected, to press on to Beho-Beho hospital camp (Beho-Beho Chogowali) and occupy it on the 2nd or 3rd.

General Sheppard himself was ordered to assume command of all forces south of Kiderengwa should the enemy be cut off there and to press in from all sides.

To General Beves was assigned a special mission.

Moving from Kissaki with the Force Reserve he was to reach Kirengwe on December 31. From this point Pretorius, with 25 Askaris, was to be sent towards the Rufiji and procure information.

On the morning of January 1, Beves was to send his engineers and pioneers forward to put the road in order for light transport and was, with the rest of his force, to follow the same route, dropping adequate posts on the line of his advance.

He was ordered to arrange, if possible, that one double company with engineers should reach the Rufiji below its junction with the Ruaha, cross in Berthon boats and establish a position on the south bank.

The whole of his leading battalion would then cross the Rufiji, and Pretorius, with his intelligence scouts, would investigate the country eastwards towards Kibambawe and Luhombero.

On the following day, 5th, Beves was to send all his force over the Rufiji, leaving a double company to hold the crossing.

He was then to hold his hand and was advised that his further movements would depend upon the devolpment of the general situation and upon such information as he himself might send to the Commander-in-Chief after he should have effected the crossing.

The extreme importance of early information was emphasised and he was ordered to keep a sharp look out towards Beho-Beho and Kidatu on the Ruaha (see map number twenty-one) near which place the presence of an enemy detachment had been verified.

Cunliffe from Dutumi, supported by artillery, was to demonstrate against the front of the enemy position with a view to drawing attention from the other movements.

(xiii) THE COLUMNS MOVE FORWARD.

In pursuance of these orders the initial movements were carried out.

Lyall reached Kiruru on December 31 at 2 p.m. unopposed, bridged the river and sent over the Kashmirs to occupy the further bank.

Dyke (130th Baluchis) crossed the Mgeta on the same day and made some distance in the direction of Wiransi by dark.

Beves reached Kirengwe on the same day.

On January 1 the operations began.

Cunliffe, whose command had been allotted to the holding attack, as, in its march to the scene, the Nigerian Brigade had outstripped its transport, had secured all the enemy trenches to the north of the Mgeta river by noon.

A heavy artillery bombardment had induced the enemy to retire.

Later, 5 p.m., the 4th Nigerians secured a position over the river, and the force remained in position for the night.

Sheppard crossed the Mgeta close to Kissaki in the early morning of the 1st and moved against the enemy left flank and reached the Wiransi road after slight opposition. Hearing of Lyall's engagement near Chimbe, Sheppard decided to move on Beho-Beho Chogowali and marched in the night of January 1-2 towards Wiransi.

Meanwhile Lyall had moved on from Kiruru in a generally south-westerly direction striking the Kiderengwa–Beho-Beho road in the afternoon of the 1st near Chimbe where small enemy parties were observed moving to the south. Placing himself astride the road facing to the north, Lyall awaited any enemy detachments which might follow this route to the south.

(xiv) LYALL ENGAGED.

Shortly afterwards was encountered a strong enemy detachment retiring southwards, and an engagement ensued—the Nigerians skilfully capturing a 4.2″ howitzer by utilising the cover of the bush—and the enemy (Otto with his detachment) was repulsed. After an abortive attempt at counter-attack, Otto retired to the east and rear of Lyall's position and contact was lost. Lyall remained in his position for the night of January 1-2.

253

During this night Sheppard was on the march to Wiransi, as related, in an endeavour to head off Otto.

He reached Wiransi in the early morning of January 2 and there met a double company of the 130th Baluchis detached by Dyke on December 31 to Wiransi.

(xv) DYKE ENGAGED.

This movement was in execution of an intention by Dyke to deny the Wiransi road to the enemy by blocking it to the north of Wiransi, while Major Moore with the double company should seize the latter place.

Dyke, with the remainder of his battalion, on January 1 reached the Dakawa-Wiransi road and moved up it in a north-westerly direction to the rear of the original position of the enemy on the Mgeta.

On his march he came against a strong enemy detachment (von Chappuis' with three companies) retiring from the left of the German Mgeta position.

A severe engagement ensued, the Baluchis, outnumbered, putting up a fine fight in the course of which they sustained a loss of 36 killed and 29 wounded. Many of the casualties occurred in hand to hand bayonet fighting. The enemy, hearing the sound of Sheppard's firing approaching nearer, withdrew at midday and Dyke established contact with Sheppard a little to the north.

On the evening of January 1 Beves was 3 miles south of Hobola on the way to the Rufiji, having met with no opposition, Sheppard was moving on Wiransi, Cunliffe with 1,200 yards south of the Mgeta, Lyall was at Chimbe astride the Dutumi–Beho-Beho road and Moore was at Wiransi.

Casualties, except in the case of the 130th Baluchis, had been slight and the enemy had retired and was temporarily out of touch.

(xvi) FURTHER MOVEMENTS.

On January 2 both Sheppard and Lyall reported the retire-ment of the enemy to east of Wiransi.

Sheppard was ordered to move so as to reach a ridge south of the Chogowali river west of the Wiransi–Beho-Beho road by daybreak on the following morning (3rd) and thence to send scouts along the Kipalala mountains to overlook the road between Kibambawe and Beho-Beho. Lyall was instructed to reach Beho-Beho-Kwa-Mahinda by the evening of the 2nd and there await orders.

Cunliffe was ordered to withdraw to Dutumi after establishing touch with Lyall at Chimbe, and remained at Dutumi for the rest of the operations.

In view of the retirement of the enemy to Beho-Beho the necessity for speed was urged upon Beves.

At midday a report of an enemy company on the road between Kiderengwa and Chimbe was received.

Accordingly Lyall was ordered to turn north from Chimbe and with 500 rifles, Nigerians sent from Cunliffe, to endeavour to surround the reported enemy party.

The latter proved to be a party of irregular intelligence scouts who had been mistaken for German troops and been fired upon by such British troops as came in contact with them and eventually reported them as the enemy.

This involved delay for Lyall who was then ordered to reach Beho-Beho-Kwa-Mahinda early on the 3rd.

The position on the evening of January 2 was as follows:—
Lyall moving on Beho-Beho-Kwa-Mahinda, Sheppard advancing on Beho-Beho-Chogowali. Beves was at Mhumbi and still without opposition.

(xvii) BEVES REACHES THE RUFIJI.

On the following day, January 3, Beves' advance party reached the Rufiji after an unusually arduous march of 28 hours over dry and roadless country. Beves seized both banks and began the crossing of his force.

During this day Sheppard, who was between Fuga mountain and the Wiransi–Beho-Beho road, the night before, made little progress through thick difficult country.

(xviii) LYALL, DYKE AND SHEPPARD ENGAGED.

At 4.30 p.m. Lyall became engaged with the enemy, close to Beho-Beho-Kwa-Mahinda, the junction of the Dakawa and Dutumi roads, who were " in strength and in a good position ".

He was joined after dark by Dyke who had marched to the sound of the firing.

On the night of the 3rd the positions of the forces were as follows:—

Lyall and Dyke at Beho-Beho-Kwa-Mahinda opposed by what, in view of an apparent intention to stand, might be assumed to be Otto's concentrated force, 8 companies. They planned to encircle the enemy position on the following morning.

Sheppard, to the north-east of Hatambulu mountain, moving from Beho-Beho-Chogowali to the main road below the junction.

Beves at the Rufiji. He had tapped the enemy wire according to instruction and from intercepted messages reported that the enemy had probably retired over the Rufiji leaving a small detachment as rear guard.

On January 4 Dyke, who had assumed command of Lyall's column and his own, reported the enemy as in position though probably in small numbers.

This bore out Beves' information and Dyke was ordered to push in and test the enemy before him and to try to join Sheppard with whom at 11.30 a.m. G.H.Q. had no communication.

Two and a half hours later Sheppard telegraphed from Beho-Beho-Kwa-Mahinda reporting that at 10.30 a.m. he had reached the main road and engaged an enemy company which had been severely handled and had retired through the bush.

His casualties had been slight but included the gallant Captain F. C. Selons who was killed by machine gun fire on stepping into the road leading his men.

This intrepid explorer, at an advanced age, had placed his ripe experience at the disposal of his country, not in an advisory capacity where his counsel would have been of the greatest value, but in a comparatively humble position as a fighting soldier. His example of determined courage and skill had been an inspiration to all with whom he had come in contact.

Except for this serious loss, Sheppard's casualties, less than a score, were light.

(xix) SHEPPARD REACHES THE RUFIJI.

Sheppard was ordered to march early on the following day to the close proximity of Kibambawe and to reconnoitre for a crossing place but to refrain from crossing except at night by moonlight.

On January 5 Sheppard reached the left bank of the Rufiji opposite Kibambawe and reported the enemy to be holding the south bank. He was ordered to cross the same night and, in reply to the order, stated his intention to endeavour to carry it out, but that the only possible crossing was 400 yards wide.

Early next day, 6th, he reported that he had a double company and two machine guns in a good position on the south bank covered by his guns. This had been effected without the enemy having become aware of the step..

Beves was now instructed to move 400 rifles to assist Sheppard's detachment across the river and in reply reported an enemy company two miles east of Mkalinso ahead of him, and indicated a reported intention by Otto to concentrate against, and attack, him.

On January 7 Beves occupied the enemy position near Mkalinso without incident, and on the same day Sheppard's increased detachment began to experience a stiffening resistance by a force which he estimated at 4 companies with one gun. The presence of Sheppard's troops on the south bank had been realised by the enemy for the first time.

Heavy fighting in thick high grass took place and Sheppard's troops retained their position at the cost of about 100 casualties.

(xx) THE SUPPLY SITUATION AND ITS CONSEQUENCES.

On January 8 General Smuts visited Beves at the Rufiji and returned early on the following morning, travelling all night by moonlight, to receive a report from his Administrative Staff.

It was not such as to encourage any hope of further immediate successful movement.

The report made after a most careful review of the position stated that the maintenance of three brigades on the Rufiji with the transport available for the purpose was impossible.

After January 20, unless a large reinforcement of drivers and Ford cars could be guaranteed, rations would begin to go down and by the end of the month the forces would be on half rations. This would come about sooner, if rain, of which there was a great probability, should fall and stop all traffic.

Among many causes contributory to this state of affairs was " rapidly increasing sickness amongst the drivers and insufficient reserves to meet the ' men ' wastage ".

The A.Q.M.G. wrote: "I honestly cannot see how we are going to feed the troops" and urged that all the forces that could be spared should be sent back to the railway.

Once more, for the last time, General Smuts, after successfully planned and well executed operations, was compelled to stay his hand in the middle of their execution and had to be content with a partial success.

The Commander-in-Chief accordingly arranged on January 10 for the return to the Central Railway of a considerable portion of Sheppard's and Beves' forces—incidentally too Major-General von Deventer and all South Africans with him were all ordered back to the Union on the score of health—and the hope of achieving, before the rainy season, anything more substantial than what had already been done, was abandoned.

(xxi) GENERAL SMUTS LEAVES FOR EUROPE. THE ACHIEVEMENTS DURING HIS COMMAND.

At this point the narrative ends.

General Smuts, called to the Councils of the Empire, responded to a request—the idea had been in contemplation for some months—that he should represent the Union of South Africa at the Imperial Conference to be held in London, and was formally ordered on January 8 to hand over his command as soon as possible to Major-General A. R. Hoskins the Commander of the 1st Division.

This exchange was effected on January 16 and General Smuts sailed from Dar-es-Salaam on January 20, 1917.

It was then barely 11 months earlier that he had landed at Mombasa to find the British forces in their own territory, though prepared to advance, and the enemy on British soil near Taveta.

In the period of his command the enemy had first been ejected from British territory, driven to the Central Railway, hustled out of the Uluguru mountains, thrust across the Rufiji and pushed into a tract of country representing about a quarter of the area of the German Protectorate. All the important towns, the whole of the railways and all the seaboard with its ports were held and held *permanently*.

It is in no forgetfulness of the immense difficulties left to be faced by his successors, and perhaps even less in lack of recognition of the magnificent work still to be done by the troops that the view is expressed, as was stated in the preface, that the third clear-cut phase of the whole campaign, that of war of a guerilla nature, began after General Smuts' departure.

With no special strategic objectives to protect, the elusive enemy became free to wander as he would, and the smaller his strength became, the more nearly did the work of finding him and bringing him to account resemble the proverbial task in a bundle of hay.

The Secretary of State for War telegraphed his congratulations " on the ability and uniform success with which you have conducted the campaign in the face of great natural difficulties ".

No general ever attained any military success in war without the loyalty, courage and self sacrifice of his soldiers, though soldiers have from time to time won battles in spite of their generals.

What of the gallant men who from every quarter of the Empire came to serve under General Smuts in East Africa?

There is a temptation, with the knowledge of what these men suffered and achieved, to use extravagant language.

If, however, the story that has been told in these pages has been set out clearly enough it may stand as their tribute.

In the words of their Commander: " eulogy seems unnecessary and misplaced. The plain tale of their achievements bears the most convincing testimony to the spirit, determination and prodigious efforts of all ranks. Their work has been done under tropical conditions which not only produce bodily weakness and unfitness but which create mental languor and finally appal the stoutest hearts. To march day by day and week by week through the African jungle or high grass in which danger lurks near but seldom becomes visible, even when experienced, supplies a test to human nature often in the long run beyond the limits of human endurance ".

In such conditions the South African soldiers who fought for General Smuts in the centre of the African continent showed a spirit worthy of their hardy forbears, the Settlers and the Voortrekkers, and added many stirring pages to the history of their nation.

CHAPTER XV

(i) NATURE OF THE LESSONS OF THE CAMPAIGN.

THE lessons of a war or campaign may be divided into those which lend added emphasis to former lessons and those which, in consequence of the employment of new appliances or the experience of unfamiliar conditions, suggest a change or modification of methods before considered as effective.

In other words—

> (a) those which affect or reaffirm basic principles, and
> (b) those which indicate the need for special arrangements in detail.

The lessons afforded by General Smuts' campaign in German East Africa may be conveniently classified as follows:—

Under (a)—

> The need for preparation in war.
> The difficulty of strategic surprise.
> The strength of a defensive-offensive system of tactics in bush country.

And under (b)—

> Administrative lessons.
> Tactical lessons.

(ii) THE NEED FOR PREPARATION IN WAR.

There is no more important direction in which preparation for war is essential than in collecting and keeping up to date all information which can be acquired as to the topography, climate and generally characteristic features of all possible theatres of war in which the military forces of a state may be called upon to fight.

Allowing that when hostilities became a reality to be faced in East Africa in 1914, heavy commitments elsewhere made the provision of everything needed for a campaign in that country a matter of extreme difficulty, if not, for a time at any rate, even of impossibility, there is no apparent reason to suppose that the British Government had ever realised what would be entailed by the prosecution of a campaign in such country, or that adequate efforts had been made to find out.

The figures quoted at the end of the preface bear out this contention, for though the strength of 111,731 is the ration and not the fighting strength, the latter at the end of the campaign was very largely in excess of what had been considered to be enough to subdue the German forces, when they were *ten times as numerous* as they were when General von Lettow surrendered.

A proper estimate of what would be required for active military operations in East Africa with its dense bush, unfordable rivers, swamps and huge mountains would have saved many lives, the health of tens of hundreds of soldiers, large sums of money expended on hasty extemporisation and much useless material, and would almost certainly have shortened the duration of the operations.

Though the names of military commanders are long remembered in the light of their success or failure in war, it is not soldiers but Governments that are primarily responsible for lack of preparation for that ordeal.

A nation, however, relieved to come to the end of an exhausting struggle, takes little heed of the extent to which the vast sums of money which have gone to the conduct of a war may be swollen by expenditure directly due to omission to prepare in time of peace, and only comparatively few of those concerned in the waging of war realise the enormous waste of money which unreadiness causes.

War is inherently a wasteful business, and, with the acceptance of that aphorism, goes that of what is practically unlimited expenditure.

To-day the army of a nation is no longer an army of professional soldiers paid to fit themselves for war, but includes the whole manhood of its civil population which may be fit for military service. A country thus has a personal interest in its soldiers which was wanting before.

A people which neglects to prepare to the full measure of its capacity for the defence of its possessions before actual defence may become necessary must be prepared to take a serious risk of being beaten.

To-day, Great Britain, with a long record of the evils of unpreparedness behind her, is taking steps to defend herself before the need for action in that direction may arise. At the back of her preparations must bulk largely the two last considerations given above and they are certainly potent influences in the nation's acceptance of the heavy financial burden which will have to be shouldered in consequence of the present measures.

The army of South Africa is composed *entirely* of her male civil population of military age.

Her permanent force, in respect of numbers, is negligible, and her citizen forces trained in peace will have to be very largely increased to deal with any situation (which is not of a minor character) which may call for active military measures.

The principle of universal military service in defence of their country is traditional with South Africans.

But—apart from all military considerations—men who are taken from the civil occupation which gives them their livelihood and the means of keeping and providing for those dependent upon them have a clear right to expect that a Government in support of whose policy they may be called to arms shall omit no single precaution which it can take to enable them to render their military service as efficiently as possible, and that what *can* be done in the way of preparation to reduce the risk and discomfort of that service *shall* be done.

It may be well here to emphasise that any suggestions or comments which the author may offer are propounded solely with the *defence* of the Union in mind.

That South Africa will embark upon a war of aggression or expansion alone, or in conjunction with those with whom she is at present in alliance, is improbable enough to be dismissed from calculation.

Defence of her independence and territory, however, is a very different matter.

It is most unlikely that, should the Union become involved in war, and such a possibility must be taken into account, the military advisers of a South African Government would find themselves in a position to recommend that any of its soldiers who could be held to military service should leave the continent of Africa for any other theatre of operations.

If the scene of hostilities be confined to Africa the correctness of this view is self-evident.

In hostilities over a broader field, which would connote a struggle of, or approaching, world dimensions, such strength as South Africa could spare would exercise no practical influence whatever, though the same strength might at any time turn the scale on the African continent.

The Cape of Good Hope, always of strategic importance, may, in a variety of possible situations, at any time become a vital link in the chain of communications, and the protection of her own seaboard and territory may well prove to be a task which will call for the employment, to the limit of her capacity, of her military forces and to be the greatest service which it is in her power to render to her associates in the British Commonwealth of Nations.

There is another important consideration.

South Africa, by virtue of her geographical position, nationhood and wealth, has become the chief political factor south of the Equator.

This implies prestige and responsibility, and both these conditions compel the Union to be prepared to bring its full influence to bear upon any question affecting the territory in the area referred to.

Military situations cannot be excluded, and thus the continent of Africa south of the Equator and any possible theatres of war which lie within that country must be the object of attention by the Union General Staff. And this, be it emphasised again, *for the security of the Union.*

One of the theatres mentioned above is that with which this volume deals.

Some of the grave consequences of embarking upon a campaign without preparing for it have become clear in the foregoing pages, and the first and most important lesson of the campaign in German East Africa is that preparation for war is the surest guarantee of waging it successfully, and the lesson is ages old.

Generally, in view of the position of South Africa, such preparation might well include:—

1. An understanding with local British Colonies for mutual defence.
2. An arrangement for co-operation with a view to supplementing each other's deficiencies and avoiding overlapping.

3. Reconnaissance by means of civil surveys of all country of which a knowledge is decided to be desirable for military purposes, and the provision of maps. Much good may be done if those charged with civil surveys are made aware of what is needed by the military authorities.
4. Exchange of information as to climate, roads, diseases and resources; as to hospitals, transport and food supply.
5. As regards communications, in any plans of road making for ordinary purposes a consideration of probable military requirements might prove of much benefit later.
6. Free and regular interchange of views and information with a view to making military co-operation for defence as effective as possible.

In the pages which follow some more definite indication will be given of the direction which preparation might take in the light of the experiences of the campaign.

(iii) THE DIFFICULTY OF STRATEGIC SURPRISE.

" A commander who succeeds in surprising his opponent gains a moral superiority which gives him an initial advantage in his operations and helps considerably to counter-balance any superior resources the enemy may possess."

Field Service Regulations, 1929; Vol. II, page 59.

A military commander in war is constantly at pains to take his opponent by surprise and to protect himself from any similar enterprise.

To refrain from the obvious as a rule, and to endeavour to attack or advance from a quarter least likely to be suspected is the first aim of the attacker, who must carry out his plan by rapid movement and without any check which has not been foreseen and taken into calculation.

It was just this essential rapid movement without interruption which proved to be so consistently difficult, indeed almost impossible, in the campaign of 1916.

The move on Kondoa Irangi, it would now seem, was a surprise, for General von Lettow appears for some time to have regarded it as impossible, and accordingly took a chance and left the provision of an adequate force for the protection of the place until too late; and the action of the Lukigura barely missed complete success.

The movement round and through the Uluguru which had most substantial results in a very short space of time was not a surprise, though its rapidity enabled General Smuts to take full advantage of a temporary decline in the *moral* of the forces opposed to him.

All other efforts to surprise the enemy failed, and that any attempts achieved such measure of success as attended them was due to the persistent resolution of the troops in the face of immense difficulties.

The main factors which prevented success were:—

    (1) The impossibility of relying upon supplies reaching the troops in sufficient quantity and in time to keep them fit to move.

    (2) As a consequence, the necessarily indeterminate pace at which any enveloping movements were carried out beyond a very short period.

    (3) As a further consequence, the impossibility of relying with any degree of confidence upon a sustained movement over any given period.

    (4) The knowledge of the country possessed by the defending and retiring enemy and the want of such knowledge experienced by the advancing forces.

    (5) The great strength of the tactical defence in such country as German East Africa, and,

    (6) Occasionally, at regular seasons, rain which was conclusive in its consequences when it operated.

Of the above factors (1) was due to inadequacy, and, in the earlier part of the operations at all events, often the unsuitability of transport, to the casualties among the administrative personnel concerned from disease, and to the abnormally rough and difficult nature of the terrain and the almost entire absence of roads fit for anything but porter transport. Breakage was in consequence constant and heavy.

These are difficulties which may be substantially reduced by attention to the teaching of experience and will be dealt with later.

(4) May be remedied by reconnaissance of all likely theatres of war which may be available for the purpose during peace. The co-operation already suggested would produce valuable results.

(5) The strength of the tactical defence will be dealt with later, but, in its relation to strategic surprise, it operated in the following manner.

In defence it was possible to allow an enemy turning movement, of which information was always received before it reached a dangerous stage in its development, to proceed for a long time without interference, for a small force in a selected position could hold up far stronger forces long enough to make its own withdrawal possible at its choice without inconvenience or loss.

As von Lettow says, it was always possible for " the enemy to execute flanking movements but their effectiveness was greatly reduced by the difficulty of the country ", and again " these outflanking tactics of the enemy in thick bush demanded great exertions and used up his strength " and " the short range of visibility always enabled us to avoid the danger or to attack the troops outflanking us in detail ".

In such conditions unless the attack itself was delivered as a surprise—for to surround an enemy force, unless the movements against it were rapidly executed and were possible within a short period of time, was impossible*—there was no chance of cornering such a mobile force as General von Lettow commanded.

(6) Rain put an end for all practical purposes to all movement of mechanical vehicles and animal drawn transport and to the movement of infantry except under conditions of great hardship and at a rate which put anything like surprise of an enemy quite beyond possibility.

Some movement, however, was undertaken by troops even in bad weather, but they were mounted troops, and here we may perhaps well consider the employment of such troops in tropical Africa. It is a question of much importance for the military forces of the Union and will repay investigation.

(iv) THE EMPLOYMENT OF MOUNTED TROOPS IN TROPICAL BUSH COUNTRY.

The value of a *national* military system is universally admitted. Such a system takes full advantage of any special

---

* Van Deventer's action at Lolkissale fulfilled these conditions. The capture of Hübner by Murray mentioned on page 234 was due to the immobility of the former caused by the slow progress of oxen drawn heavy artillery.

aptitude of a people for war, and in it strategy and tactics are determined with due regard to national characteristics and needs.

Up to the present the national military arm of South Africa has been the mounted rifleman, whether in the commandos or the mounted regiments of the country, and it behoves a writer whose experience of active service for the past half century has been in Africa to be careful to give no ground for suspicion of a sentimental preference for that arm.

But let the facts speak for the mounted rifleman.

As recently as 1915, in the Great War, the mounted troops of the Union captured German South-West Africa.

Merely as a physical feat it was remarkable; performed under the conditions of active service in difficult country it was an example of the ideal use of extreme mobility with striking result.

When it is said that mounted troops captured German South West Africa it is well remembered that the infantry in their support bore their full share in the campaign, and that one brigade performed a march of 200 miles within a period which the enemy regarded as impossible.

The achievements of the South African mounted troops in German East Africa were perhaps more remarkable than the record of their work given in these pages may have suggested.

Here again, with full recognition of the magnificent work of the infantry of all nationalities.

First, to take the movement on Kondoa Irangi, of which the capture of Lolkissale formed a brilliant feature.

The advance to Kondoa Irangi, nearly 200 miles from the main body, which resulted in the capture of that important place, was carried out by the 1st S.A. Mounted Brigade under the command of van Deventer—the rest of his Division, except his two South African batteries which accompanied him, came up later—and was effected in 18 days after his start from Aruscha. Of these, 4 days were occupied at Lolkissale, dealing with the enemy there.

Only 650 rifles of his brigade actually took Kondoa Irangi, the rest had fallen sick or lost their horses which died in numbers along the route, but the place was captured in an incredibly short time, for torrential rain fell throughout the movement, and the brigade was engaged with the enemy from day to day.

267

The importance of Kondoa Irangi—von Lettow describes it as " an extremely dangerous point " from which action was possible against his communications—has been made clear, as has the effect of its capture.

The point which it is desired to emphasise here is that mounted troops *alone* could have carried it out.

The infantry was strung out all along the 200 miles behind van Deventer, manfully, but slowly, toiling through mud, while, as far as mechanical transport was concerned, the position has already been described by Commander Whittall, see page 7, where he says a journey along the same route which would, under ordinary conditions, have taken " a day " occupied " five weeks ".

Then there was the movement through the Nguru mountains to Mhonda by the 2nd S.A. Mounted Brigade which compelled Kraut immediately to detach in some strength from his main force at Tulo. Enslin was held on reaching Mhonda by the defence and any hope of cutting off the enemy disappeared, but the detachment of enemy forces weakened the opposition to Sheppard who consequently reached the Wami, after passing through very difficult country, unopposed.

Here again, this movement in the time in which it was effected could only have been completed by mounted troops. The route followed by the Brigade was impossible for any kind of wheeled transport. The latter was all sent back.

Enslin reached Mhonda on August 7, and it was not until the 12th that the leading infantry on the same flank overtook him.

In the same month, on August 23, Enslin reached Mlali on the Central Railway having been detached from General Smuts' main force to aid van Deventer, held up at Kilossa, to clear up the situation in front of him.

At Mlali, by the occupation and retention of a suitable position, Enslin denied the road round the west of the Uluguru mountains to the enemy who was forced to retire by the rough tracks through the hills. It was for this purpose that the movement had been ordered and of course infantry could not have reached Mlali in time.

Mechanical transport in this instance might have done so, for the weather was fine, but there was no such transport available.

There is little doubt, too, that the rapidity of the movement tended to affect the *moral* of some of the enemy at this time.

The use of his mounted troops by van Deventer between Njangalo and Kilossa has already been referred to—see page 187.

The rapidity of the enemy retirement before van Deventer was due to the outflanking movements by the South African mounted troops in as formidable terrain as was to be found in this difficult country, and to these flanking movements must be attributed the relatively small loss to the infantry to whose lot fell the final advance against postitions of unusual strength.

Brigadier-General Nussey, who commanded the 1st S.A. Mounted Brigade, writes: " The wide turning movements caused the enemy to divide his forces and at no place was he strong enough to withstand our advance ". He adds: " It was the horse which kept the enemy's retirement on lines which we could always anticipate ".

One final instance of valuable work by the mounted troops.

On October 30, in view of the grave situation caused by the severance of Northey's communications, van Deventer was ordered to assume command of the Iringa area and to send to that quarter all available reinforcements. The state of the troops of the 2nd Division in consequence of sickness and exhaustion and the want of transport to keep them supplied prevented them from being sent forward, and the horse was used for the last time in the campaign to fill the gap.

On October 31 and November 4 Nussey marched from Morogoro with what was left of the personnel of the two S.A. Mounted Brigades and with 800 horses and 60 mules, " all in splendid condition ". " I arrived ", he writes: " with 32 horses and 6 mules and these were dead within a week ".

But 400 rifles had reached Iringa at a time when their presence was vitally needed there, and this could have been achieved by no other agency, and, as mounted riflemen fight on foot, the accession of strength was of full value.

Thus, even in a country where such toll is taken of animal life on active service, the mounted troops gave invaluable aid when no other troops could have done so, and it would seem that their employment under such conditions should be decided upon in each instance, after taking the cost into consideration, in the light of what they may achieve.

A single success may alter the whole aspect or even the result of a campaign, and it might be well worth while to use an efficient body of mounted troops on an isolated enterprise, provided the result may be expected to be commensurate with the cost. Even if in the execution of the task they lose their mobility.

Once on the scene of action, which he can reach at far greater speed, the mounted rifleman is the equal of the infantry-man.

There are other advantages besides the admittedly highly important one of mobility.

The horse, with good horsemastership and grazing, can do without supply trains to a considerable extent; its rider is far more self contained than a man on foot and can carry no inconsiderable amount of food for himself; and, again to quote General Nussey, it " enables men to forage far and wide ".

These are great advantages when the supply question is acute.

The communications of an enemy, especially of an enemy with modern equipment calling for aerodromes, repair shops and dumps of inflammable fuel, offer objectives for raids of a practical value.

Mobile horsemen could do much damage in such circum-stances.

On the general question of mounted troops, and apart from that of their employment in any special theatre, it would seem advisable to consider whether they should be retained in view of the general tendency to mechanisation, and in this connection the position of the Union as regards the supply of modern means of warfare must be taken into account.

Assuming that mechanisation is to be relied upon for providing any extra mobility beyond that possessed by infantry, and disregarding the fact that, as has been shown, in certain terrain and circumstances the use of motor vehicles is from time to time rendered impossible, can the vehicles and their accessories be readily supplied to all the units which are to take the place of the mounted rifleman and supply the essential mobility which he has hitherto provided? They will be needed not on mobilisation alone but in sufficient numbers for training in peace.

Assuming that they will be available in the quantity needed, will their replacement in war be possible?

Unless the answer to these questions can be given in the affirmative, the necessary mobility must be sacrificed if the mounted rifle arm be prematurely abandoned.

Mechanisation to the necessary extent to replace the horse will also be an extremely expensive undertaking.

Therefore, until South Africa can produce and maintain the equipment for an adequate number of mechanised units, *in peace and war*, any reduction of the mounted troops who have up to date served the country so well and established a fine tradition in the process would seem to be undesirable.

The commando is still the time honoured instrument of conveying the respect of a country community to a distinguished visitor, and, provided care be taken to maintain the spirit of the old mounted soldiers of South Africa, their successors may continue to serve their country until the time when a modern and compeletely efficient substitute shall replace them.

(v) THE STRENGTH OF THE TACTICAL DEFENCE.

The strength of the tactical defence in tropical bush country has been remarked upon from time to time in the foregoing pages.

Clausewitz says the defence aims at " keeping possession. But this keeping possession is no mere holding out, not passive endurance; its success depends upon a vigorous reaction. This reaction is the destruction of the attacking force ".

In other words the defence—and the posture implies a watchful attitude in consequence of the impossibility or inexpediency of purely aggressive tactics—should be so arranged that counter-attack may be made full use of. The counter-stroke has been described as " the soul of the defence ".

In German East Africa the country lent itself peculiarly to an obstinate defence.

As has been explained, surprise by any considerable attacking force was almost impossible.

An advance by an army requiring modern equipment and all that such equipment entails and an elaborate system of supply, must in such country be slow and liable to frequent interruption.

It is confined to one line which can only be changed after long further delay and much rearrangement, and a change would come to the knowledge of the defender long before any resumption of movement.

Both General Smuts and General van Deventer experienced the disadvantages mentioned above, as indeed did all commanders advancing.

In consequence, General von Lettow, well aware of the direction of his opponent's forward movements, was able to select suitable positions for resistance from which, after preparation, he could deliver effective *counter-attacks*, very often at will, with troops which were extremely mobile and *knew the ground* over which their attack was to be launched.

Their comparatively simple and light encumbrances in the way of supplies and transport (by porter) enabled them to retain a position (long after a more hampered force would have been compelled to extricate itself) and then retire, again aided by a knowledge of the previously arranged route they would take and the nature of the country, which would compel a pursuing force to move with caution.

Four considerable enemy detachments were captured by the British forces during the period of the war in East Africa.

Rothert at Lolkissale, Gravert at Likuyu, Hübner at Ilembule and Tafel on the Rovuma.

Rothert was practically in garrison at Lolkissale, and was in a situation—guarding the important road to Kondoa Irangi—where he was compelled to receive attack, and was unable to move without testing the strength of any movement against him, but even then, General von Lettow considered that the fact that Rothert was severely wounded was the cause of the surrender and evidently regarded a withdrawal, after van Deventer had attacked, as feasible.

He also is of opinion that Gravert exaggerated the difficulties of his supply situation and need not have surrendered, and points to the escape of a detachment in each case to support his view.

The action of Hübner is not criticised by his Commander-in-Chief, and here it was the loss of his *mobility* in consequence of being saddled with the protection of ox-drawn heavy artillery which was his undoing.

Nor is any stricture passed upon Tafel who was completely without supplies and therefore immobile.

Field Service Regulations lay down that " The defensive battle must be fought in advance of localities the retention of which is vital to the defender ".

The position of South Africa, if compelled to fight on Union territory for its protection, would be grave, and it must be accepted that her defence against any overland attack should be undertaken as far to the north of her boundaries as her military strength and resources and the situation may permit.

This will mean fighting in country presenting many of, if not all, the features which were met with in the campaign which has been described.

The Union troops will be on the defensive, but in circumstances which, if they are trained with the object in view, should enable them to deal very effectively with a large, and in many respects unwieldy, force presenting many vulnerable spots in a long drawn line of communications.

Broadly, their training should aim at mobility and flexibility with an organisation calculated to confer the maximum possible of these necessary conditions.

Training for the counter-attack is also essential.

The Republican Forces in 1899-1902 in the earlier days of the Anglo-Boer War lost chance after chance from failure to recognise the value and the opportunity for counter-attack.

Colenso and Stormberg were notable instances of this.

Had a counter-attack been delivered against Hart's Irish Brigade at Colenso when, after sustaining 400 casualties in 40 minutes, it retired from the loop of the Tugela, which, as a result of an error in the map, it had entered, few of the Brigade would have left it.

In point of fact General Botha *did* send an order to attack to the Commandants on that part of the field, but they replied— obviously with the view that defence need accomplish nothing but repulse of an enemy—that they had already beaten their opponents.

Again at Stormberg, when, after a little more than an hour's fighting, General Gatacre's force retired, demoralised and worn out for want of sleep, any attempt to head it off or do more than occupy successive ridges behind it would have turned a defeat into a spectacular disaster.

So that counter-attack should form a definite part in the training of South African troops, and, in order that it may be used to the greatest advantage, careful reconnaissance of likely theatres of war should be carried out wherever it may be possible.

A military commander who neglects the chances offered by counter-attack in defence in the bush, if the experiences of 1916 go for anything, sheds a valuable ally.

(vi) ADMINISTRATIVE LESSONS.

(a) Transport.

A steady and sufficient stream of supply is the life-blood of an army, and a shortage of supply means loss of strength.

To maintain the stream, transport of a type and in quantity suited to the purpose must be available.

Neither the right type in the first instance, nor, at any time, a sufficient quantity of transport was provided in German East Africa to the British forces in 1916.

It is quite obvious again that the question of transport for any considerable campaign in East Africa had received no attention before war broke out.

Even porter transport, the normal means of conveyance of stores in the African bush and available on the spot, had to be hurriedly organised *after* hostilities had begun.

It was sought to make up the deficiency in mechanical transport from the Union and all the motor vehicles which could be scraped together and repaired and reconditioned were sent up.

They included every kind of make and model, and the first consequence of this catholicity was that repairs were always extremely difficult and often impossible owing to the lack of spare parts, and this would have been avoided if some standardisation had been possible.

Scores of motor vehicles were abandoned because they could not be repaired in a country where appallingly bad tracks caused endless breakage.

That in such circumstances all the vehicles provided would be suitable for the work for which they were intended was too much to expect, and in the matter of type such information as had been procured was apparently most unreliable.

The following extract from Colonel Beadon's " History of Transport and Supply in the British Army " is here of interest. He writes: " On the advice of one who stated that pneumatic tyres were of little use owing to *the roads being covered with mimosa thorns** 30 cwt. lorries were provided . . . but these vehicles proved quite unsuitable after a month's experience in the country; in dry weather they quickly ground the surface of such tracks as existed into dust which rendered them impassable where constant traffic passed over them; in the rains they sank axle-deep ".

Late in 1916 light cars were provided in some quantity but their lift was of course comparatively small, 600-1,000 lb., and, to equal the load of a 30 cwt. lorry with one driver, five were required for the extra light cars, and again the question of personnel arose.

The gap between the abandonment of the heavy lorry and the advent of the light car was bridged largely by the use of oxen of which 28,000 died at the work.

Enough has been recorded to show that much care and investigation is necessary to determine the best type of mechanical transport for use in tropical Africa and it is here apt to quote Beadon again. He writes, giving reasons for the study of the campaign, " it demonstrates the bringing into use of mechanical transport on a large scale and under conditions which would appear ill suited to its capabilities ".

Mechanisation of the South African forces should therefore be undertaken with caution and only after careful estimation of its limitations as well as of its effectiveness.

Reference was made on page 238 to Colonel Murray's use of mechanical transport for the conveyance of troops rapidly to any point of danger, and the instances of such movements are of interest.

On November 11 Murray left Lupembe by car with a detachment to relieve the garrison at Malangali, 120 miles away. He reached the vicinity of Malangali the same evening. From Malangali he proceeded on the 13th to Njombe (80 miles) where he arrived the following day, and finally moved 50 miles on the 20th to meet Hübner.

---

* Brigadier-General Hazelton, Director of Supplies and Transport in the campaign, has stated with regard to this " information " that the purveyor of it assured his auditors that the thorns punctured pneumatic tyres every 100 yards. And the " information " was acted upon!

On each occasion the rapid movement produced most valuable result.

But 50 light cars—they were recently arrived mechanical transport for supplies used for the special occasions—could carry no more than 130 rifles and 4 machine guns. 500 such cars on this basis would be required for the conveyance of 1,200 men and would need 500 drivers.

Therefore, unless suitable vehicles, combining lightness with considerably greater carrying capacity can be provided, the use of mechanical transport for the quick transfer of troops in such country must be confined to small bodies.

There are two classes of transport which may be relied upon to keep pace with troops.

In the case of infantry, carrier, and in that of mounted troops, pack.

Carrier transport was resorted to largely on both sides.

In the case of the Germans, except for a few ox waggons, it would seem to have been the only transport which was made use of. It was an integral feature of their local military system and had been carefully organised in peace. To each company of 160 rifles were allotted 250 carriers trained to military service, and the latter were not only a potential reserve of Askaris, but were accustomed to military conditions and therefore not liable to panic, a most important point when a stampede of non-military porters was often the accompaniment of a sudden emergency in action.

Von Lettow refers to the hundreds of thousands of carriers who were employed by his force, and in the first half of the year 1917—when objections of the civil authorities to recruitment ceased—150,000 carriers were in the ranks of the British forces.

The employment of porters in large numbers will be necessary in military operations in tropical Africa for long to come, and the organisation, supervision, feeding and medical care of such numbers of raw natives represent a very big undertaking.

So long as the infantryman can move, however, the carrier can do the same

General von Lettow appears to have used several hundred pack donkeys in his hurried retreat to Kissaki but presumably this was to meet an emergency. Pack transport with General Smuts' force was confined to the wireless on occasion and to the mountain batteries.

Pack transport can keep pace with mounted troops if it is trained, and upon any occasion where mounted troops *can* be used its employment might be considered. Training is, however, essential.

(b) Supply.

Supply difficulties in East Africa were due solely to the impossibility of getting them forward to the troops and not to a lack of supplies reaching the country, and this was on account of the transport position, complicated often by the climate.

With this difficulty in mind one point suggests itself.

If it had been possible to issue a highly concentrated ration, light in weight and small in bulk, but sufficient to maintain bodily strength without other food and only to be used when the normal ration was unobtainable much physical discomfort and loss of health might perhaps have been avoided.

It is possible that expense or other considerations may prevent such a step from being carried out, but, if it is a practical suggestion, such an emergency ration would have been of the utmost benefit in East Africa.

(c) Medical Services.

" The medical history of the East African campaign has outstanding points of interest peculiar to itself. . . . actions for the most part consisted of wide turning movements entailing long marches and great physical fatigue. It became more and more a campaign against climate, geographical conditions and disease ".*

Deaths in the campaign were: battle casualties 3,443, non-battle casualties 6,558, a total number of say 10,000.

Of these 1,929 were South Africans.

The total ration strength of the British force in 1916 was 98,580, in December, 1916, the actual number of sick in hospital for one week was 10,700.

Malaria and dysentery were the principal diseases which affected the forces.

---

* Medical Services, General History, Vol. IV.

The abnormal sick rate is attributed in the Official Medical History to " failure on the part of the responsible military staff to recognise the importance of preventive measures against disease ".

Prevention meant the regular use of quinine and the use of mosquito nets. Admirable as both these precautions were, it may be well imagined that in the field under the conditions which have been described earlier, quinine was often not available. Mosquito nets went with the troops' clothing, torn to shreds in the bush, and, assuming their value to be as great as the medical authorities appear to think, were for weeks irreplaceable in consequence of the deficiency of transport and difficulty of supply. Men who are on quarter rations are not likely to be enthusiastic about the arrival of a consignment of mosquito nets.

Mosquito nets too are of small value when men have to move through swampy areas at night or do sentry duty there.

General von Lettow writes that he slept under a mosquito net on the ground and " had malaria ten times for in the field it is not always possible to employ preventive measures to the extent that is desirable from a hygienic point of view ".

The history states too that " orders were given to destroy mosquitoes ". It can hardly be supposed that this injunction was intended for troops in the field, for, if it were possible of execution in their circumstances, East Africa would be a far more salubrious locality than it is.

It is also recorded that a D.A.D.M.S., medically inspecting a division in the field, emphasised the need for " the selection of suitable camps, the value of incineration, the most suitable hours for marching and other elementary details important in preserving the health of troops in the field ".

These excellent measures are all desirable when they are possible, but in the field the site of a camp and the hour for marching are not seldom mainly settled by the enemy.

A more correctly estimated preventible cause of the heavy incidence of disease is indicated in the following observations: " rations and equipment were generally inadequate and there can be no doubt that men who are *underfed, exposed to hard fighting and unsuitably protected against weather conditions fall easy victims to disease* ".

278

Failure rightly to appreciate the full implications of such a campaign and neglect to prepare for it were the main causes of the heavy toll taken by disease.

The history continues: "There were not sufficient medical units* and when the medical staff became depleted young and inexperienced medical officers with little knowledge of tropical medicine or sanitation were sent out".

It has already been stated that the absence of a senior medical officer from advanced G.H.Q. in dealing with the responsible medical officers of formations was a handicap, and the official history comments upon the fact and notes that the D.M.S. "had his headquarters too far away, resulting in lack of association" with the combatant staff.

In August, 1917, the year following the period of General Smuts' command, Major-General Pike and Lieut.-Colonel Balfour were sent out by the War Office generally to report upon the medical situation, and drew attention to "the deficiency of the scientific and sanitary branches of the medical administration"† and stated that there had been "lack of initiative and driving power in the personnel of the medical staff".

It was shown that men of middle age were more immune from climatic diseases than younger men of 28 and less. Nevertheless, the climate of East Africa is not such that men whose physical energy has begun to decline in consequence of advancing years can be expected to show much bodily activity nor are they able in the circumstances which obtained in the campaign to do full justice to themselves.

Some were undoubtedly handicapped by their age, but, as a rule, all ranks of the medical services did their work, as did all other branches of the forces, occasionally under most dispiriting conditions, in a manner which redounded highly to their credit.

(d) Communications.

Communication—always essential for the proper combination of detachments in war—is extremely difficult in mountainous bush country where, as General Sheppard, whose name has often appeared in the foregoing pages, has written "a man separated from his fellows 20 yards away in the bush felt himself alone in Africa".

---

* Of these, many were without their full transport.
† Official Medical History.

Difficulty of inter-communication was one hindrance with which, after the early stages of the campaign, General von Lettow had to contend. If he had been able freely to communicate with Wahle during the latter's movement from the north-west, Northey's position, dangerous as it occasionally was, would have been more so. As it was, from July 27, when a detachment of the S.A. Motor Corps from van Deventer occupied Dodoma, until November 22 when Wahle joined Kraut in the Mnyera valley the former had no communication with German G.H.Q.

And if Tafel, who surrendered because he was without any supplies, had been in touch with Goering, a day's march away from him, he would have become aware that the latter had captured a well-stocked Portuguese camp, and had ample supplies for both of them.

The signal services under Lieut.-Col. H. C. Hawtrey were by him brought into order in January, 1916, from, to use his words " the chaotic condition in which they had grown up ".

This condition was of course general throughout the forces to begin with, and was due to the want of original appreciation and preparation which has so often been mentioned.

At this date, that of the assumption of command by General Smuts, 1,700 miles of telegraph lines were under military control along the lines of communication and 200 miles of field lines were in use.

The wireless sets available, stationary, waggon or pack, were " spark " and of " *little or no use in bush country* ".

The various nationalities represented in General Smuts' command and the happy-go-lucky entry into the campaign combined to produce a signal service " of men of different nationalities—of different training—speaking different languages, *with equipment of varying patterns thrown together without any co-ordinated training to carry out an important operation in unknown country* "—a state of affairs which added enormously to the inevitable difficulties imposed by the nature of the country and operations which entailed the movement of widely separated columns.

While General Smuts was moving on the east to the Central Railway and van Deventer to the west was moving on the same objective, a length of 600 miles was developed over which communication had to be maintained " with no prospect—in bush country and with spark wireless—of reducing the distance until the Central Railway should be reached ".

The main strategy was repeated in the case of detachments, and communication between columns and H.Q. had to be assured.

" Wireless being quite unreliable, visual signalling impossible, and despatch riders most vulnerable, there remained cable which had to be laid with each advancing column.

For this porters were necessary and time and time again the porters bolted when firing broke out—time and time again the cable was broken by troops in the column, by bush fires or disturbed game."

The lack of cross tracks through the bush and of accurate maps made it impossible generally to lay loop lines to reduce the length of cable which in almost every instance had to follow the route of the column.

Experience showed that it was wise to carry at least half as much cable as was estimated to be necessary. This sometimes " proved to be inadequate so inaccurate were the maps " and the native idea of distance.

As the cable had to be laid near the head of the column, and ahead of the column commander, the whole column passed along it during the march and it was found best to peg the cable down in the centre of the bush path in full view " until happily it might become buried in the dust and sand ".

A lineman moved behind the column to repair damage.

Efforts were made to lay the cables under the top soil by means of a kind of plough but as a rule the process was too slow.

The difficulties in connection with columns sent out enormous distances were far greater, for the work was hindered by the eternal transport situation.

Though visual signalling and wireless were occasionally helpful, one hand line at least was found to be needed for each force. Motor cyclist despatch riders who operated along each line of communications were efficient auxiliaries.

In giraffe country wires had to be raised to a height of 24 feet to be safe from destruction.

Natives, camp followers and sometimes troops, cut out pieces of cable to tie up loads or mend saddlery, while the wire used by signals was the object of attention by the local native for making into ornaments.

In consequence of transport difficulties one single wire was all that could be provided to link up posts along several hundred miles of lines of communication. The single wire was used as a telegraph circuit with telephones superimposed upon it to serve both purposes.

Language was a source of difficulty as well.

In one instance of complaint of inadequate facilities it was found that telephone orderlies only spoke their own language and were British, Afrikaners, Nigerian, Indian, Gold Coast and Swahili.

Colonel Hawtrey writes: " The use by us of abandoned German wires often of the ' barbed wire on bottles ' type proved in many cases of doubtful value owing to the misplaced zeal of our troops who, despite repeated orders to the contrary, would insist on tearing down and destroying the ' enemy communications '; men of one unit, newly arrived in the country, were found to be doing this three hundred miles behind our front line ".

The signal services were as liable to disease as any other. Taking good stations with bad the average proportion of signal inefficients in hospital was over 20 per cent., while in low lying country it varied from 40 per cent. to 80 per cent.

(e) The Lines of Communication.

These have been indicated from time to time, and ran by rail, road, track, mountain path, through heavy dust or seas of mud according to the season, and often through dense trackless bush. For many hundreds of miles the " roads " were made by the advancing forces and splendid work was done by the Engineers and Pioneers concerned.

It included the constant making and repairing of bridges which went by the board wholesale as soon as rain fell.

In other respects most of the problems which face an Inspector-General of Communications were present here, and, with the complications due to climate and disease, gave Brig.-General W. F. S. Edwards who held the appointment much hard and anxious work.

It may be well, however, to mention several important operations undertaken by the I.G.C. for a variety of objects. They were not included in the normal activities of an officer on the Lines of Communication.

Instances of these were the military operations in connection with *all* the coast towns in conjunction with the Navy; the measures taken against the enemy to counteract his interference with the lines of communication to the west of the Korogwe-Handeni road; and the occupation of Mssanga, the post south-west of Dar-es-Salaam between the Central Railway and the Rufiji.

To disengage any considerable number of forward troops committed to an enterprise and divert them to a distance was—as has been made clear—a very difficult, and, if it could be avoided, undesirable step.

Its march alone would probably mean that it would at once begin to shrink in numbers, for it would be a hurried movement, the provision of its transport would entail drawing out the necessary vehicles from a quarter where there were never enough of them, and it was hardly ever possible to contemplate with any degree of resignation the transfer of fighting troops from the advancing columns because of their constant and heavy diminution of strength as the advance went on.

All along the lines of communication were troops, some in posts, many on their way forward and others, such as engineers and pioneers at work on the railways and roads, and, as a rule, comparatively near the scene of trouble.

It was therefore found necessary, at the risk of adding to the burdens of an already harassed I.G.C., to place the conduct of such operations in his hands and let him find the troops and transport for the venture.

This General Edwards invariably did, and conducted all the operations with energy and skill to the great advantage of the general plan.

It was an unusual, but, in the circumstances, a most effective rôle of the I.G.C.

(vii) TACTICAL LESSONS.

Such comments as have suggested themselves in connection with tactical operations have been submitted in the course of the narrative, but it may be well to summarise some of the special lessons which appear to be deducible from this campaign and which may be usefully applied in training.

(a) Artillery.

In the thick bush and primeval forest which was the setting of almost every engagement in East Africa in 1916, observation of a target for, and the effect of, artillery fire was impossible.

Every additional arm which needed personnel, transport and food, and *did not fulfil an unmistakably effective rôle which was calculated definitely to aid the progress of operations* was merely an encumbrance and a source of anxiety.

Any weapon which could not be easily transported was of no use because it could not reach a scene of action in time.

Much of the heterogeneous collection of artillery which was in East Africa in 1916 failed to fulfil either condition of effective use or comparative mobility, and would have been far better left behind.

The transport which it needed would have been invaluable for general use.

The campaign was one of movement, and mobility and light weight were essential conditions for anything on wheels, if it was to be of use.

Some field artillery, light howitzers and mountain batteries in limited quantities were all that were needed.

Anything in the nature of heavy artillery was unsuitable and unnecessary.

Even in the six weeks at Msiha camp, when the enemy had an unrestricted power of observation from the Nguru mountains, the casualties caused by the Königsberg gun under the most favourable conditions exercised not the slightest effect upon the operations. The guns of the Königsberg, dragged about at infinite trouble, were all abandoned in due course, and did no harm to the British forces except at Msiha under conditions which were hardly ever possible in this country.

Mountain guns, with pack mules, are suitable for the terrain, and in 1915 a section of each of the Indian Mountain Batteries (27th and 28th) were furnished with carriers to take the place of mules in fly-country.

(b) Machine Guns.

These are admirably adapted for use in bush country.

Handed boldly and promptly as they were at first by picked German crews they may be used with great effect, and the same applies to any light automatic gun.

On the flanks of prepared positions where they were occasionally sited in rear of an attack with serious result to it, in counter-attack, and to deal with a retiring enemy they were consistently effective.

Their teams should be carefully picked for sound tactical sense, initiative and bodily fitness. The enemy Askaris were not good shots, but the machine guns, the value of which was fully appreciated by the Germans, were often deadly in the bush. They usually had a substantially greater number in action than the British forces.

(c) The Bayonet.

The Askari was not a good shot, but he was an extremely brave soldier and readily came to close quarters when he could, and hand to hand fighting was frequent. Any native has the advantage of an untrained European in such combat, and, if the conditions of 1916 are to be repeated, European troops should be well trained to the use of the bayonet.

(d) The need for close touch between the Command and the Troops.

It was essential that the Commander-in-Chief should be close up with the main fighting force; an attempt to conduct operations from a distance would have resulted in failure, and the same held good of all detachment and column commanders.

The great difficulty of keeping touch and control and the suddenness of events in the dense bush make the close presence of the commander advisable. He alone can decide upon the employment of reserves and their effective use may be a matter of minutes.

(e) The selection of suitable positions for halts for the night.

In the event of a halt for the night during any operations the latter should whenever possible be broken off early enough to allow deliberate choice of a position and reconnaissance of its vicinity. The extraordinary strength of the defence was enhanced by the fact that the ground was known to the enemy and his defensive positions were all carefully selected.

(f) A deployment means a risk of loss of control.

Every extension should be well watched. Touch and therefore control are easily lost in the bush, and it is necessary always to keep reserves.

(g) *Reserves.*

A reserve should be as strong as possible especially in attack, when an enterprising enemy can—and in German East Africa did on every possible occasion—launch a counter-attack with little warning. Such an enterprise can only be dealt with by the prompt use of reserves which, in view of the suddenness with which situations arise in bush fighting, should be under the hand of the commander.

(h) *Lateral communication.*

This is always a matter of great difficulty in thick bush, and was experienced on almost every occasion in action. Runners were used as early as Tanga for the purpose, and the suggestion made in Chapter VI that parties of selected natives under European supervision with pangas (native knives) should be allotted to formations for cutting paths may possess some value perhaps.

(i) *The Air Service.*

The work of the Air Force in East Africa involved the additional hazards imposed by the nature of the country which over by far the greater portion of its surface was covered with large mountainous areas, thick forest and bush, swamps, lakes and broad rivers—all impossible for a forced landing.

The hard work put in by the members of the force was not productive of results to satisfy them.

The bush—and it was in the bush that all the enemy encampments were in 1916—gave *complete* cover from view from the air, and observation and bomb action were quite ineffective.

The only positive information which was brought back was of towns, railways, roads and rivers and such features as could be detected, and, sometimes, confirmatory evidence of the movements and whereabouts of their own columns, though these were often hard to trace and were often better known from other sources.

Detection of the enemy and damage to his troops—the two most valuable features of assistance to the ground troops in such a country—were denied to the aviators.

In these circumstances, however, what it was possible to do was done and well done.

(vii) CONCLUSION.

The phase of the Great War that was fought out in German East Africa was essentially a war of attrition and it followed the course usual in such a contest.

As a rule this begins with the meeting of two forces on a more or less regular basis with several strategic objectives available.

While this condition obtains, operations follow a course which is the consequence of a definite training of each force for war.

This is succeeded by a second condition—usually styled guerilla warfare—when one army, still maintained on a regular basis, furnished with the means of war and preserving an orderly form, endeavours to subdue the weaker opponent who, deprived of such normal aids to fighting and compelled by force of circumstances, resorts to a "hit and run" policy, and seeks assistance from natural aids to resistance, adopting special tactics suitable to the country and his own circumstances to avoid defeat and prolong hostilities.

The first condition obtained in German East Africa until the time—early January, 1917—when General Smuts relinquished his command there.

The second ensued after his departure and the disappearance of any objective for the British forces save the enemy force in the field.

The use of the term "guerilla" in this instance is by no means indicative of the possibility of cessation of effort or of diminution in its scope, for at the beginning of 1917 some of the most severe fighting and most trying hardship was still to come. The term is used to denote the nature of the struggle.

German East Africa was peculiarly adapted for such a mode of defence by a weaker force, and General von Lettow took full advantage of the fact.

There seems to be little doubt now that such a campaign had been foreseen and prepared for by the Germans in East Africa.

It would appear that there is a two-fold moral to this tale.

First, and this is borne out by history over and over again, the army that can keep the field regularly supplied and in orderly shape will always *in the end* beat that which is compelled to resort to a guerilla form of fighting.

The Anglo-Boer War of 1899-1902 is a notable example of this truth which is of the greatest interest to any student of the military history of South Africa who must find himself constantly speculating as to what course that struggle would have taken in its early stages if the splendid fighting material of the Republican Armies had been directed by trained leaders with an expert professional staff.

General von Lettow was still in the field at the end of the war but his force had been reduced from 2,700 Europeans and 12,000 Askaris to 155 and 1,168 of each, respectively, and the end of this gallant remnant was in sight when the Armistice intervened.

Preparation and training—of which perhaps enough has already been said—are needed to maintain an army as such in war.

Second, and this may be no less important to the Union than the first part of the moral, a smaller army of good soldiers well led may, if aided by the conditions and features of a country with which they are familiar, resist a greatly superior force long enough to take advantage of a favourable issue at a decisive point elsewhere.

This, in the position of South Africa, one of several members of a powerful alliance, may, in circumstances which are by no means impossible, prove to be a form of resistance of the greatest value.

The Duke of Wellington at Brussels before Waterloo, discussing the chances of victory in a battle with Napoleon and seeing a British soldier staring at the statues in the park said: "There, it all depends upon that article whether we do the business or not. Give me enough of it and I am sure ".

The quality was sound, the quantity doubtful.

The soldier of South Africa has won an enviable reputation on many fields. His achievements in this hitherto little known campaign in the heart of the African Continent suffer no whit in comparison with the finest exploits of his countrymen elsewhere. The same resolution, fortitude and courage went to the establishment of their common fame.

The quality again is sound, the quantity small in view of possible situations which may have to be faced.

Leaders trained to higher command and staff officers able to give full effect to the plans of those leaders must be found if the soldiers of the Union are to fight to the greatest advantage possible.

In neither direction is training easy in a force which is without higher formations and where full regimental training—an indispensable condition of the proper training of a staff officer—is not available.

If in this book there is to be found anything which will help the successors of the fine soldiers who fought under General Smuts in 1916 to emulate their predecessors' example, the purpose of its author will have been served.

INDEX

INDEX

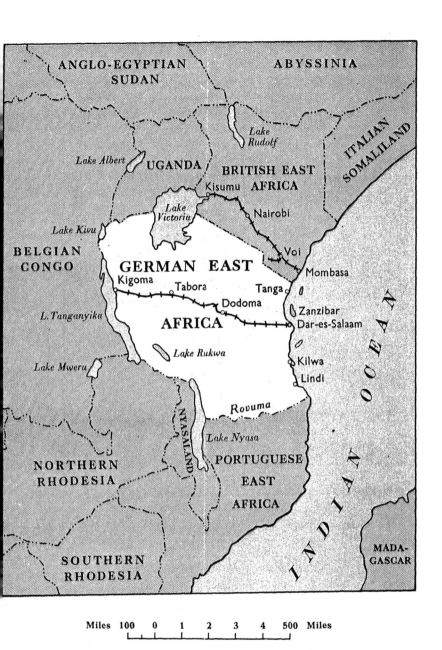

GERMAN EAST AFRICA IN 1914

SURROUNDED BY ENEMY TERRITORY

BRITISH, BELGIAN, AND PORTUGUESE.

$\boxed{1}$

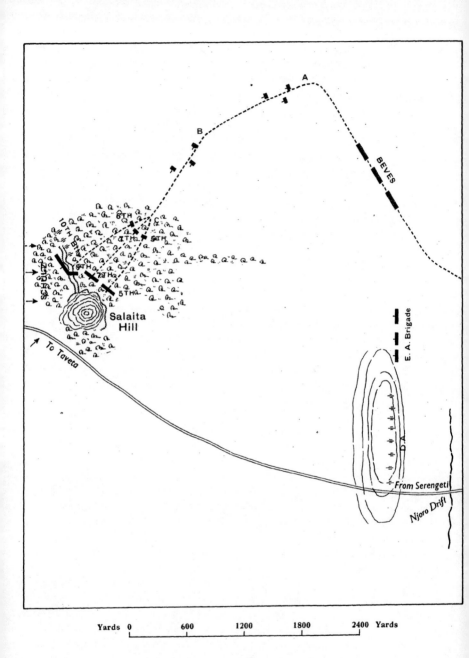

SALAITA HILL ACTION
12TH FEBRUARY, 1916.

Yards 0   600   1200   1800   2400 Yards

British..............■■■   German............■■■

2

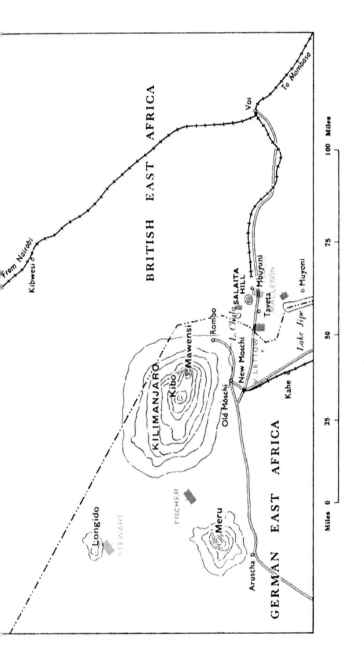

SKETCH MAP SHOWING

CONCENTRATION OF FORCES
JUST BEFORE KILIMANJARO OPERATIONS

Troops British ....
Troops German ....

3

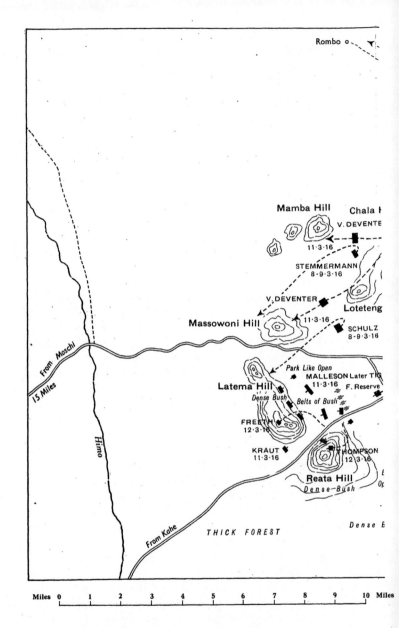

Rombo o

Mamba Hill   Chala H
                    V. DEVENTE
                    11·3·16

            STEMMERMANN
            8-9·3·16

    V. DEVENTER
                11·3·16   Loteteng

Massowoni Hill   SCHULZ
                            8-9·3·16

                Park Like Open
                MALLESON Later TIC
Latema Hill   11·3·16   F. Reserve
    Dense Bush   Belts of Bush

FREETH
12·3·16
        KRAUT   THOMPSON
        11·3·16   12·3·16

            Reata Hill
            Dense-Bush   Op

                            Dense B
From Moschi
15 Miles

Himo

From Kahe   THICK FOREST

| Miles | 0 | 1 | 2 | 3 | 4 | 5 | 6 | 7 | 8 | 9 | 10 Miles |

SKETCH MAP ILLUSTRATING

OPERATIONS EAST OF TAVETA

FROM MARCH 7 TO MARCH 11 CULMINATING IN ACTION AT LATEMA AND REATA MARCH 11-12 1916.

Troops British..............
Troops German............

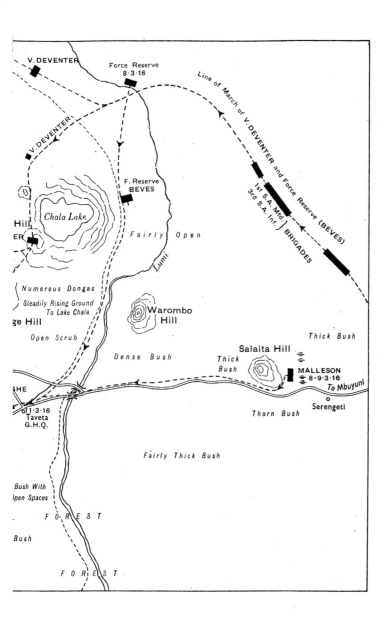

V. DEVENTER

Force Reserve
8·3·16

Line of March of V. DEVENTER and Force Reserve (BEVES)

V. DEVENTER

1st S.A. Mtd.
3rd S.A. Inf. } BRIGADES

F. Reserve
BEVES

Chala Lake

Hill
ER

Fairly Open

Lumi

Numerous Dongas
Steadily Rising Ground
To Lake Chala

ge Hill

Open Scrub

Warombo
Hill

Thick Bush

Salaita Hill

Dense Bush

Thick
Bush

MALLESON
8·9·3·16
To Mbuyuni

HE

Serengeti

6|1·3·16
Taveta
G.H.Q.

Thorn Bush

Fairly Thick Bush

Bush With
)pen Spaces

F O R E S T

Bush

F O R E S T

4

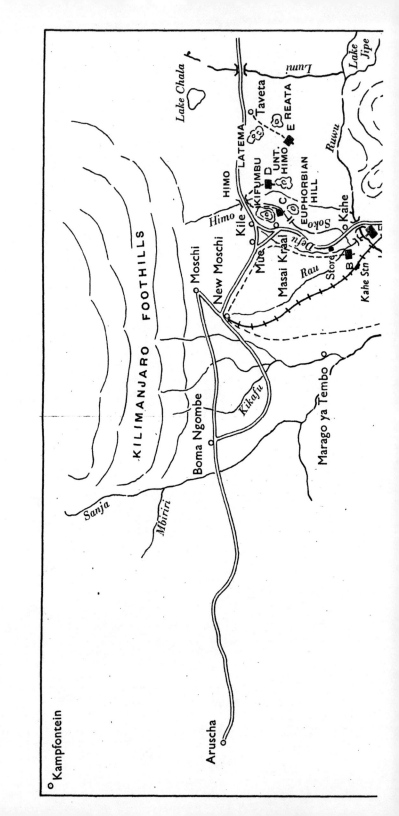

A. VAN DEVENTER
B. SHEPPARD
C. BERRANGE
D. BEVES
E. DET. from TAVETA
F. VON LETTOW

NORTH PARE

Kissangire

KAHE HILL

BAUMANN HILL

Pangani

Miles 0   5   10   15   20   25   30 Miles

SKETCH MAP TO ILLUSTRATE

OPERATIONS for the OCCUPATION of the
RUWU RIVER LINE after the ACTION of LATEMA - REATA

MARCH 11, 1916.

Troops British..........
Troops German..........

5

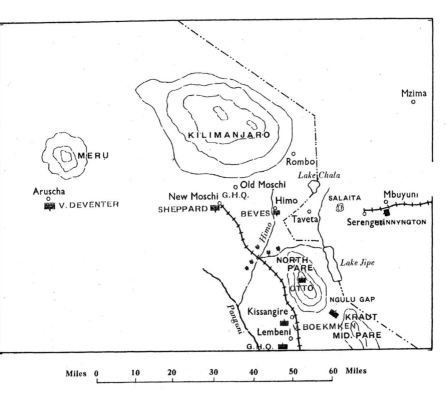

Mzima

KILIMANJARO

MERU

Aruscha
V. DEVENTER

Rombo
Lake Chala

Old Moschi
New Moschi G.H.Q.
SHEPPARD
BEVES
Himo
SALAITA
Mbuyuni
Serenge INNYNGTON
Taveta

Lake Jipe
NORTH
PARE
OTTO

Pangani
NGULU GAP
KRADT
Kissangire
V. BOEKMKEN
Lembeni
MID. PARE
G.H.Q.

Miles 0   10   20   30   40   50   60 Miles

SKETCH MAP TO ILLUSTRATE

QUARTERS TAKEN UP FOR RAINY SEASON
1916.

Troops British ....
Troops German ....

6

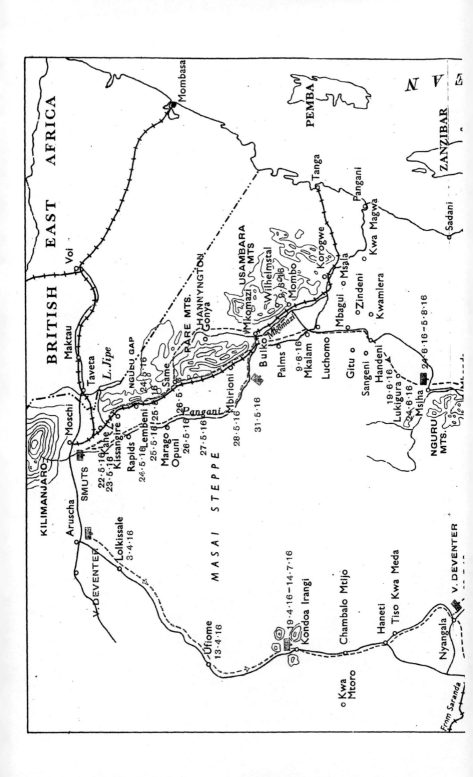

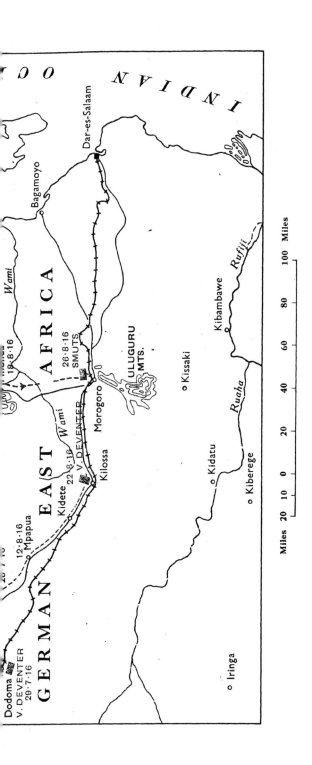

MAP ILLUSTRATING

ADVANCE OF GENERAL SMUTS AND GENERAL VAN DEVENTER

TO

CENTRAL RAILWAY VIA PANGANI RIVER AND KONDOA IRANGI RESPECTIVELY

7

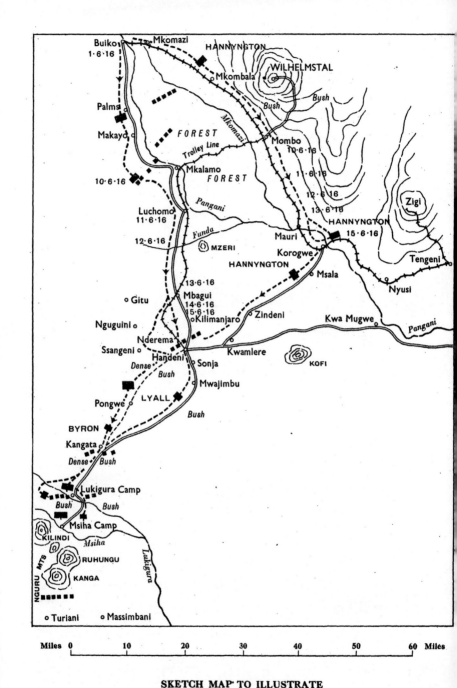

SKETCH MAP TO ILLUSTRATE

GENERAL SMUTS' ADVANCE from BUIKO to MSIHA CAMP

Gen. Smuts' Advance......◼◼◼

German Positions ....◼◼◼◼

8

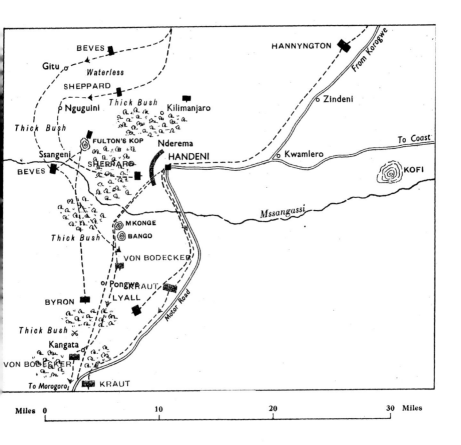

Miles 0   10   20   30   **Miles**

PLAN SHOWING

ADVANCE ON HANDENI AND MOVEMENT ON KANGATA

Troops British............ ■
Troops German......... ▧

9

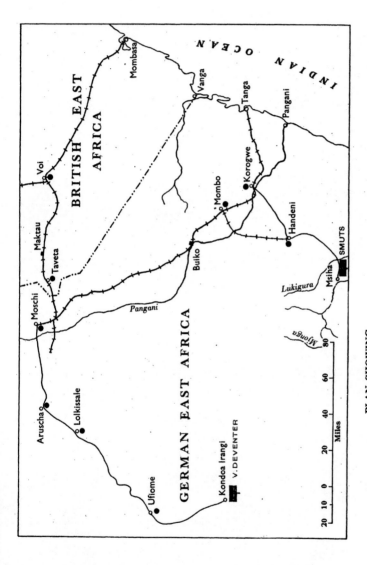

PLAN SHOWING
COMMUNICATIONS OF THE FORCES OF
GENERAL SMUTS AND GENERAL VAN DEVENTER
AT END OF JUNE 1916.

Rail ....
Road ....
Field Troops.....
L. of C.

10

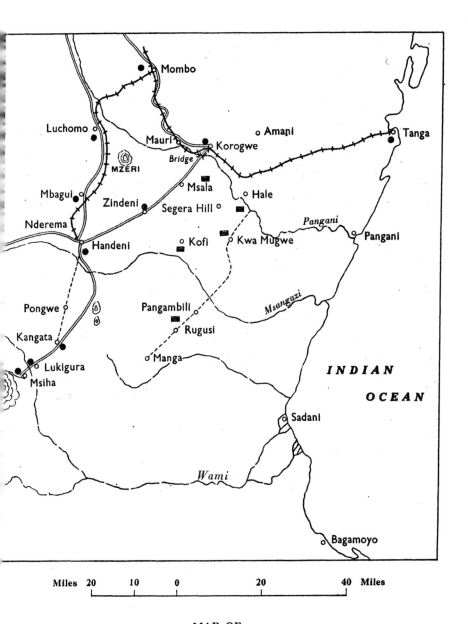

Mombo

Luchomo

Amani

Tanga

Mauri

Korogwe

MZERI

Bridge

Msala

Mbagui

Hale

Zindeni

Segera Hill

Pangani

Nderema

Kofi

Kwa Mugwe

Pangani

Handeni

Pongwe

Msangazi

Pangambili

Kangata

Rugusi

Lukigura

Manga

INDIAN

Msiha

OCEAN

Sadani

Wami

Bagamoyo

Miles 20   10   0   20   40 Miles

MAP OF

AREA FROM WHICH ENEMY OPERATED
AGAINST L. OF C. JULY 1916.

British Posts .... ●
German Detachments ...... ▰

11

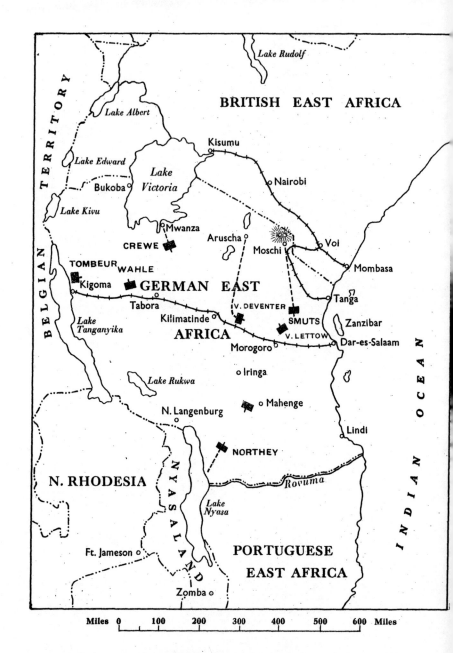

BRITISH EAST AFRICA

Lake Rudolf

TERRITORY

Lake Albert

Kisumu

Lake Edward

Lake Victoria

Bukoba

o Nairobi

Lake Kivu

Mwanza

Aruscha

Voi

CREWE

Moschi

BELGIAN

TOMBEUR

WAHLE

Mombasa

Kigoma

GERMAN EAST

Tabora

V. DEVENTER

Tanga

Lake Tanganyika

Kilimatinde

SMUTS

Zanzibar

AFRICA

V. LETTOW

Morogoro

Dar-es-Salaam

o Iringa

Lake Rukwa

o Mahenge

INDIAN OCEAN

N. Langenburg

Lindi

NORTHEY

N. RHODESIA

Rovuma

NYASALAND

Lake Nyasa

PORTUGUESE

Ft. Jameson

EAST AFRICA

Zomba o

Miles 0   100   200   300   400   500   600 Miles

MAP TO ILLUSTRATE

STRATEGIC SITUATION AT THE END OF JULY, 1916.

Forces British..........
   ,,   Belgian.........
   ,,   German........

12

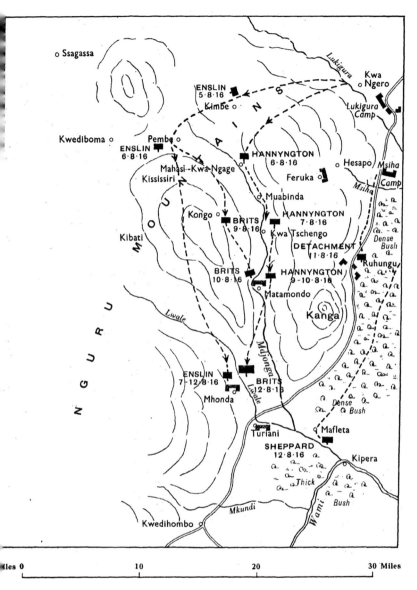

MAP TO ILLUSTRATE

GENERAL SMUTS' OPERATIONS
IN NGURU MOUNTAINS

Troops British........ ■
Troops German.,..... ■

Positions British........ ⌐
Positions German...... ⌐

13

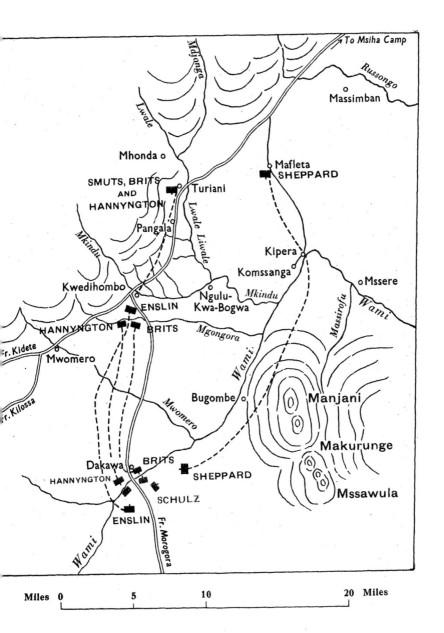

Miles 0   5   10   20   Miles

SKETCH MAP OF

GENERAL SMUTS' OPERATIONS BETWEEN
TURIANI AND THE WAMI RIVER

Forces British...........
Forces German.........

14

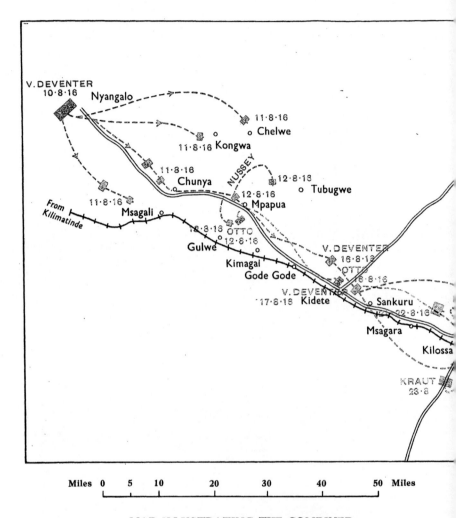

Miles 0   5   10   20   30   40   50 Miles

MAP ILLUSTRATING THE COMBINED

OPERATIONS OF GENERAL SMUTS
WITH GENERAL VAN DEVENTER
IN SECURING CENTRAL RAILWAY

Forces British...........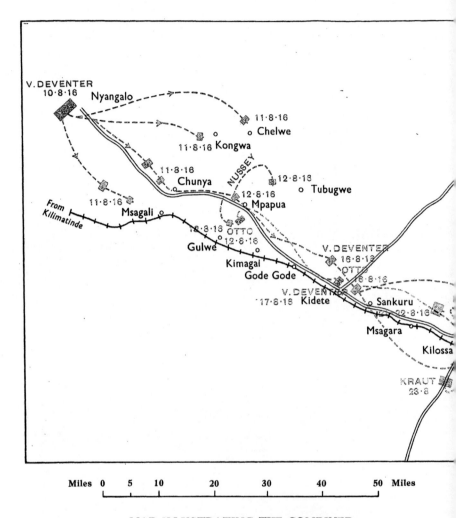
Forces German.........

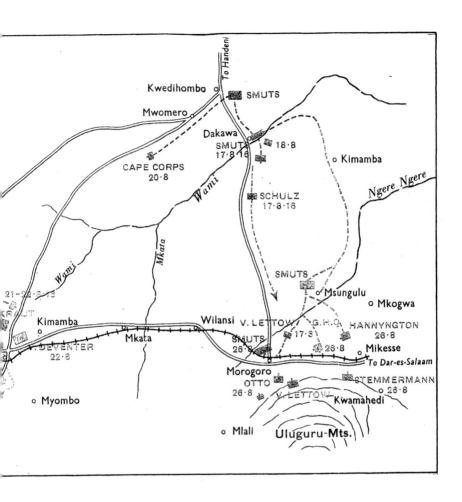

To Handeni

Kwedihombo
Mwomero
Dakawa
SMUTS
SMUTS 17·8·16
18·8
CAPE CORPS 20·8
Kimamba
Ngere Ngere
Wami
SCHULZ 17·8·16
Mkata
Wami
SMUTS
Msungulu
Mkogwa
21-22·8·16
KRAUT
Kimamba
Wilansi
V. LETTOW
G.H.Q.
HANNYNGTON 26·8
V. DEVENTER 22·8
Mkata
SMUTS 26·8
17·8
26·8
Mikesse
To Dar-es-Salaam
Morogoro
OTTO 26·8
V. LETTOW
STEMMERMANN 26·8
Kwamahedi
Myombo
Mlali
Uluguru-Mts.

15

ENEMY TERRITORY OCCUPIED
AT END OF MAY 1916.

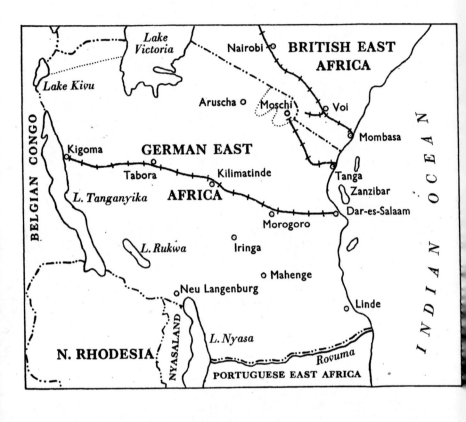

PLAN SHOWING

THE RESULTS OF THE OPERATIONS OF

GENERAL SMUTS DURING THREE MONTHS, JUNE, JULY AND AUGUST 1916.

Enemy Territory Occupied......
Allied Forces.........................

16

ENEMY TERRITORY OCCUPIED
AT END OF AUGUST 1916.

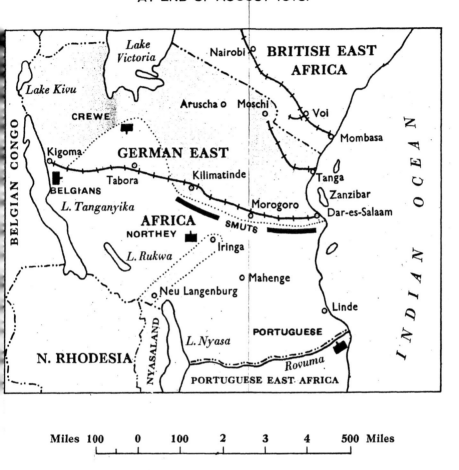

PLAN SHOWING
THE RESULTS OF THE OPERATIONS OF
GENERAL SMUTS DURING THREE MONTHS,
JUNE, JULY AND AUGUST 1916.

Enemy Territory Occupied......
Allied Forces......................... ▬   16

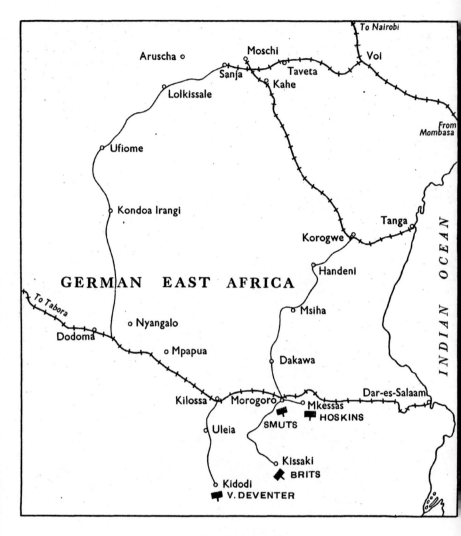

Miles 20 0 20 40 60 80 100 Miles

PLAN SHOWING

LINES OF COMMUNICATION OF
GENERAL SMUTS AND GENERAL VAN DEVENTER

IN EARLY SEPTEMBER 1916.

17

Rail ....+++++++   Road ...... ─────

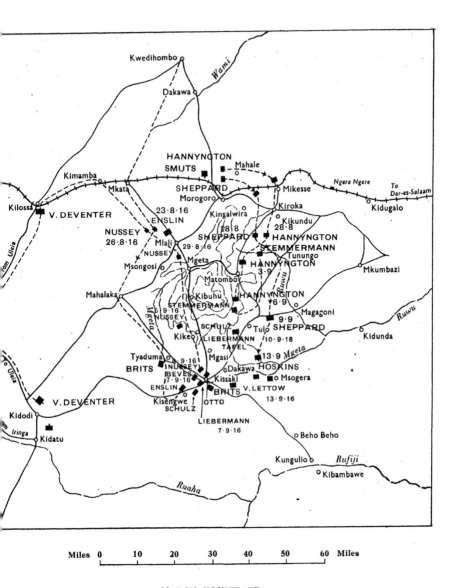

Kwedihombo ○

Wami

Dakawa ○

Kimamba ○   Mkata   HANNYNGTON
Kilossa ○   SMUTS   Mahale
           V. DEVENTER   SHEPPARD   Mikesse
                              Morogoro   Kiroka   Ngere Ngere   To
                              23·8·16   Kingalwira   Dar-es-Salaam
                  ENSLIN   Kikundu   Kidugalo
           NUSSEY   Mlali   28·8   28·8
           26·8·16   NUSSEY SHEPPARD   HANNYNGTON
                    Msongosi ○   Mgeta 29·8·16 STEMMERMANN
                                           HANNYNGTON   Tunungo
                                                  3·9   Mkumbazi ○
           Mahalaka ○   Matombo   HANNYNGTON
                              Kibuhu HANNYNGTON 6·9   Ruwu
                          STEMMERMANN
                          NUSSEY SCHULZ Tulo SHEPPARD Magagoni
                                      LIEBERMANN 9·9
                          Kikeo   TAFEL 10·9·16   Kidunda ○
                    Tyaduma ○ 9·16 Mgasi 13·9 Mgeta
                    BRITS NUSSEY Dakawa HOSKINS
                       BEVES 17·9·16 Kissaki Msogera ○
                       ENSLIN   BRITS V. LETTOW
           Kidodi   Kisengwe OTTO   13·9·16
                       SCHULZ
           Iringa Kidatu ○   LIEBERMANN
                              7·9·16   Beho Beho ○

                                    Kungulio ○   Rufiji
                                         Kibambawe ○

                    Ruaha

Miles 0   10   20   30   40   50   60 Miles

MAP TO ILLUSTRATE

GENERAL SMUTS' OPERATIONS SOUTH OF MOROGORO
FROM SEPTEMBER 1 TO SEPTEMBER 20 1916.

18

Forces British ....
Forces German ....

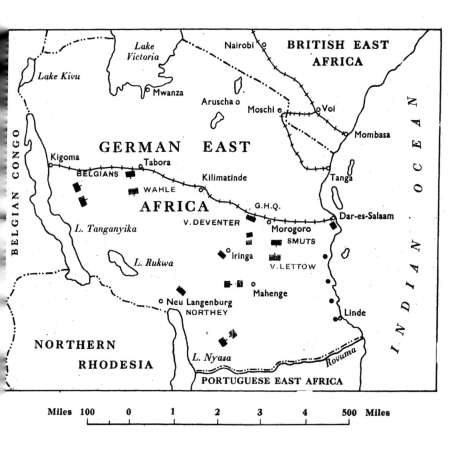

Miles 100   0   1   2   3   4   500   Miles

PLAN SHOWING

STRATEGIC SITUATION AT END OF
SEPTEMBER 1916.

Forces Allied.............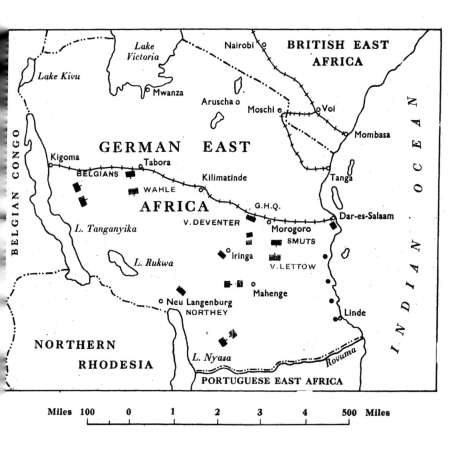
Forces German.........

19

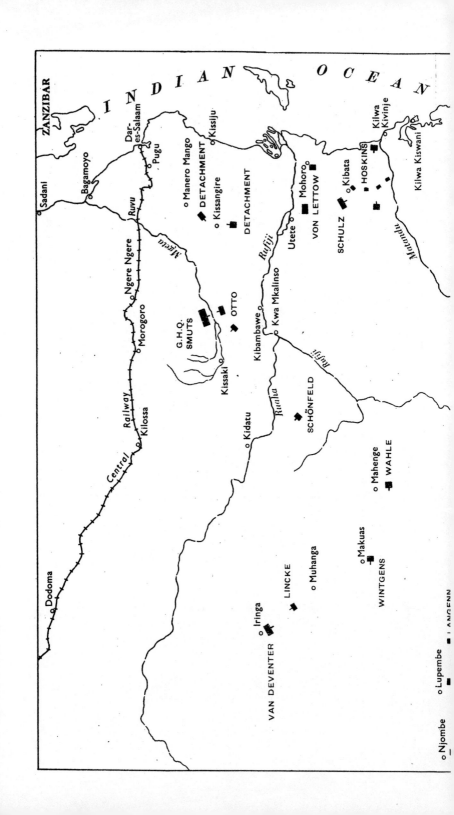

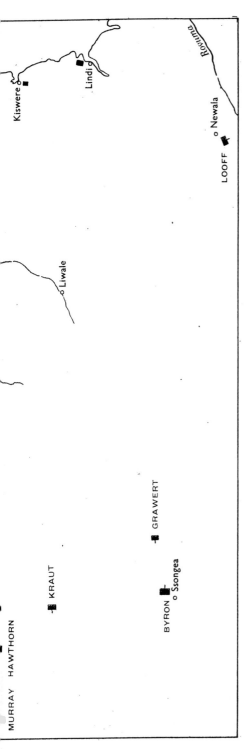

MAP ILLUSTRATING

STRATEGIC SITUATION

AT THE RESUMPTION OF THE GENERAL ADVANCE
DECEMBER 1916.

Miles 0   50   100   150   Miles

Forces British..........
Forces German..........

20

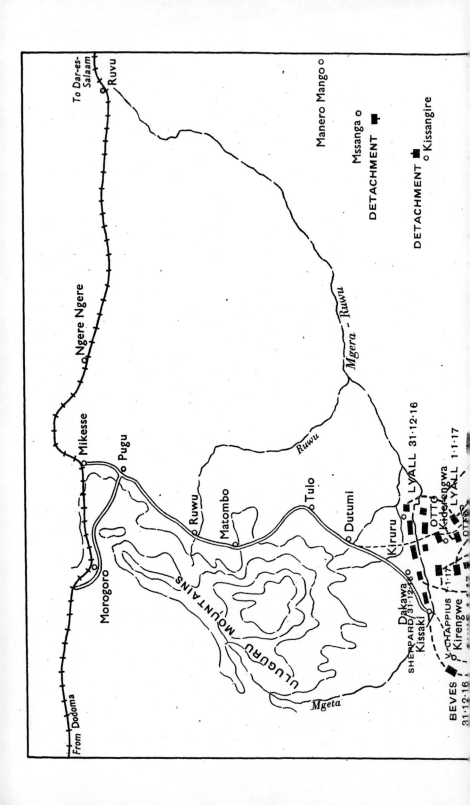

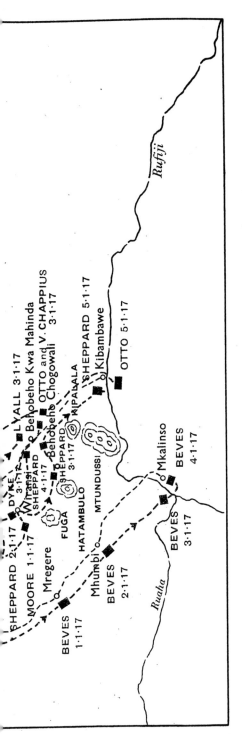

MAP TO ILLUSTRATE

GENERAL SMUTS' OPERATIONS
ON THE RUFIJI, JANUARY 1917.

Miles 0   10   20   30   40 Miles

Forces British..........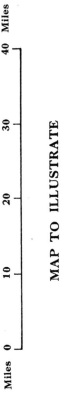
Forces German..........

21